WEST POINT

THE BICENTENNIAL BOOK OF THE
UNITED STATES MILITARY ACADEMY

WEST POINT
Two Centuries of Honor and Tradition

Edited by Robert Cowley
and
Thomas Guinzburg

WARNER BOOKS

An AOL Time Warner Company

Page 2: The Color Guard of the United States Military Academy represents West Point's commitment to Honor, Duty, Country.

The bicentennial logo and the terms "United States Military Academy" and "West Point" are registered trademarks of the Department of the Army. Used with permission.

Warner Books, Inc., 1271 Avenue of the Americas, New York, NY 10020

Visit our Web site at **www.twbookmark.com**.

An AOL Time Warner Company

Printed in Canada

First Printing: May 2002

10 9 8 7 6 5 4 3 2 1

ISBN: 0-446-53018-2
LCCN: 2002100280

For Inge, with much admiration and affection.
TG & RC

Produced for The West Point Project, LLC by Koerner Kronenfeld Partners, LLC.
Carl Seldin Koerner and Ivan S. Kronenfeld, Executive Producers

    West Point
    Two Centuries of Honor and Tradition

Edited by Robert Cowley and Thomas Guinzburg

Picture research: Linda Sykes Picture Research, Hilton Head, SC
Art Direction and Design: Marleen Adlerblum Design, New York, NY
Principal Photography: Inge Morath
Timeline: COL (R) Kenneth E. Hamburger
Assistant Producer, The West Point Project: Nathalie Casthely
Project Co-ordinator: Candice Koerner
Assistant to the Editors: Victoria Anstead

The editors would like to particularly acknowledge the contributions of Alan Aimone.

Acknowledgments

The editors have endeavored to be as accurate as possible with respect to the hundreds of names, dates, ranks and other citations. In a volume with so many writers and sources, mistakes will almost surely have crept in. All such errors of omission or commission are ultimately the responsibility of the editors, RC and TG.

The editors are particularly grateful for the leadership of
MG (R) Joseph P. Franklin, BG (R) Peter Stromberg, Bill Raiford

WEST POINT PROJECT, LLC
Rand V. Araskog, James E. Arnold, John D. Bergen, LTG (R) Daniel W. Christman, John Delaney, Paul B. Firstenberg, Richard and Annette Graf, Curtis A. Harris, BG (R) James V. Kimsey, James Kiss, Jane Lahr, Herbert Lichtenberg, Richard Marek, William F. Murdy, Pamela Newman, Patrick O'Neill, Bernard F. Reynolds, William H. Roedy, Elihu Rose, Patricia Savino, Bonnie Schweppe, Richard Stolley, Ambassador William J. vanden Heuvel

UNITED STATES MILITARY ACADEMY AT WEST POINT
Leadership of the Academy: Superintendent, LTG William J. Lennox, Jr.; Dean of The Academic Board, BG Daniel J. Kaufman; and Commandant of Cadets, BG Eric T. Olson. Public Affairs: LTC James E. Whaley, III and staff; USMA Library/Archives: Director Joseph M. Barth, Suzanne Christoff, and staff; West Point Museum: Mike Moss, David Reel, and staff; Dr. Stephen B. Grove; COL (R) Kenneth E. Hamburger

ASSOCIATION OF GRADUATES OF USMA
Jack Hammack, Tom Dyer, COL (R) Seth Hudgins, COL (R) John Calabro, LTC (R) Freed Lowrey, COL (R) Morris Herbert, and staff.

USMA BICENTENNIAL CELEBRATION OFFICE
COL Pat Kane, MAJ Scott Weliver, and Kris Fox

Contents

14   Introduction by General H. Norman Schwarzkopf

Chapter 1
16   A NEW COUNTRY STARTS A SCHOOL FOR SOLDIERS
by Thomas Fleming

Chapter 2
46   THE GOLDEN AGE: 1834-1860
by Cecelia Holland

Chapter 3
76   WEST POINT IN THE CIVIL WAR
by Stephen W. Sears

Chapter 4
106   FROZEN INTERVAL: 1866-1915
by Carlo W. D'Este

Chapter 5
146   THE GREAT WAR AND AFTER
by Robert Cowley

Chapter 6
178   THE ACADEMY GOES TO WAR AGAIN
by Tom Wicker

Chapter 7
208   INTO THE COLD WAR: 1946-1964
by Dennis E. Showalter

Chapter 8
232   FIELDS OF FRIENDLY STRIFE
by Geoffrey Norman

Chapter 9
254   FOUR DECADES OF TUMULT
by Brian Haig

Chapter 10
284   WEST POINT TODAY
A photographic portfolio by Inge Morath

296   Photo Credits
298   Index

Opposite: This print from the early 1900s shows cadet officers in full dress, foreground, and in regular dress and service uniforms, rear left. The Victory Monument is in the background, right.

In a turn-of-the-century photograph, plebes line up in front of their summer camp tents for rifle inspection.

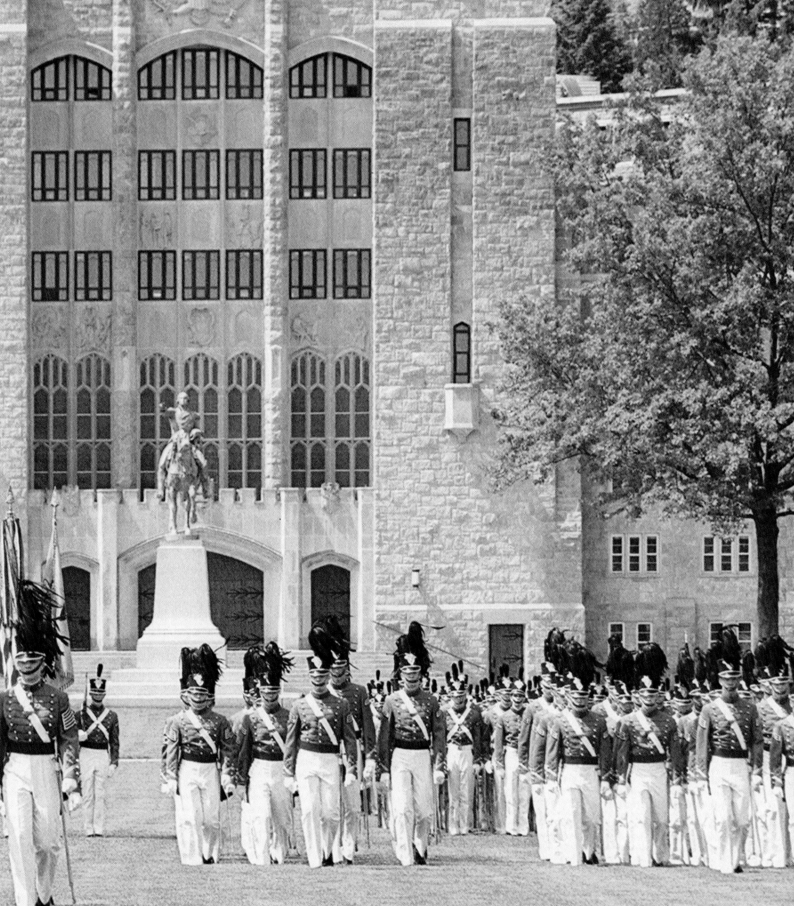

At ceremonies for the 2001 graduation, the Corps of Cadets parade on the Plain in front of the equestrian statue of George Washington and Washington Hall.

*H. Norman Schwarzkopf '56
as a cadet.*

Introduction
by General H. Norman Schwarzkopf

Nearly from the day I could walk I wanted to be a West Pointer. I never had a shred of doubt. My father was a West Pointer and he always told me the Academy shaped his entire life. "Duty, Honor, Country" was his creed and in time it came to be mine as well.

I reported in on June 1, 1952, like so many thousands before me, clutching an athletic bag that contained a razor, a toothbrush, and a $300 check to cover the cost of toiletries and other incidentals. Four years later, I carried away a system of values to live by, and a lifelong calling.

Ask any West Pointer what day they remember best and almost all of them will say it's that first day. It's scorching hot and you find yourself standing in a long line of other reporting cadets, nervously glancing around at the imposing gray fortress, at the other faces, and worrying whether you'll measure up. Suddenly, there's nobody in line ahead of you. Suddenly, an upperclassman in a gleaming white uniform fixes you with a hard stare and harshly barks, "You, Mister, step forward. Stand at attention. Get your shoulders back. Pull in that chin. Get that chest up. Drop that bag. No, wrong. Not fast enough. Pick it up. When I tell you to drop your bag, you drop your bag right away."

You know in that instant you've entered another world: You know your life is going to be immeasurably changed. By the end of that day, you haven't been given a single instant to stop and think. You've been run ragged. You've been outfitted with uniforms, been taught to march and salute, been given your first severe lessons on military etiquette, and are standing in packed ranks with the rest of your classmates, waiting to take the oath that makes you a cadet. You are unsure, proud, and awed all at once. Your heart is racing. Suddenly, you raise your right hand and commit your life to serving your country. It's a profoundly moving moment.

West Point doesn't have fraternities, or sororities, or secret societies. Its graduates think of themselves as part of one Long Gray Line that stretches right back to that very first Class of 1802. They are part of a huge extended family that finds unity in a common experience and the character and purpose molded by that experience. To West Pointers, those three words, "Duty, Honor, Country," are more than a motto; they're immortal ideals that guide your life.

A day I will never forget came shortly before my retirement, after all the parades and celebrations that welcomed home the troops from Desert Shield and Desert Storm. The Academy invited me back to West Point to be honored in a full dress review, a singular privilege that's bestowed on very few. Having marched in a few of these special parades in my days as a cadet, I had always wondered what it must feel like to be on the receiving end of such a great honor. As I stood on the Plain, the entire corps of cadets arrayed in perfect ranks, I finally learned. It is profoundly humbling. You feel boundless hope for the future, knowing that your days in service may be ending, but that within those anonymous ranks of gray are more great leaders who will step forward and do great deeds when America requires it.

Academy professors like to say that at West Point you are taught the history made by its own graduates. It happens to be true. We spent countless hours studying those who went before us. We looked back to Ulysses S. Grant and Robert E. Lee as the fathers of modern warfare; to Blackjack Pershing and Dwight Eisenhower for the skills to lead coalitions in battle; to George Patton and William Tecumseh Sherman and Stonewall Jackson for how to campaign; and Douglas MacArthur for how to build upon victories just won. And this is only the tip of the iceberg; heroes are something West Pointers have in awesome abundance. But the Academy's contributions haven't been limited to wars; an equally impressive history exists away from the roar of the battlefield. West Pointers mapped this country and discovered the routes that carried us westward. They built the railroads that connected us together; the great dams that tamed our waterways; the Panama Canal that married the two mighty oceans on our flanks; and the atomic bomb that ended World War II. They led great corporations that changed how Americans live, from Henry DuPont who made his family's chemical company a household name, to Jim Kimsey, who co-founded America OnLine.

The professors and tactical officers of my cadet days were nearly all World War II and Korean War veterans. Chests cluttered with ribbons are one of the things that make the Academy's faculty unique. We were always looking for sly ways to rush them through our lesson plans and coax them into telling us what it was like to be a tank commander sweeping across France and Germany under George Patton, or an infantryman battling back up Pork Chop Hill under Matthew Ridgeway. Our curiosity had nothing to do with the glories of battle; I didn't know many cadets foolish enough to have romantic notions about war. We wanted to prepare ourselves for what lay ahead. We wanted to be ready for the fiercest duty a nation can ask of it citizens: To lead soldiers in war; to win battles without wasting the precious lives placed in our trust. When my generation later came back from the jungles of Vietnam to serve faculty duty, I felt the same intense curiosity from my cadets.

Two hundred years have now passed since West Point was founded. For a young nation that revolted against Great Britain in large measure to halt the abuse of English soldiers against our citizens, it was a hard step to found an Academy to train professional officers. Not surprisingly, there was great resistance. Would it create a permanent military caste? Would it create a pool of elitist officers? Would such a school prove destabilizing to a frail democracy that was still struggling to find its moorings?

This book is a look back at that 200 years. It's an inspiring narrative that is expertly told in a series of chapters by some of America's most prominent and respected writers and historians. It's a celebration of the wisdom of George Washington, who advocated the Academy, and of Thomas Jefferson, who gave it life. Reflecting back, it truly was one of the bright and shining instances of political farsightedness. When you think of how much of America's history and how many of its proudest moments were the result of leaders forged inside the Academy's walls, you cannot help but be thankful. West Point is today the finest military academy on earth, a model for other nations to emulate; not an impediment to American democracy—an invaluable guardian.

It would be terrifically naïve, though, to think all this happened without birthing pains and turmoil and sometimes, disillusionment. Within sixty years after the founding, West Pointers were forced to choose sides in a civil war that pitted classmates against classmates in a bitter struggle for the country's future. They were sent to fight in agonizingly unpopular wars, against Mexico, and later in Vietnam, that strained the trust and affection that must exist between the Army and its society. Twice in the last century, West Pointers helped mobilize and lead America through global wars against powerful enemies. They saw us through the long, tense years of the Cold War, and its occasional lapses into real war. It's no exaggeration to say that the fate of the world hung in their hands. And throughout, the Academy had to make never-ending changes to adapt to a continuously changing world, most recently the thrust to achieve racial and sexual equality.

America is now the most powerful nation on earth. We have obligations and alliances that span the globe. The responsibilities that fall on the shoulders of our senior military officers are mind-boggling. Warfare is staggeringly more complex, faster-paced, and lethal than when I first pinned on my lieutenant's bars. Military leadership is not an undertaking for amateurs: it takes highly trained professionals who are willing to dedicate full careers to the study and practice of arts that are not taught in any other university but West Point.

The barbaric attacks on the World Trade Center and the Pentagon, and all that has followed, have underscored again our reliance on our men and women in uniform. As we have so often in the past, we are calling on them to defeat our enemies and ensure our safety. Scattered in their ranks are thousands of West Pointers. America needs to know their history. America needs, more than ever, to contemplate the unique national treasure we call the United States Military Academy.

1
A NEW COUNTRY STARTS A SCHOOL FOR SOLDIERS

BY THOMAS FLEMING

"The Establishment of an
Institution of this kind
[a military academy], upon a
respectable and extensive basis,
has ever been considered
by me as an object of
importance to this country."

—George Washington, 1799

■ Washington writes Alexander Hamilton two days before his death: "The establishment of a military academy upon a respectable and extensive basis has ever been considered by me as an object of primary importance in this country."

■ July 1: The Secretary of War directed that all the Cadets of the Corps of Artillerists should report for instruction at West Point.
■ September 1: A school opened at West Point with four army officers and a civilian as administrators and instructors.

■ March 16 :Thomas Jefferson signs bill establishing USMA
■ July 4: Formal opening of United States Military Academy.
■ Joseph Gardner Swift [later Chief of Engineers and Superintendent of USMA] and Simon Magruder Levy graduated, both after only seven months attendance.

■ Three cadets graduated after stays at USMA from ten to thirteen months.

■ Hannibal Montesque Allen graduated, son of Revolutionary War hero General Ethan Allen.

■ Alden Partridge entered West Point. Later acting Superintendent 1815–1817; founded seven military schools including Norwich University, Northfield, Vermont.

On March 1, 1802, the Congress of the United States authorized President Thomas Jefferson to create a corps of engineers for the American army. It was to be "stationed at West Point . . . and shall constitute a military academy." This terse establishment of America's most important school has left readers and not a few historians puzzled about why it happened in 1802—and not in 1790 or some earlier date. Why did it take so long for Americans to apply the lessons of the eight-year war for American independence?

One explanation, uncovered by scholars who have explored what happened at West Point before 1802, emphasizes the little-realized fact that there already was a school of sorts in operation at the site of the future academy. Colonel Henry Burbeck, the army's chief of artillery, was giving rudimentary engineering and gunnery instruction to junior officers and cadets—and had written the secretary of war, Henry Dearborn, urging him to create a military academy. Jefferson, in short, was formalizing an idea that had already taken shape.

Why did the president do it in 1802? A look at what was happening in America and the rest of the world offers a likely explanation for Congress's—and Jefferson's—decision. Americans had just made the unnerving discovery that the First Consul of France, Napoleon Bonaparte, the most ambitious, power-hungry ruler on the globe, had acquired the immense territory of Louisiana from Spain—and had shipped an army to Saint Domingue (present day Haiti) to reestablish French rule there and then garrison New Orleans. Even more unnerving was the news that the Spanish, presumably acting on Napoleon's orders (it turned out they weren't) had revoked Americans' right to export cotton and grain through New Orleans, stirring a furious shout for war in the Mississippi Valley.

For ten years America had been struggling to stay neutral in a world aflame with the passions ignited by the French Revolution. England and France had been locked in global combat, making it more than clear that it was a dangerous world for an undeveloped country with and political parties that violently disagreed on which way to tilt the nation's neutrality. Alexander Hamilton's Federalists, forerunners of today's Republicans, favored England; Thomas Jefferson's Republicans, forerunners of the modern Democrats, backed France.

From 1798-1800 the United States had fought an undeclared war with the French on the high seas to stop them from inflicting ruinous damage on the nation's commerce in retaliation for our refusal to side with them against England. Hamilton, the acting commander of the 10,000-man army raised during this contest, had written to George Washington, urging him to lend his support to a military academy. In one of his last letters before his death in 1799, Washington replied that he considered the proposal "of primary importance to this country."

When Jefferson became president in 1801, he immediately dismantled Hamilton's "provisional" army. But the idea of a military academy stayed alive, not only because of the world situation, but because Jefferson had decided an academy was a good way to alter the political composition of the American officer corps. He wanted officers loyal to his political party and he

PRECEDING SPREAD: Left: In this View of West Point from Philipstown *by Victor DeGrailly, 1840, the Academy is on the left and the mountains of Storm King and Breakneck loom beyond. Right: Sylvanus Thayer took over a ragtag discredited Academy in 1817 and made it the most progressive school in the country. Robert Weir, the Academy's most famous art instructor, painted several portraits of him.*

| 1806 | 1807 | 1808 | 1809 | 1810 | 1811 | 1812 |

■ Fifteen cadets graduated, including John Duncan Wyndham, a British Army officer before entering West Point.

■ Justus Post graduated, later surveyor of Illinois and Michigan Canal.

■ Sylvanus Thayer, "Father of the Military Academy," graduated after an eleven-month stay at West Point. Born in 1785 in Braintree, Massachusetts, he had already graduated from Dartmouth. Built coastal fortifications in New England and Virginia.

■ Seven cadets graduated between January and June after study at West Point averaging just over nine months each; the longest any one of them stayed was fifteen months. There were fifty-two graduates between 1802 and 1810.

■ Academy was deprived of nearly all means of instruction because of lack of appropriations by Congress. There was no Class of 1810.

■ George Ronan graduated; he was killed in fight against Indians at Fort Dearborn, 15 August 1812, becoming the first USMA graduate to be killed in action.

■ No instructors remained.
■ April 29 : Academy Reorganization Act: corps of professors authorized; 250 cadets authorized.
■ Colonel Joseph G. Swift named Superintendent.

Mount Vernon December 12, 1799

Sir,

I have duly received your letter of the 28th ultimo, enclosing a copy of what you had written to the Secretary of War, on the subject of a Military Academy.

The Establishment of an Institution of this kind, upon a respectable and extensive basis, has ever been considered by me as an object of primary importance to this Country;— and while I was in the Chair of Government I omitted no proper opportunity of recommending it, in my public Speeches, and otherways, to the attention of the Legislature:— But I never undertook to go into a detail of the organization of such an Academy;—leaving this task to others, whose pursuits in the paths of Science and attention to the Arrangements of such Institutions,—had better qualified them for the execution of it.

For the same reason I must now decline making any observations on the details of your Plan;—and as it has already been submitted to the Secretary of War, through whom it would naturally be laid before Congress, it might be too late for alterations if any should be suggested.

I sincerely hope that the subject will meet with due attention, and that the reasons for its establishment, which you have so clearly pointed out in your letter to the Secretary, will prevail upon the Legislature to place it upon a permanent and respectable footing.

With very great esteem & regard,
I am, Sir,
Your most obedt. Servt.
G.Washington

General Hamilton

George Washington (above pictured as Commander of the Revolutionary Army) first proposed a military academy in 1783. His handwritten letter of December 1799 (left, with transcription) advised establishing the Academy at West Point.

made sure the young men sent to West Point during his presidency came from staunchly Republican backgrounds.

At the same time, the 1802 law testified to Jeffersonian doubts about the very idea of a military academy. It was connected in too many minds with the idea of a standing army, which was considered a perpetual danger to the liberties of the people. That was one among several reasons why the president preferred to leave the school at West Point remote from any and all centers of political power.

Another reason was West Point's historic role in America's triumph over England in the struggle for independence. After the site was fortified in 1778, George Washington called it "the key to America." Its numerous cannon in forts high on

West Point commands the Hudson where its course narrows into a dogleg turn; during the Revolution the string of American forts built here constantly frustrated British efforts to isolate New England from the rest of the young Republic. This aerial view of Ft. Putnam, left, on the west bank, shows the magnificent defensive position. Above: The remains of Redoubt No. 4 at West Point on the summit of nearby Rock Hill. Below: A Revolutionary War cannon on the redoubt overlooks the Hudson.

Captain Molly

DURING THE REVOLUTIONARY WAR, many women followed their husbands into the Army, to cook and care for them while they fought. One such was Margaret Corbin, who was twenty-five years old when the British attacked the fort where she and her husband John were stationed.

This was Fort Washington, one of a pair of strongholds General George Washington threw up on the banks of the Hudson in the grim year 1776, when he was fighting desperately to keep control of New York. Fort Washington, and Fort Lee on the New Jersey side, could control the great river whose valley made a highway due north toward the Saint Lawrence.

General Washington could not win the battle for Manhattan Island, and as he retreated north the British swung around and attacked Fort Washington. John Corbin manned a gun on the walls of that fort, his wife by his side, and when his chief gunner was killed Molly Corbin rushed in to help her husband use the rammer and the sponge and load and fire the gun.

The battle was furious. Soon John himself was killed. Molly took over the gun, cleaning it, loading and firing it by herself, until a round of grapeshot struck, shattering her left arm and shoulder. Other soldiers got her to the rear where she was bandaged up, but Fort Washington soon fell, and Molly was taken prisoner.

She was paroled, but she never used her left arm again. In 1779 the Continental Congress gave her a pension, noting her bravery under fire, and she went to live in Buttermilk Falls, near West Point. In 1926 the Daughters of the American Revolution had her reburied at West Point and built a monument to her, a fitting triumph to a woman soldier. The Corbin Seminar, for women cadets of the service academies, continues the tradition of courage and service that Molly Corbin embodied so well.

—*Cecelia Holland*

the frowning cliffs above the Hudson made it virtually impregnable. The river made two right angle turns, forcing square-riggers to lose headway directly under these batteries. A massive chain was stretched across the river to make passage even more difficult for an enemy warship attempting to run the guns. West Point frustrated British plans to control the Hudson and cut off New England, the heart of the rebellion, from the rest of the nation.

In 1780, West Point became the scene of a drama with large symbolic overtones for the future military academy. The commander of the post, Major General Benedict Arnold, offered to betray it to the British for 10,000 gold pounds and a general's commission in the royal army. A combination of luck and vigilance revealed the plot, only days before it was to be put in motion. The adjutant general of the British army, Major John André, was seized with incriminating documents from Arnold, who escaped to a British warship waiting a few miles below the fortress. The importance of duty and honor was underscored in the starkest imaginable way.

In 1782, in another tantalizing bit of foreshadowing, West Point saw the arrival of the first woman to serve in the ranks of the American army. Her name was Deborah Sampson. She was, of course, wearing a man's uniform, and using the alias Robert Shurtleff. Born in Massachusetts of an old colonial family, Deborah apparently enlisted because she was bored with teaching school. On patrol along the Hudson, she gave a good account of herself in a skirmish with loyalists. Not long after that encounter, she was badly wounded in the thigh when her company was ambushed. She somehow managed to avoid detection while the wound healed but a few months later a bout of fever sent her to an army hospital where a doctor soon discovered her secret. Washington arranged for her to receive an honorable discharge.

Ironically, by the time West Point became the U.S. Military Academy, the Americans had, by one of those tricks of historical memory, lost contact with George Washington's "Continental" Army of Regulars. The next generation became convinced that the militia—untrained citizen soldiers summoned for sporadic emergencies—had won the long struggle. The battle of Bunker Hill, fought before the Continental Army was created, became the cynosure of Jeffersonian politicians, who doubled as military theorists. One of the cornerstone's of Washington's strategy, the need for a regular army "to look the enemy in the face," had been forgotten along with the battles the regulars had won at Trenton, Guilford Court House, and Yorktown. Even dimmer was the memory of the Revolutionary army's corps of engineers, headed by France's Colonel Louis Duportail. Without their skill in building fortifications and positioning artillery, the war for independence might have had a very different outcome.

Hence the vague and contradictory nature of the military academy's original charter. How and when the corps of engineers would constitute a military academy was left for others to decide. It took them a while. In the beginning, the faculty numbered two. The cadets ranged in age from ten and a half to thirty-four. No attempt was made to screen them for anything beyond their political connections. The regular army officers on the post refused to take orders from Jonathan Williams, the first superintendent. Williams, a gifted scientist and grandnephew of Benjamin

Franklin, resigned in disgust within a year. His successor was even more disenchanted with the so-called academy and he too quit in short order. A discomfited President Jefferson persuaded Williams to return but he was a reluctant and often absent leader, who found other tasks, such as building forts, more interesting.

Typical of the anarchy that reigned was the arrival of Joseph G. Swift, who would earn some retrospective fame as the academy's first graduate. When Swift showed up in 1802 his manly demeanor won the admiration of several regular officers, who invited him to join their mess. Captain William Amhurst Baron, one of the two faculty members, ordered him to dine with the other cadets. Swift refused and Baron called him a "mutinous rascal." Cadet Swift attempted to inflict bodily harm on Professor Baron, who fled to his quarters.

Ordered to apologize, Swift refused. The officers of the garrison meanwhile court-martialed Baron for conduct unbecoming an officer—he had a habit of entertaining ladies of ill fame in his quarters—and drove him off the post. Small wonder that one cadet morosely noted that "all order and regulation, either moral or religious" had vanished.

In 1808, a discouraged Superintendent Williams suggested the academy be moved to Washington D.C. where it might attract some attention from the federal government. He pointed out that the entire U.S. Army only had sixteen engineers and they were constantly detailed to all points of the national compass to build forts and make surveys, leaving no one to teach the cadets. Williams gloomily described the school as "a foundling, barely existing among the mountains . . . almost unknown to its legitimate parents."

Adding to West Point's intellectual desuetude was a dismaying lack of textbooks and scientific equipment. When Sylvanus Thayer, who had graduated first in his class at Dartmouth, arrived in 1808 to embark on a military career, he found himself staring at Hutton's Mathematics, a book he had used teaching grade school in New Hampshire, and Enfield's Natural Philosophy, an elementary physics book that he had used at Dartmouth. The acting superintendent, Joseph G. Swift, graduated Thayer within a year, tacitly admitting the military academy had nothing to teach him.

By 1810, the number of cadets had dwindled to forty-four, although Congress had raised the ceiling to two hundred because it looked more and more as though England and the United States would soon be at war. That year Secretary of War William Eustis decreed that no cadet could be younger than fifteen or older than twenty and they should be skilled in reading, writing, and mathematics. This got rid of some obviously useless, if not quite dead, wood but solved none of the academy's major problems.

Eustis, a doctrinaire Jeffersonian Republican, was hostile to the academy and reduced the number of new cadet appointments to a trickle. He also transferred faculty and cadets all over the map, bringing the school to a dead stop for the better part of a year. When war with England exploded in 1812, anyone who could carry a gun was hastily graduated, reducing the corps to one lone cadet. Congress belatedly decided it might be a good idea to have a decent military academy and passed a law raising the number of cadets to two hundred and fifty. They also mandated professorships in engineering, mathematics, and natural philosophy, independent of the corps of engineers.

These new appointees did little teaching. The flustered administration of James Madison rushed a swarm of new cadets to West Point for minimal instruction and ordered them graduated as fast as possible to join the U.S. Army, which needed all the help it could get. Congress had called up 100,000 untrained militia, with equally untrained officers elected by the ranks, to conquer Canada and sweep the British off the continent of North America once and for all. The regulars numbered a pathetic 3,000.

The war swiftly became a fiasco. American generals were inept, the militia refused to obey orders and frequently ran away at the sight of a British bayonet. In Detroit, one general surrendered his 2,200 man army to a besieging British army of 2,000. In northern New York, another general did nothing while the British burned the town of Plattsburg before his eyes. In 1814, another militia army ran away and a British force of 4,500 men marched unopposed to the nation's capital and burned the White House, the Capitol, and other public buildings.

West Pointers provided the few bright spots in this dismal performance. They used their engineering skills to build forts that stopped several British offensives. Not a single fort constructed by a graduate was captured by the enemy. They also demonstrated an ability to lead men. Captain Eleazer Derby Wood '06 commanded a sortie

MANŒUVRES

OF

HORSE ARTILLERY,

BY

GENERAL KOSCIUSKO;

WRITTEN AT PARIS IN THE YEAR 1800, ...

AT THE REQUEST OF GENERAL WM. R. DAVIE,
THEN ENVOY FROM THE UNITED STATES TO FRANCE.

TRANSLATED, WITH NOTES AND DESCRIPTIVE PLATES,

BY JONATHAN WILLIAMS, ...
COL. COMDT. OF THE CORPS OF ENGINEERS, AND PRESIDENT OF
THE U. S. MILITARY PHILOSOPHICAL SOCIETY.

PUBLISHED BY DIRECTION OF THE SOCIETY.

NEW-YORK:

SOLD BY CAMPBELL & MITCHELL.

1808.

from Fort Erie that routed the besieging British army. Wood died at the head of his column, as did James Gibson '08. Of the 47 graduates who saw action, ten were killed on the battlefield or died of wounds. Graduates won eleven brevets—temporary advances in rank for bravery or exceptional services—ten percent of those awarded—though they were little more than 1 percent of the wartime army's 3,495 officers.

Studying the war in retrospect, President Madison drew some conclusions that deviated from the military thinking of Thomas Jefferson. Madison informed Congress that the war had demonstrated the importance of "skill in the use of arms and the essential rules of discipline"—qualities that the "present system" of reliance on militia was unlikely to inculcate in the American army. He urged an expansion of the military academy. Congress did nothing so the president decided to act on his own. He created the office of Permanent Superintendent of the military academy. No longer would the job be a sideline for the overworked chief of the Engineering Corps. He gave the assignment to the man who ran the academy during the war years, Captain Alden Partridge.

Thaddeus Kosciusko, the Polish artillery officer and engineer who volunteered in the Revolution, supplied one of the Academy's first texts, an artillery manual, left. Jonathan Williams, the first superintendent of the Academy, translated it into English. Kosciuszko, seen above in a contemporary portrait, built many of the fortifications at West Point.

While he was living at West Point Kosciusko planted a garden around a natural fountain just below the edge of the plateau. This monument to him, seen above in a 19th century view, still stands at West Point.

The war had spurred a rush of construction, creating for the first time separate barracks for the cadets (previously they had been bunking with the post's enlisted men) as well as a mess hall and a combination library, lecture hall and scientific laboratory. Congress also ordered the superintendent to inculcate discipline in the corps by drawing up regulations for their daily routine. During the summer months they were supposed to live in tents, learning the duties of the army's lower ranks by daily practice.

Superintendent Alden Partridge instituted a regime that would more or less prevail at the academy for the rest of the two centuries we are celebrating in this book. Cadets rose at 6 a.m., answered roll call and returned to clean their rooms, make their beds, and stand inspection. They marched to the mess hall in formation and maintained "perfect order" at the tables. The rest of the day was devoted to classroom work, followed by an hour of drill, followed by an evening parade and supper. Uniforms had to be scrupulously neat and misconduct, such as gambling, swearing, and scuffling, was forbidden. To add zest to the daily drills, Partridge persuaded the army to supply the post with a band.

A new uniform was also one of the war's legacies. When U.S. regulars commanded by Brigadier General Winfield Scott won America's first significant victory at Chippewa in 1813, they wore improvised gray uniforms because the government had run out of regulation blue cloth. Captain Partridge decided to turn in the cadets' blue coats for gray ones to express pride in the regulars' achievement. It was the beginning of "the long gray line."

Unfortunately, along with these positive contributions to the rudiments of a genuine military academy, Captain Partridge did much to destabilize the school. "Old Pewter," as the corps called him, played favorites, permitting cadets he liked to ignore the regulations, go to New York when they felt like it, and graduate without bothering to take examinations. He loved to

Right: The Long Barracks, a vast U-shaped building with stairs on the outside, housed cadets, enlisted men, and their families. Probably built during the Revolution, it burned down the day after Christmas 1827. Below: The blockhouse under Kinsley Hill was another of the string of forts defending the Hudson at the end of the 18th century. Kinsley Hill lay on the road south of West Point, halfway to the hamlet of Buttermilk Falls.

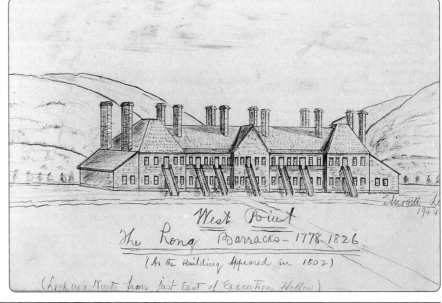

The War of 1812

In his depiction of the repulse of the British at Ft. Erie, E. C. Watmough painted one of the first actions in which West Pointers played a role. Here Eleazar Derby Wood '06 and James Gibson '08, on the wall, lead the defense against the charging British. Wood and Gibson were among the first graduates to die in their country's service. The West Pointers' primary duty was to build forts, and during the War of 1812 not a single one built by a West Point man fell to the enemy. Above, right: In the Battle of Chippewa, painted by H. Charles McBarron Jr., General Winfield Scott leads his regulars to victory over the British on July 5, 1814. Before this battle Scott's men ran out of blue cloth for uniforms, and switched to gray. A similar shortage of blue dye led West Point Superintendent Alden Partridge to change cadets' uniforms to gray, thus originating the long gray line. That new uniform is seen on the lower right.

drill the cadets personally, often commandeering them when they were supposed to be in class or studying. Partridge also had an overbearing side to his personality, which led to collisions with members of the faculty—disputes he solved with peremptory arrests.

Worse, Partridge had numerous friends and relatives on the academy payroll. His nephew was the commander of the regular army company on the post and his uncle was the steward. Both made money in various extra-legal ways such as chopping down trees on the reservation and selling the wood. The steward maintained a flock of stinking sheep on The Plain—the academy drill field. The cadets threatened mutiny when mutton was served for supper.

Complaints from the faculty and rumors of loosened discipline brought President Madison and Chief Engineer Joseph G. Swift to the school in 1816 and President James Monroe made his own personal investigation in 1817. Although a court martial board acquitted Partridge of most of the charges brought against him by his critics, President Monroe decided the superintendent had to go. There seemed to be more than a little truth to the faculty's claim that Partridge preferred "drill and mechanical maneuvers" to a thorough course of study.

To replace Partridge, Monroe chose Major Sylvanus Thayer. His ability as an engineer had

impressed the future president when Thayer designed and commanded a fort that saved Norfolk from a British amphibious attack in 1813. Chief Engineer Swift had chosen Thayer and Lieutenant Colonel William McCree to tour Europe in 1816 to study the military schools and coastal fortifications of France, considered the best in the world, and purchase books and scientific equipment for the academy.

No one had any overmastering sense of destiny when the slim thirty-two-year-old engineering officer headed up the Hudson to take over West Point in July of 1817. Choices that later become historic often appear mundane and even routine when they are made. Thayer was not enthusiastic about his new job. He knew the school was a mess and a subject of constant political contention. His European touring partner, William McCree, had been offered the appointment and politely refused it. But Thayer told his sister he had taken the job "as a solemn duty" and he was "determined to perform it whatever the personal consequences to myself."

The hostility Thayer met from the ousted Partridge and the cadets would have made any man wonder if the school had a future. The few cadets on hand acted more like spoiled brats than soldiers. Thayer was dismayed to discover that most of the corps were on a long summer vacation—and five members of the faculty were under arrest.

The new superintendent went to work on organizing the school for the coming academic year. Absent cadets were told to report by September 1 or else. The faculty members were freed from arrest and urged to draw up courses of study for their departments. Thayer assured them that there would be no more invasions of their classrooms for impromptu drills and other martial exercises. They were further heartened to learn that the books Thayer had bought in France would soon arrive, putting the school in touch with the latest thinking in military and civilian science.

As a semblance of system took shape, Captain Partridge returned, paraded the cadet corps and announced he was resuming command of the school. The cadets cheered. Mostly teenagers, they preferred "Old Pewt's" haphazard style, with its minimal demand for headwork, to the rugged program Thayer was devising. Thayer wisely made no attempt to challenge Partridge. The result might well have been a mutiny and the collapse of the school. Instead, he reported the situation to the Secretary of War and took the first available steamboat to New York to confer with Chief Engineer Swift.

Swift had protected Partridge from his numerous critics but this latest gambit removed any and all lingering affection for the man. He ignored Partridge's plea to come to the academy and take personal charge. Instead, he sent an aide with orders to put Old Pewt under arrest. Thayer returned with the aide but took no part in arresting Partridge. However, he made sure a message from Swift, ordering "implicit obedience to the orders of Major Thayer" was read to the cadet corps. This warning did not prevent the cadets from giving Partridge a raucous send-off at the steamboat dock. "Old Pewt" was court-martialed and dismissed from the army but a plea for clemency from Chief Engineer Swift won him permission to resign.

New York's newspapers, on the brink of the tabloid age, printed sensational stories about a mutiny at West Point. Thayer ignored them and went to work on bringing order out of semi-chaos. He ordered a general examination which revealed forty-three cadets—a fifth of the corps—were virtual ignoramuses. Twenty-two of these laggards had been at the academy for three years without advancing beyond the first year's course. Twenty-one others had been at the school for as long as four years without making "any progress whatever." The numbers were vivid proof of Partridge's indifference to academic standards—and the dangers inherent in Jefferson's emphasis on political connections in cadet appointments.

Thayer permitted half of these dawdling cadets to enroll in the first year's course. He sent the rest home—risking the wrath of their often powerful friends and relations. No less a personage than General Thomas Pinckney of South Carolina, Revolutionary War hero and former governor, was told that his son Edward was among those who had wasted four years at the academy. Thayer tried to soften the blow by assuring the father that Edward's moral conduct had "always been very commendable."

Meanwhile, what would soon be called "the Thayer system" was taking root at West Point. It was nothing less than a quiet revolution in American education. The classes were divided into small sections, with the head of the department teaching the first section, which included the most gifted students. Other sections were taught by assistants, who moved at a slower pace but made sure the essentials of the subject were well learned. In the rest of American colleges, the professorial lecture to an entire class was the standard educational technique. That meant the slow learners controlled the pace, leaving gifted students with "a great deal of idle time," noted one early critic.

Thayer bolstered his system, which was based on his observations at France's L'Ecole Polytechnique, with the closest possible supervision from the top down. Each week, professors were required to hand in reports noting cadets who

An anonymous artist painted the first known portrait of a West Point graduate, Washington Wainwright '21.

were neglecting their studies. Any cadet who received too many negative reports would be dismissed from the school. From these reports, a cadet's standing in his class was computed and published each week, encouraging a very American spirit of competition in the corps.

Equally close attention was given to cadets' conduct and military training. The corps was divided into two companies and they acted as

Superintendent's House, 1820

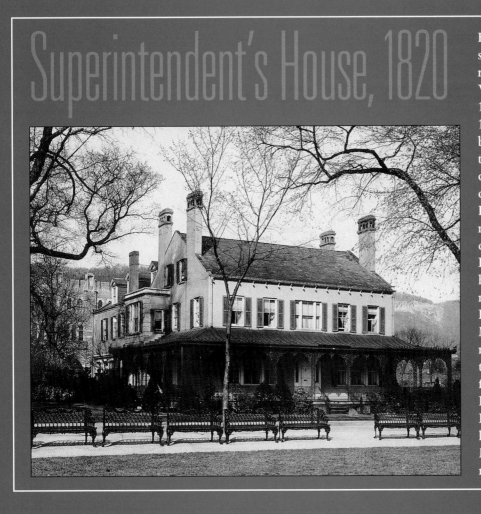

FEW HOUSES IN AMERICA have seen as many famous men under its roof as the Superintendent's House at West Point. Also known as Quarters 100, the original structure dates to 1820, making it the second oldest building now standing at the Academy; the Commandant's House next door, or Quarters 101, is just a few months older. Made of brick in the Georgia Farmhouse style, which featured chimneys flush with the exterior walls and a central hallway, the house cost $6,670. Besides Sylvanus Thayer, whose portrait hangs above the fireplace in the room named for him, the house sheltered Robert E. Lee, Douglas MacArthur, Maxwell D. Taylor and other military notables during their tours as Superintendents of the Academy; among the famous guests were the Marquis de Lafayette, Abraham Lincoln, and Dwight D. Eisenhower. The house is allegedly haunted, primarily by Thayer's maid, Molly, who slips around the house mussing up bedcovers. —*C.H.*

their own officers, on a rotating basis. One of the Army's best drillmasters, Captain John Bliss, was brought to the school to supervise this vital branch of cadet life. Unfortunately, Bliss proved to be a mixed blessing. His short fuse and his aggressive style were better suited to raw recruits than gentleman cadets. When Bliss physically assaulted one recalcitrant cadet, the corps exploded.

Five ringleaders presented Thayer with a list of complaints against Bliss, backed by a round-robin petition signed by over a hundred other cadets. Alden Partridge had encouraged this sort of unmilitary communication. Thayer briskly informed the ringleaders they were flirting with mutiny. When they ignored his warning and returned the next day with a new petition, he ordered all five off the reservation before sundown. They retreated to Washington D.C. and spent the better part of the next year using all the political influence they could muster to ruin

Thayer. Fortunately, President Monroe stood behind the new superintendent and after lengthy hearings, a congressional committee concurred. Thayer emerged from this potentially ruinous clash with his authority reaffirmed and even strengthened.

The military academy soon settled into Thayer's system, which he continued to develop and improve. He replaced drillmaster Bliss with Captain William C. Worth, one of the heroes of Chippewa. "Haughty Bill" looked and acted like a man who was proud to be a soldier. Other tactical instructors were soon added, and Thayer decided they should live in the barracks with the cadets to bolster discipline and a military spirit. The "tacs" as they were soon called—and cadet officers—became responsible for reporting cadets who broke the regulations. Worth, soon designated commandant of cadets, was the court of last resort to which the "skinned" cadet could

Sylvanus Thayer, the Father of West Point, sits at his desk in this portrait by Robert Weir. His tour of European military schools inspired Thayer with ideas he carried back to the banks of the Hudson, where in the face of shrill opposition he laid down a foundation of high standards and progressive policies that has endured for 200 years.

■ Some cadets received "short muskets" or carbines of .54 caliber after frontier settlers objected to the government giving them to friendly Indians. Younger cadets sometimes used them, but they were generally disliked.

■ Cadet uniform: coat and pantaloons of blue cloth, round hat with black silk cockade and gilt eagle, and Jefferson shoes—single breasted coat with one row of bullet buttons and standing collar—black belt and army musket. Little attention, however, was paid to the prescribed dress.

■ Alden Partridge named Superintendent.
■ "Cadet Gray" adopted as standard color for USMA. Partridge's nickname became "Old Pewter" because of the color of the uniform.

■ Uniform further modified: A coatee of gray satinette, single-breasted, three rows of eight yellow gilt bullet buttons in front, and button holes of black silk cord in the herringbone form, with a festoon turned at the back end, a standing collar to rise as high as the tip of the ear.

■ Sylvanus Thayer named Superintendent.
■ September 15: Cadets were organized into a battalion commanded by Lieutenant G.W. Gardiner; the position being the precursor of the Commandant of Cadets.

■ Professor of History, Geography, and Ethics authorized.
■ November 22: Cadet mutiny over discipline.
■ Richard Delafield, future Superintendent, graduated at the head of his class.

■ Oliver Gridley takes over a public house easily reached through well-marked holes in the plank fence marking the south boundary of the post.
■ Colonel Thayer tried to have the government buy the tavern.

appeal—with the stern expectation that he would truthfully answer any direct question. As Thayer explained in a letter to Secretary of War John C. Calhoun, he wanted graduates to leave West Point with a strong sense of honor as well as intellectual achievement.

Reacting against Partridge's attempts to establish a camaraderie with the corps by calling cadets "my young friends," Thayer maintained an aloof, stern, rather distant style most of the time. But he could unbend, especially with new arrivals. Each was greeted with a handshake and a long personal interview. Some of these youngsters got away with conduct that Thayer would never have tolerated in a cadet. One raw young Kentuckian asked: "Old man, are you colonel or captain or whatever-you-call-um Thayer?" He survived to graduate.

In 1825, Thayer added another element that more or less completed his system. Henceforth, when a cadet broke a regulation, a certain number of "demerits" were debited to his name. These became part of the computation of his class standing. Thayer could also point to the numbers when he decided a repeated indifference to the regulations called for dismissal. It was not merely added control that Thayer wanted—he was constantly aware that he might have to defend his decisions against hostile politicians in Congress.

Thayer's cadets were not allowed to receive any money from home. Virtually every minute of their fifteen-hour days was filled with classwork, study, drill, and policing their rooms. They slept two to a room on mattresses thrown on the bare floors. In winter the only heat came from small fireplaces which did little to ward off temperatures that were frequently below zero. Cadets often studied wrapped in blankets, their numb feet pressed against the fender around the fireplace. Thayer abolished summer vacations. Only once in four years, between sophomore and junior years, were cadets permitted a visit home. In other years they camped on The Plain and learned to be soldiers.

In spite of this spartan regime, the school's popularity grew with remarkable speed. In 1818-19, Thayer worried about whether he could fill the 250 openings. By 1823, as word of the quality of the academy's education circulated around the nation, applications leaped to over 1,000 a year. Thayer could take not a little credit for this quiet transformation. He created a Board of Visitors, distinguished academics and government officials who examined the cadets annually. Their glowing reports testified to the excellence of the new system.

Among those who won a place in the corps during these years were names that would loom large in American history. One of the first was a young man with an air of command about him: Jefferson Davis of Mississippi. He soon demonstrated a rare ability to give Superintendent Thayer gray hairs. There were few regulations that Jeff Davis did not feel compelled to break, from making noise during study hours to—in the words of an outraged tactical officer—"improper conduct: firing his musket from the window of his room."

Davis also became an enthusiastic patron of a tavern in Buttermilk Falls, two miles from the academy, run by a genial Irishman named Benny Havens. Caught by a prowling tactical officer, Jeff was court-martialed and dismissed; but Commandant Worth, impressed by his enthusiasm for the military side of cadet life, persuaded Thayer to reinstate him.

Davis seems to have learned nothing from

■ Graduates 1802–1820: 261; 1811–1820: 209.

■ Course in Natural Philosophy [today known as physics] prescribed.

■ In the early 1820s, Benny Havens opened a tavern near West Point, off-limits to cadets.

■ The Corps of Cadets marched to Boston during the summer, encamped on Boston Common, and visited ex-President John Adams at Quincy on August 14.

■ Albert Sidney Johnston entered West Point as a member of the Class of 1826, where he would graduate eighth of forty-one. Killed in the Civil War at Shiloh 1862.

■ George Sears Greene graduated second in his class, Founder and President of the American Society of Civil Engineers. Engineer of many public works in New York City.

■ Jefferson Davis entered with the West Point Class of 1828, where he graduated twenty-third of thirty-three cadets. With the onset of the Civil War, he would be elected President of the Confederacy.

■ Cadets authorized to have wine on banquets at Christmas and Independence Day. On July 4, 1825, Colonel Thayer witnesses drunken behavior and forbids alcohol.

■ December 24: The "Egg-Nog Riot" occurred involving most of the cadets including Cadet Jefferson Davis. Cadets chased officers at sword point, threw missiles through windows, and destroyed stairs and railings. Several cadets were court martialed.

this close call. He was soon back at Benny's, hoisting a glass, when a cadet lookout bellowed "Old Hant!"—their nickname for Worth. Davis and a friend raced out Benny's back door and fled through the night along the edge of the cliff above the Hudson. Stumbling on a root or rock, Jeff went headlong into space—to be rescued, forty feet down, by some outjutting trees. He spent some time in the hospital recovering from this caper but escaped another court-martial since "Old Hant" had not seen him at Benny's.

On Christmas Eve, 1826, Davis proposed to indoctrinate the corps in "the mysteries of eggnog." Eluding the post's sentries with his usual skill, Jeff smuggled the vital ingredients from Benny Havens. When tactical officers heard rumors of the party and tried to seize the "nog" early on Christmas morning, a riot exploded that soon escalated into a veritable mutiny, wrecking the North Barracks and leaving most of the tacs in need of medical treatment for bruises and cuts from flying objects. Nineteen

cadets were dismissed but Davis, ordered to his room as the upheaval began, escaped with a reprimand and numerous demerits.

By way of consolation, one might almost think, the South sent Thayer another cadet who was as close to perfection in conduct and academic achievement as anyone in West Point's two centuries. His name was Robert E. Lee. His flowing dark hair, his superb physique, soon had some cadets calling him "the marble model." In stark contrast to Jeff Davis, Lee went through four years without a single demerit. He managed this without arousing any recorded envy among his classmates. One later said he never met any other youth or man who "so united the qualities that win warm friendship and command high respect."

Another cadet bound for future fame failed to graduate from the academy: Edgar Allan Poe. For a while he flourished, finishing seventeenth in his class after the first six months of his plebe (freshman) year, 1830. But a falling out with his guardian and a falling in with some of the most

By 1820 several substantial buildings already stood at West Point; The Long Barracks is on the left. The plume on the sentry's shako is perhaps exaggerated.

George Catlin, famous for his portraits of Native Americans, visited West Point in 1826. This painting shows artillery drill on the Plain.

dissolute members of his class turned Poe into a dropout. He was repeatedly absent from evening parades and reveille calls and even from classes. On February 8, 1830, he was dismissed for gross neglect of duty. His sympathetic classmates donated enough money to help him publish his first book of poems, hoping it would be a rhymed assault on the military academy. They were vastly disappointed by lyrics such as "To Helen" and "Israfel" which are now considered classics.

Poe's failure was a symptom of a major problem in Thayer's merit system—one he ruefully identified in a talk with President John Quincy Adams. Most of the time, the men at the head of a class were outstanding both in the classroom and in their conduct. But every so often, a top man was a rebel against the system and he frequently led alarming numbers of his classmates in the same direction. Many of these young gentlemen were convinced it was their God-given right to drink Benny Havens' dry whenever possible.

This fondness for John Barleycorn—and resisting discipline in any shape or form—was not confined to the military academy. The cadets were reflecting the expansive liberty-infatuated spirit of "Young America." At Harvard, Yale, and

In the summer of 1821 the Corps of Cadets marched to Boston, where former President John Adams received them. At the ceremony the City of Boston presented the Corps with a stand of colors, of which the cadets chose this one, depicting Minerva, Mars, and the Statue of Liberty, to be the standard of the battalion.

Cadet Edgar Allan Poe

Edgar Allan Poe was painted in 1845 at the height of his career.

AS IT WAS FOR SO many young people, West Point was a crucial moment in the life of Edgar Allan Poe. Twenty-one years old when he entered West Point, Poe had already studied at the University of Virginia and served two years in the Army; his first published poems were attracting the kind of shocked and amazed attention that has pursued them ever since. His appointment to West Point was a last-ditch effort to please his rich and distant guardian—to choose a respectable, manly career over the contemptible perversions of poetry. The effort was an all-around disaster.

It must have seemed promising at first. Poe had certain romantic aspirations toward a military life: he was a boy in 1824, when the Marquis de Lafayette toured America to widespread acclaim, and when the old hero came to Richmond, Poe and a friend formed a volunteer company to greet him, marching up and down in uniforms with gilt braid, flourishing guns and swords. Later, when he enlisted, Poe had done well enough, his clerical skills winning him promotion, and allowing him to avoid a lot of tedious marching and guard duty.

Arriving in June, 1830, at West Point, he passed the entrance examinations with no trouble. The other cadets looked on him with some awe, because he was older, and because Poe surrounded himself with an aura of mystery. He told stories of travels and adventures in Arabia and the Mediterranean, tales so full of color and detail his classmates soaked up every word as truth.

Legends and rumors collected around him. For a while the notion circulated that he was the grandson of Benedict Arnold (Poe's mother's maiden name was Arnold), a story Poe refused to confirm or deny. He hardly studied, although he read constantly. He wrote just as constantly, spinning outlandish and romantic visions. He spent a lot of time at Benny Havens' tavern, trading everything he could find, his candles, his clothes, for drink. The story (almost certainly false) persists that, ordered to turn out for drill armed and in crossbelts, he appeared in the belts and carrying his rifle and wearing not a stitch otherwise.

But his guardian gave him no money—Poe had run deep into debt already—and the harsh life of the plebe, the endless marching, the miserable food, and the hazing by upperclassmen, broke down his health, at the same time convincing him that he could only live as a poet. By January of 1831, he claimed he was too sick to continue as a cadet. He left West Point that February 19, with his life set implacably on its tragic and extraordinary creative course.

—*C.H.*

Princeton, getting drunk, rioting, and setting fire to buildings were standard responses to attempts by the college president or tutors to enforce order. In 1830, the agitated president of Princeton, Ashbel Green, lamented his students' "fixed irreconcilable hostility" to study, moral conduct, and religion.

Thayer grimly resisted this national tendency to youthful misbehavior. He felt the academy had a right to insist on strict discipline, because cadets were preparing to be army officers. Those who broke the rules were dismissed with a ruthlessness that inevitably rebounded on Thayer and the academy. No less than sixty percent of the cadets admitted during the ten central years of his superintendency failed to graduate, with dismissals for bad conduct accounting for almost half that number. Many of these ousted cadets made their way to Washington or had fathers who wrote angry letters to congressmen protesting their treatment.

Soon ambitious politicians scented an issue.

Engineer Cantonment
Feb 1820

Opening The Great West

West Point topographical
engineers helped to explore
the West. One of the earliest
and most important was
Stephen Long '11, upper
left, who led several westward treks. Other West
Point graduates on his
expeditions were John F.
Bell '12, J.D. Graham '17,
and W. H. Swift '19. Long
took artists with him who
documented his voyages.
Samuel Seymour drew
both Long's meeting with
the Pawnee near Council
Bluffs, above right, and
the view of Long's Peak,
14,255 feet high, across
the Colorado plains.
Left is Long's steamboat,
The Western Engineer,
on the Missouri River, by
Titian Peale.

"Benny Havens, Oh!"

Benny Havens himself is seen, above right. Paul McElroy's mural "Lt. O'Brien under the influence, 1838," hangs in the West Point Club.

IN 1824, A SUTLER NAMED BENNY HAVENS and his wife opened a public house in Buttermilk Falls, on the bank of the Hudson just below West Point. It was an instant success, specializing in buckwheat cakes and flips, and serving a wide variety of spirituous liquors. It was, of course, off limits to cadets, who formed nonetheless a large percentage of its custom.

Cadet life was boring, an endless round of drill, guard duty, and study, and the food was uniformly ghastly—boiled potatoes, boiled fish, boiled beef, boiled pudding. No wonder a steady parade of young men in gray found the path down to the riverside and the comforts of Mrs. Havens' cooking.

Benny himself was obligingly flexible in the matter of compensation, taking not only cash money but also candles, blankets, and odd bits of furniture in payment for his wares.

When wayward cadets were caught—and Captain of Cadets Ethan Allen Hitchcock, for one, led many a fell swoop into the tavern in search of his wandering charges—they faced court-martial. In 1831, once he had determined to have himself dismissed, Cadet Edgar Allan Poe began a campaign of disobedience, cutting classes and walking in broad daylight to Benny Havens' tavern, where he made a drunken spectacle of himself. Jefferson Davis, caught there with five other young men well into their cups, tried to defend himself on the grounds that he was only drinking beer, which he did not understand to be a spiritous liquor. The court, unimpressed, found the future Secretary of War and President of the Confederacy guilty as charged, and dismissed him from the Academy.

He was promptly reinstated, as most such young men were, another reason why Benny Havens retained its popularity with cadets at West Point for more than fifty years.

Henry Flipper, class of 1877, the ostracized black cadet, reported an elaborate drinking ceremony (which he, of course, was never allowed to join) centered on the Benny Havens song. "A group of cadets sitting or lounging around the room. One at table pouring out the drinks. As soon as he is done he takes up his own glass, and says to the others, "Come, fellows," and then all together standing:

Come fill your glasses, fellows, and stand up in a row.
To sing sentimentally we're going for to go.
In the Army there' sobriety, promotion's very slow.
So we'll sing our reminiscences of Benny Havens, Oh!

CHORUS:

Oh! Benny Havens, Oh! Oh! Benny Havens, Oh!
We'll sing beside our reminiscences of Benny Havens, Oh!

To our kind old Alma Mater, our rockbound highland home.
We'll cast back many a fond regret as o'er life's sea we roam.
Until on our last battlefield the light of heaven shall glow.
We'll never fail to drink to her and Benny Havens, Oh!

May the army be augmented, promotion be less slow.
May our country in the hour of need be ready for the foe,
May we find a soldier's resting place beneath a soldier's blow.
With room beside our graves for Benny Havens, Oh!

■ Colonel Thayer visited Washington to enlist President John Quincy Adams in helping the Military Academy. He confides in the President his concerns about "the moral condition of the institution, in particular "a habit of drinking [that] had become very prevalent among [cadets]."

■ Professor of Chemistry authorized.

■ Robert E. Lee graduated second in his class of forty-six. He became the first cadet at West Point to receive no demerits.

■ Graduates 1802–1830: 628; 1821–1830: 367.
■ West Point recognized as the premier engineering school of the United States.

■ Cadet Edgar Allan Poe court-martialed and separated. At his court-martial, he was cited for his duty absences and two counts of disobeying the officer of the day. Details of his allegedly showing up naked for formation were not part of the official transcript.

■ With the reelection of Andrew Jackson, relations with Thayer reach a crisis point. Jackson raged that "Sylvanus Thayer is a tyrant! The autocrat of all the Russias couldn't exercise more power."

■ July 1: Thayer leaves West Point for good.
■ The Class of 1837 entered, one that included a number of individuals who would rise to high rank during the Civil War: Joseph Hooker and John Sedgwick for the Union and Lewis Armistead [who did not graduate], Braxton Bragg, and Jubal Early for the Confederacy.

They began to say West Point was not being run for ordinary mortals. It was establishing a "military aristocracy." Alden Partridge, still hungry for revenge, took up the slogan in a vitriolic pamphlet. Congressman Davy Crockett of Tennessee said the school was educating "the sons of the rich" and called for its abolition. In an era when the word "aristocrat" was a political smear, regularly used by the rapidly growing Democratic Party, this was a very alarming development. Thayer realized it could destroy the school.

Thayer's woes multiplied when Andrew Jackson became the nation's first Democratic president in 1828. The crusty warrior was soon telling visitors that Sylvanus Thayer was a tyrant. Cadets who appealed their dismissals to him were regularly reinstated, threatening the fabric of the academy's discipline. Many people tried to tell Jackson he was wrong about Thayer but Old Hickory was not one to change an opinion once he adopted it.

Ironically, while Thayer fought this losing guerilla war with the president, the military academy was achieving new intellectual heights. In the 1830s, "Thayer men" began taking charge. Dennis Hart Mahan became professor of engineering, a post he would hold for the next four decades. The stumpy brilliant Virginian, who had stood at the head of the class of 1824, was handpicked by Thayer for the job. He even arranged for him to enjoy a mind-expanding tour of Europe's military schools and libraries, similar to the one Thayer had cut short to take over the academy. Mahan was matched by professor of mathematics Charles Davies, who became the first man in America to make the subject comprehensible and popular. Almost as brilliant and Davies' equal as a teacher was Edward H. Courtenay, professor of natural and experimental philosophy. He had

graduated first in the class of 1821.

By this time, Thayer himself had become a personage. VIPs journeyed to West Point to see the school and enjoy his hospitality. He spent most of his army salary entertaining these visitors in the superintendent's quarters that still stands on the west side of The Plain. There was little doubt that he enjoyed the job—and the superintendency was his for the rest of his army career. But the growing feud with President Jackson cast a fateful cloud on this pleasant future.

Not long after Old Hickory rumbled to another electoral triumph in 1832, Jackson reversed the dismissal of a cadet named Ariel Norris, with a long record of courts-martial and reprimands, including a previously reversed expulsion. Thayer decided the feud with the president had become personal—and the future of West Point was more important than his remaining permanent superintendent. With an absolute minimum of rhetoric, he sent a twenty-eight word letter to his immediate superior, Chief Engineer Charles Gratiot:

"I have the honor to tender my resignation as superintendent and to request that I may be relieved with as little delay as practicable."

The flustered politicians asked Thayer to stay until the end of the academic year. He agreed. That year—1833—the Board of Visitors was headed by Joel Poinsett, former ambassador to Mexico and a Jackson ally. He was tremendously impressed by the cadets' performance in their annual examination. He remarked that it was hard to believe no one had told them the questions that would be asked.

A faculty member reported the remark to Thayer. He immediately summoned the entire first (senior) class and told them their honor had been impugned. While Poinsett tried to protest

DAVY CROCKETT HATED WEST POINT

In the young American Republic memories of the arrogance of British soldiery still smarted. Early opposition to the establishment of the Military Academy sprang largely from fears that it would give rise to just such a professional officer caste, and thus represent a dire threat to the very foundations of the Republic. All through the 1820s, '30s and '40s the Academy was easy pickings for populists, especially the backwoods variety, who attacked what they saw as the school's elitism and latent aristocracy. In this opposition West Point had no worse enemy than Davy Crockett. In 1830 the roughhewn Congressman from Tennessee, hero of the Seminole Wars and staunch Jacksonian, led a campaign to defeat the appropriations bills and shut West Point down.

His arguments were invariably anti-establishment:

"That if the bounty of the government is to be at all bestowed, the destitute poor, and not the rich . . . are the objects who most claim it . . .

"That each and every institution, calculated at public expense, and under the patronage and sanction of the government, to grant exclusive privileges except in consideration of public services, is not only aristocratic, but a downright invasion of the rights of citizens, and a violation of the Constitution . . .

"That the Military Academy at West Point is subject to the foregoing objections . . . the sons of the rich and influential . . . are able to educate their own children, [w]hile the sons of the poor . . . are often neglected, or if educated . . . are superseded in the service by cadets educated at the West Point Academy."

Crockett's fiery oratory far exceeded his political abilities, and the Academy's friends in Congress were able to outmaneuver him. Increasingly, the need for trained civil engineers was overriding his concerns. Graduates from West Point were building the railroads and the canals and roads so vital to the new country. West Point was proving its usefulness. Still, some in the Congress had listened to Davy Crockett's alarums at first, but his shrill unrelenting attacks soon lost him more votes than they attracted.

Nonetheless, the Tennessean could not pass up the chance to do the Academy damage. When another appropriations bill came through Congress, Crockett tried to have struck down one item calling for building workshops at West Point. His resolution was thrown back in his face, voted down by a landslide.

In 1831, Davy Crockett was defeated for re-election, and set off on the road to a more glorious defeat at the Alamo. After his departure, West Point still drew an occasional wave of Congressional criticism, one of which led to the resignation of Superintendent Sylvanus Thayer in 1833, but with Davy Crockett gone, the Military Academy could feel a little more secure.   —C.H.

he meant his remark as a compliment, Thayer insisted on another examination, to cover the entire course. Challenged, the cadets performed superbly and Poinsett had to eat a large chunk of humble pie. On July 1, when the class graduated, every cadet came to Thayer's office to say good-bye to him.

Thayer remained at the academy for a few more weeks, assembling his papers and otherwise preparing for his departure. He sternly declined an attempt to give him a parade or any other kind of sendoff reminiscent of Alden Partridge's riotous farewell. One night, he went down to the dock along with several other faculty members to greet the night steamboat to New York. The rendezvous had become something of a summer custom. The dock was cool and a pleasant place to chat. As the boat prepared to depart, the superintendent held out his hand to those present and said: "Goodbye gentlemen." Up went the gangplank. In minutes the long white boat vanished into the gathering darkness.

Behind him Thayer left a school that had become world famous—a model that other American schools of science and engineering would imitate as the century advanced. The Thayer system, with its emphasis on academic excellence and personal honor, is still a force in the modern academy, which has broadened Thayer's curriculum beyond science and engineering. His statue on the edge of the Plain, saluting him as the father of the academy, is not a merely sentimental tribute. Sylvanus Thayer's life remains a monument to the commitment to duty, honor and country that is at the core of West Point's mission. The rest of this book is living testimony to what this quiet man achieved in his sixteen years as superintendent of the U.S. Military Academy.

Sylvanus Thayer's Later Years

In later years Sylvanus Thayer went on to great achievements as an army engineer; he donated money to help found an engineering school at Dartmouth College.

AFTER HIS LOW-KEYED DEPARTURE in the summer of 1833, Sylvanus Thayer never visited West Point again. In fact, he scrupulously avoided any public contact with the military academy. He did not even solicit letters from his favorite graduate, Dennis Hart Mahan, now professor of engineering and the school's guiding spirit. But Mahan nevertheless kept him well informed about the academy's situation. Each year Mahan paid a visit to Thayer in Boston, where the ex-superintendent was building a series of formidable forts around the harbor. For days Mahan and Thayer discussed the current state of the cadet corps, possible changes in the curriculum, how best to deal with Congress and other perennial problems.

In 1843, Thayer made another tour of Europe, sending back reports on topics such as new types of cannon, percussion locks for muskets, and the design of new fortifications at Metz, Antwerp and Vienna. He shipped a vast quantity of the latest books on military history and science to the the War Department. Many of these volumes found their way to the U.S. Military Academy Library.

Thayer followed with intense interest the exploits of the military academy's graduates in the Mexican and Civil Wars. In the latter conflict, he was a fierce advocate of the Union, and deplored the number of graduates who fought for the South. But he declined to offer any advice on who should command the North's armies. "I could name some who might do," he said. "But the war must develop that. Our best friends may not make the best generals." He accurately predicted it would take three years to create a good army.

In the midst of this tremendous conflict, on June 1st 1863, Colonel Sylvanus Thayer retired after forty-five years in the U.S. Army. His active duty "sons" found time to make him a brevet brigadier general "for long and faithful service." Thayer spent the last years of his life in his native Braintree, Mass. By wise investments, mainly in railroad stock, the general had accumulated a substantial fortune. He donated $70,000 (the equivalent of well over a million dollars in today's money) to his first alma mater, Dartmouth, to found the Thayer School of Engineering. He left the school an additional $30,000 in his will. To Braintree he left $300,000 to found the Thayer Academy, which is still flourishing.

Thayer died in 1872 at the age of eighty-seven. A few years earlier, when he was seriously ill, his old friend, Harvard professor George Ticknor, wrote to West Pointer George Cullum, beautifully summing up Thayer's life. "He has been from the first, the same man; —good tempered & gentle: clear-minded, far-seeing, —decided, —always firm and in matters of principle unyielding: putting his country before every thing else except his honor."

—*C.H.*

2

THE GOLDEN AGE: 1834-1860

BY CECELIA HOLLAND

"To West Point.
But for its science,
this army multiplied by four
could not have entered the
capital of Mexico."
—— Winfield Scott,
offering a victory dinner toast, 1847

■ Robert W. Weir became Professor of Drawing [until 1876]. An important American artist in his own right, Weir instructed a generation of cadets in the discipline of drawing, a critical skill for army officers in the era before photography.

■ The Class of 1835 was the first to have class rings. They were massive, with a drum and cannon on one side and a shot and sword on the other. The stone was a shield-shaped amethyst, engraved with the class seal.

■ Montgomery C. Meigs graduated: Supervisor, Washington Aqueduct and National Capitol; Union Quartermaster General in Civil War where he spent one billion dollars with all moneys accounted for.
■ William Tecumseh Sherman arrived at West Point from Ohio.

■ John Sedgwick graduated; as a Major General commanding VI Corps at Spotsylvania in 1864, he was killed by a sharpshooter. His last words were, "They couldn't hit an elephant at this range."

■ Pierre Gustave Toutant Beauregard graduated second in a class of forty-five. Beauregard was named Superintendent of West Point in 1861, but the appointment was rescinded and he soon joined the Confederacy, where he commanded the attack on Fort Sumter.

■ A sergeant "riding master" and twelve horses were provided for first cavalry instruction.
■ Ulysses S. Grant entered the Military Academy as a member of the class of 1843. Arriving at West Point at the end of May, he passed the entrance examinations "without difficulty, very much to my surprise."

■ Graduates 1802–1840: 1,058; 1831–1840: 430.
■ Richard S. Ewell [1817–1872], a future Confederate general who lost a leg at Second Bull Run, graduated thirteenth in the USMA class of '41 cadets.

The years from Sylvanus Thayer's resignation to the beginning of the Civil War have often been called the Golden Age of West Point. During this period, Academy graduates would build the new nation's infrastructure, win a war that took the country to the Pacific, and, ultimately, conduct both sides of what was in its time the greatest war in American history.

Ironically enough, however, the period began with demands to shut the Military Academy down. Jacksonians in power in Washington called the school aristocratic and elitist, an insult to the common man; other critics pointed out that as many as half of all Academy graduates resigned from the Army as soon as they could, to go into private business, and questioned why the country should pay for their educations.

Despite the honorable performance of Academy graduates in the Seminole War of 1835, Congress viewed the school with heightened suspicion. Through these years, the notion always lingered in the background of the cadets' daily routine that the school might shut down at any moment.

Still, they came, these young men, most from the East, which had the best preparatory schools, but many from the South and a small but steady stream from the West. New cadets arrived at West Point each year in the spring, generally taking the steamer up the Hudson from New York. Some, like aristocratic George McClellan, who was only fifteen when admitted, breezed in as if to a birthright; others had to struggle. Shy and awkward Thomas Jackson, an orphan, a backwoods Virginia boy, went all the way to Washington to beg for his appointment—and received it, although he had almost no education. Others, like Ulysses Grant—whose middle initial was accidentally changed to S, or U.S. Grant, thus inevitably earning him the nickname Sam—reached West Point through family connections.

On their arrival the young men went into the "beast barracks," tents set out on the Plain, where they were plunged at once into the endless discipline and military order of the Academy. Wearing whatever clothes they had come in, because they would not be issued uniforms until they had passed the entrance examination, they were mercilessly marched, drilled

PRECEDING SPREAD: The Mexican War proved the worth of West Point training as well as the value of mobile artillery, like the gun seen here in James Walker's painting Assault on Mexico City. *Right: Dennis Hart Mahan '23 was appointed by Thayer to the Academy faculty as soon as he graduated; he taught mathematics and the Art of War for nearly fifty years, profoundly influencing three generations of American officers.*

1841	1842	1843	1844	1845	1846	1847

■ Thomas Jackson Rodman graduated high in the class of 1841; innovator of artillery during and after the Civil War. He invented the Rodman Gun, cannon cast by cooling the core more quickly than the surrounding metal, thus compressing the interior of the barrel and enabling it to take larger charges of powder.

■ On July 7, the Commandant forbade "the wearing of uniform vests, cravats, stocks, and pantaloons, and the removal of the whale-bone from the caps."

■ Prescribed residence became legal qualification for admission: one cadet authorized from each Congressional District, one from each Territory, one from the District of Columbia, and ten Presidential appoint-ments from the United States at large.

■ Winfield Scott Hancock graduated eighteenth of twenty-five members of his class. He belongs to the small number of truly out-standing American combat leaders of the 19th century. Democratic nominee for President in 1880, losing to Republican James A. Garfield.

■ Thomas Jonathan "Stonewall" Jackson began his final year at West Point. Jackson struggled with academics throughout his four years. His persistence paid off: He graduated seventeenth in a class of fifty-nine.

■ Professor of Drawing authorized; Professor of French authorized [subject already taught since 1803].
■ The outbreak of the Mexican War brought West Point graduates to the attention of the nation and further entrenched USMA as a national institution.

■ Ambrose Powell Hill graduated fifteenth in a class of thirty-eight. A commander for the Confederacy in the Civil War, Hill was unsurpassed as an aggressive, fast-moving division commander. Killed during the siege of Petersburg near the end of the war.

and harassed by upperclassmen, who generally thought very little of the newcomers' prospects and said so. In June, when all the appointees had arrived, they were brought before the Academic Board for their entrance examinations.

For privileged young men like McClellan, who had already spent two years at the University of Pennsylvania, the examination was ridiculously easy—the cadet had to write a pas-sage from dictation, read a page from a book, and perform simple math on a blackboard—barely more than adding and subtraction. For Thomas Jackson, the test was torture. Witnesses remem-bered how the shy, clumsy boy stammered and sweat through the arithmetic, struggling with fractions he may never have seen before. Many of the young men failed this exam and were taken back to the steamer landing and sent back home.

Thomas Jackson passed. With his classmates, he was measured for a uniform, and spent the summer encamped on the Plain, marching and studying and standing guard duty and suffering the upperclassmen's pitiless hazing. In the fall, the cadets moved into the winter quarters, tiny rooms shared with several other young men, fur-nished with iron beds, heated by a coal grate, where a poster on the wall detailed exactly where every item was to be stowed. There was no plumbing. Cadets were ordered to bathe once a week and forbidden to bathe any more often. Officers inspected these quarters several times a day.

Soldiers ford Lake Ocklawaha in central Florida, 1838. West Point men served and died in the long and bloody, thankless war against the Seminole.

Dade's Massacre

IN 1835, EIGHT YEARS AFTER the United States assumed control of the territory, Florida was on the edge of an Indian War. For years white settlers had been steadily encroaching on the land of the Seminoles, and a series of treaties had forced this native community into an ever smaller and more barren holding. Finally a group of chiefs was tricked into signing over even that land in exchange for a much smaller piece of land in Arkansas.

The firebrand Osceola had led his people in repudiating that treaty. Everybody knew trouble was coming. When, just before Christmas, 1835, Major Francis Langhorne Dade set off with 116 men from Fort Brooke, at the top of Tampa Bay, to reinforce Fort King, 160 miles to the north, he was riding up the military road straight through an Indian country simmering with desperate rage.

At first the garrison commander, Captain George W. Gardiner '14, had been supposed to lead the unit, but his wife was sick and Major Dade offered to go in his stead. Dade's gallantry was natural to him. Scion of a family of Virginia military men, he was a spit and polish officer who impressed everybody who met him with his courage, bearing and fire. He was superbly confident, and he bragged that he would ride straight through Indian country and survive.

Later, after putting his wife safely on a ship to Key West, Gardiner caught up with the column. As they marched north they saw many signs of trouble: a store and a bridge burned, an empty Seminole village, abandoned farms. They rebuilt the bridges as they went, breaking the back of one unlucky—or not—soldier who was then left to walk by himself to Fort King. As they marched they dragged along a six pound gun; they had left Fort King with two cannon but had to give up on one entirely in the deep sand of the first day's march.

After six days' march, on December 28, they were only a few hours short of Fort King, marching in good order down the military road, when a single sniper shot blew Dade from his saddle.

A moment later, out of the high grass west of the road, a line of hundreds of Seminoles armed with muskets stood up and delivered a broadside into Dade's column. That first fusillade killed half the men in a single blast. Of those remaining many were wounded. Lt. William Elon Basinger '30 rallied these survivors and managed to get the six pounder working; for a while they exchanged fire with the Seminoles, who picked off the gun crew one by one, popping up out of the tall grass to aim and shoot, while Basinger coolly directed grapeshot at them.

Eventually the gun drove the Seminoles back, and in the momentary lull, Basinger and the remnant of Dade's column felled nearby trees, built a fort, and brought the gun inside. The Seminoles stormed this position a few hours later, killing every man but two in a systematic massacre, and hurled the six pounder, still warm, into a nearby lake. Altogether, five West Point men died in Dade's Massacre. There is a monument to their memory in the West Point Cemetery.

The Second Seminole War had begun, the bloodiest of the Indian Wars. It would last seven years, cost the United States $30,000,000 and 1,500 men, and end with most of the surviving Seminoles packed away to Oklahoma.

—*C.H.*

The Dade Monument in the West Point Cemetery commemorates the disastrous defeat that opened the Second Seminole War. Dade himself was not a West Pointer but five of the dead were.

For the next four years, from five in the morning until ten at night, the cadets marched, studied, recited, ate, drank and danced to orders. Every day they had three hours of drill and nine or ten hours of classes and study, two hours for meals and two hours for recreation. Sam Grant wrote to a cousin in the Midwest that if he had known how hard the Academy would be, he would never have come. But now that he was there, he added quickly, he would stick it out.

He didn't study very hard; he said later he never read a lesson more than once. He read a lot, mostly novels, and thought about girls. He graduated twenty-first of thirty-nine in 1843. George McClellan confessed that he studied very little; he graduated second in a class of sixty. Yet the course of study was daunting. There were no electives. The school recognized only three holidays: Christmas, New Year's Day and July 4. Under the Thayer System the professors did not lecture; instead, they presided over the recitations by which cadets proved they had studied and learned their lessons. Every cadet recited every day in each class, and every day he was graded in each subject. Twice a year there were general examinations, which many cadets flunked, to be winnowed out of the steadily shrinking corps.

In addition, a cadet had to meet a high standard of conduct; if he failed in any of a myriad matters of decorum, dress, and discipline, he got demerits, and if he got 200 demerits in any one year, he was dismissed. A cadet got demerits for not having buttons correctly buttoned, for hav-

Section on *AB*

Castle.

West Point in its early decades was primarily an engineering school. This original drawing for the insignia of the Army Corps of Engineers showed a castle with towers.

ing an item in his room in the wrong place, for striking a horse with a sword, for cooking in his room, for going to Benny Havens' notorious tavern, down on the riverbank south of the school. To the young men of Jackson's class, Robert E. Lee '29, was a legend, who in his entire career at West Point never received a demerit. Most of the others got their share.

As plebes, Jackson, Grant, McClellan, Lee, and all the rest took algebra, geometry or trigonometry every morning for three hours, their recitations consisting of working out problems on the blackboard and explaining them to the rest of the class. In French, the cadets memorized vocabulary and grammar, and read Gil Blas and Montaigne and analytical geometry. In their second year, they added English grammar,

West Point's graduates built America's railroads, and West Point's foundry, across the river from the Academy, built trains. This print from W. H. Brown, The History of the First Locomotive, 1874, shows the first of these, "The West Point."

and drawing, so that they could make good, intelligible plans for military buildings, and analyze topography and landscape.

In the third year, they took the famous science course of Professor H.C. Bartlett '26, who must have been an inspiration for young Jackson. Bartlett also had come to West Point from the backwoods, virtually uneducated, yet made himself into a renowned scholar, graduated at the head of his class, and wrote pioneering textbooks in mechanics, optics, and astronomy, used throughout the country. He sat on the Academic Board and was one of the dominant influences on the school throughout his career.

His course included electromagnetism, electrodynamics, physics, mechanics, astronomy, acoustics, magnetism, and optics. It did not include practical experiments, although the cadets learned to use sextants and surveying equipment, and Bartlett in 1840 had an observatory built at West Point. Bartlett's course was notoriously difficult, yet Tom Jackson took to the work and did well in it, studying late into the night by the light of coals heaped on the grate in his room.

In the fourth year the cadets took Dennis Hart Mahan's fabled engineering course, which covered architecture and military and civil building; they studied ethics (where Jackson also did well), chemistry (including mineralogy and geology), artillery, and infantry tactics. Throughout their tour, the cadets were expected to learn something of the art of the sword, take dancing lessons, and eventually, toward the end of this period, practice gymnastics.

In 1843, to Sam Grant's delight, the Academy began classes in equitation. Here he came into his own; young Grant was a splendid horseman. In addition to all this, the cadets marched for three hours a day on the Plain, and they stood guard duty for hours, in the rain, the snow, the sun that blistered their faces under the heavy black visors of their helmets.

In spite of this grueling schedule they managed good times, along with an endless round of pranks and jokes. Many drank in the great beauty of the place, the vistas of the mountains and the river, as a tonic to the hard work. Despite the rules against cooking in their rooms, they pilfered or bought ingredients for cadet hash, compounded over the coal grates, and many a local woman made pies for them—until the Academy cracked down. And there was Benny Havens' tavern down on the river, which specialized in hot rum flips, pancakes, and other delights. Periodically the Academy raided the place— Jefferson Davis, according to one story, fell down a cliff and nearly killed himself escaping from a raid on Benny Havens'.

In spite of all the regimen there was room for a little individuality here and there. George Pickett '46, who spent his entire career among the "Immortals" at the very bottom of the class lists, ever in danger of dismissal, earned that position in part because he insisted on wearing soft collars and ties instead of the regulation uniform collar.

Over all, this system worked. West Point was graduating a steady stream of disciplined and educated men. Although as late as 1843, Congress saw one final effort made to shut the school down, the Academy remained open for the same reasons its critics attacked it. The militia system was failing miserably, and while the United States had no obvious enemies, few sensible Americans were ready to face the world without some kind of military leadership.

Also, the Academy did produce engineers, who often left the Army and went to work for private companies, which were building the rail-

roads, the canals and bridges and roads that made possible the American surge westward. George W. Whistler '19, built railroads both in the United States and in Russia; William Gibbs McNeill, who stayed in the Army, directed the construction of railroads all over the U.S. West Point men were vitally necessary to the country.

The United States was pushing westward at an amazing pace, but newly settled lands remained backwoods and poor without efficient lines of transportation and communication. Until well into the 1840s only one other school in the country besides the Military Academy trained the civil engineers who could get such projects built, and that school, Rensselaer Polytechnic Institute, used texts written at West Point. Men trained at West Point built the Baltimore & Ohio Railroad, the harbors in Rhode Island and Connecticut, the Chesapeake & Ohio Canal, the Western & Atlantic Railroad—the list goes on and on, and the names chronicle the drive to the West. Even while politicians in Washington and elsewhere reviled the Military Academy as an elitist enemy of the people, Congress was approving the use of Army officers to supervise the internal improvements the people desperately wanted and needed.

By 1844 West Point was more of an engineering school than a military academy. Over half the graduates were going on to jobs in private industry. Who could blame men for resigning their commissions as soon as they could, when an Army officer's life offered no prospects, little money, and—in the absence of wars—no opportunity to exercise his skills? Robert E. Lee '29, was a typical example: in spite of graduating second in his class and with that spotless record, he had spent much of his professional career doing office work, and was still a captain at thirty-nine.

But for Lee, and for 542 other graduates of the United States Military Academy, including Lieutenant Ulysses S. Grant '43, Colonel Jefferson Davis '28, Lieutenant George B. McClellan and Lieutenant Thomas Jackson, both '46, all this was about to change. That same westward thrust of the young country was bringing it into a war with Mexico. West Point and the regular army were coming into their own.

In retrospect, the outcome of the Mexican War looks inevitable. At the time it was a considerable gamble. The Mexican Army was a veteran force of 32,000 men; Mexican terrain was forbidding, and guarded by terrible infectious disease as well as by its soldiers. The U.S. Army, numbering only 7,200 men, had fought a few Indian tribes, but no major armies since the War of 1812. Nearly half the enlisted men were recent immigrants, badly trained and of questionable loyalty, large numbers of whom deserted the first chance they got. When the war began in 1846, many European powers, and the Mexican government itself, believed that the United States was about to get its comeuppance.

Instead, the war was a stunning American victory, by which the burgeoning nation took possession of the entire northern third of Mexico. The victorious general himself attributed this success to the performance of graduates of the United States Military Academy.

Of the 452 promotions these men earned in the war with Mexico, including Robert E. Lee's brevet to Lieutenant Colonel, 447 were for courage on the battlefield. Forty-nine of these officers were killed, including some of the most brilliant, and ninety were wounded. Yet, in honoring them, it was not their bravery General Winfield Scott mentioned, but their educations.

"To West Point," he said, offering a toast. "But for its science, this army multiplied by four could not have entered the capital of Mexico."

The War was a double-header. The first campaign began along the disputed border between Texas and Mexico. There Zachary Taylor, with a mixed force of some 3,500 men, faced a Mexican Army of 6,000. Taylor, a rough-hewn old Indian fighter who generaled by the seat of

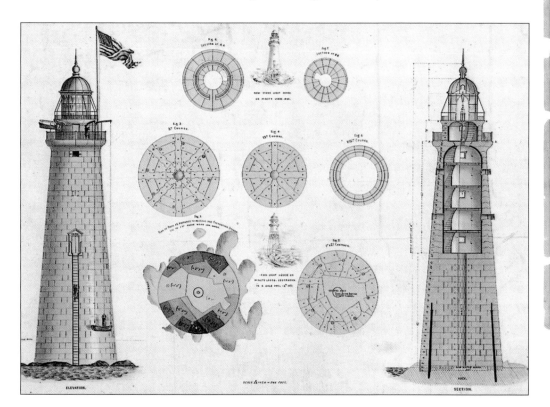

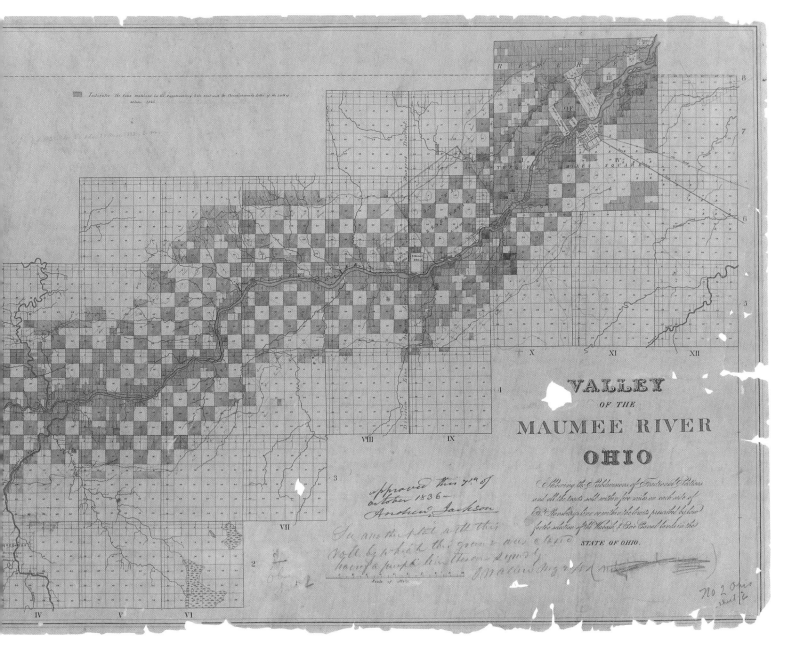

The Evolution of a Uniform

In 200 years of uniforms, the greatest change in cadet uniforms took place in the early days of the Academy. The winter dress of the class that entered in 1802 is seen top left. (The absence of a sword knot distinguished a cadet from a junior officer.) In the top center, Supt. Alden Partridge reviews cadets in their summer parade uniforms, 1815. Partridge was very fond of marching drill. Note the cockaded shakos. The blue coat of one of Samuel Ringgold's soldiers, from the War of 1812, shown bottom left, was standard before the shortage of blue cloth inspired a shift to gray. The collar and facings were red. On the top right is a sketch by Superintendent Robert E. Lee, who tried to improve the helmet, which sometimes gave cadets headaches; he drew this smaller shako with a plume of feathers. Bottom right are engineers in blue coats from the early 1820s.

Clockwise from top: By 1845 cadets' full dress gray coats sported three rows of brass buttons. Cadet Philip Sheridan '53 sits between Lt. George Crook and Lt. John Nugen. He may look as if he's holding them down but they had out-stripped him: Crook and Nugen had just graduated from the Academy and wear regulation Army uniforms. Sheridan's grades and demerits held him back a year and he still wears a cadet coat. Cadet George Custer (right) and another cadet, 1861, show off summer white trousers. The first appearance of fly-front trousers caused much controversy. The full dress cap from 1899 was nicknamed the tarbucket. The plume of shining black cock feathers was adopted in 1842. Uniforms were made in this shop at the Academy at the turn of the century.

his pants, was outmaneuvered and cut off with most of his army from his main base at Matamoros. The Mexicans swung around between them, laid siege to the American remnant at Matamoros, and dared Taylor to go to the rescue of his camp.

Across the flat saw-grass studded plain of Palo Alto, Taylor faced the Mexican army, resplendent in their uniforms, their lances by the thousands glittering against the sky, and realized he was outnumbered more than two to one. He called up Major Samuel Ringgold '18, and his "flying artillery."

Ringgold had gotten some innovative ideas from his West Point studies of Napoleon's tactics. Under the aegis of a forward-thinking Secretary of War he had re-engineered the cumbersome heavy field guns then in use, making them faster and more maneuverable. Swiftly he placed his guns before the American lines and began firing.

The Mexicans had artillery also, heavy and unmaneuverable, and firing solid shot, which hit the rock-hard ground of the plain and bounced and rolled, so slowly the Americans could usually dodge out of the way. Ringgold's batteries fired canister and explosive shells, which blew huge gaps through the Mexican lines. When the desperate Mexican generals sent lancer companies around to flank the Americans, Randolph Ridgley '37, pulled his two-gun horse-drawn battery around to meet the threat and drove the Mexicans back in a fury of canister shot.

The armies never closed. "The infantry stood at order arms as spectators," said Lieutenant Grant, who watched the day-long artillery duel with his unit. The shooting stopped at sundown, and overnight, the Mexicans fled, leaving behind hundreds of casualties. Only Americans had died. One was Sam Ringgold, the man whose

redesigned artillery had just ushered in a new era of warfare. A cannon ball had hit him in the legs; he did not live to see the triumph of his work.

Taylor pursued. The fleeing Mexican Army turned at a place called Resaca de la Palma and dug in. Taylor led 1700 men in an assault up this

ravine, choked with cactus and chaparral. Now Lieutenant Grant, and other officers, like George Meade, Class of 1835, had their hands full, leading small infantry units with bayonets and swords through high brush. As Taylor's men closed on the Mexican lines hard fighting broke out. Here American discipline and training made the difference. The Mexicans fought bravely but American units turned the flank and burst through the line, and suddenly the Mexican army was in a rout, running away. Panic spread among them and many drowned trying to swim the Rio Grande to escape.

Taylor set out for Monterrey, in the interior. On this march he took with him all his regulars but only one third of the volunteers. Young

U.S. Grant's horsemanship was famous even before he left the Academy, where in the early 1840s he supposedly set a high jump record that stood for twenty-five years. Above: He rode through a hail of shot at the Battle of Monterrey to bring fresh ammunition for his regiment. Top: Grant '43 wore his uniform proudly at first, but when some girls jeered at him he lost his taste for brass buttons.

The Mexican General Santa Anna caught Zachary Taylor by surprise at Buena Vista, but discipline and artillery won the day anyway. The painting at left is from an on-the-spot sketch by one of Taylor's aides. The Americans in the foreground are galloping up to reinforce the line. Inset: In this painting by William Carl Brown, Taylor (center) confers with his staff, including William Wallace Smith Bliss '33, Braxton Bragg '37, Joseph Horace Eaton '35, Robert Selden Garnett '41, Thomas Beasly Linnard '29 and Joseph K. Fenno Mansfield '21. Taylor's favorite horse, "Old Whitey," stands ready.

Top: Jefferson Davis carried this percussion pistol. Davis left the Army on graduation but volunteered for the Mexican War at the head of his Mississippi Rifles, who turned the tide of battle at Buena Vista. Below, in descending order, are three West Pointers who became important Civil War leaders: Robert E. Lee, George B. McClellan, and P.G.T. Beauregard.

Robert E. Lee drew this map of Cerro Gordo during the Mexican War. Scott depended on Lee's tireless reconnaissance and resourceful analysis of the terrain for the daring march on Mexico City.

Lieutenant Grant, to his immense disgust, was taken out of his infantry unit and assigned to the quartermaster corps to wrangle mules.

Arriving at Monterrey, capital of Nuevo Leon, Taylor and his engineers, including Major Joseph K. Mansfield '22, and Lieutenant John Pope '42, found the walled city heavily fortified, with 10,000 Mexican soldiers, and several strongholds built on high ground outside. With half his men Taylor attempted a frontal assault, which got nowhere and cost many lives. The new artillery was of little use against a dug-in enemy whose superior positions gave him enfilading fire.

Nonetheless, Captain Braxton Bragg '37, took his battery straight into the defenders' fire, until all his horses were shot down. His men dragged the guns to safety, while Bragg calmly removed the harness from the horses. He sent his lieutenant, Sam French '43, to retrieve the sword of a dead soldier, but when French brought back also the man's pocket knife Bragg frowned. "It is not public property, Mr. French." In spite of Bragg's boldness and punctilio, Taylor's army had stalled out in front of Monterrey.

But the other half of Taylor's army had circled around to the west; these men were making a dent against the entrenched Mexican forces, although it was not until the next day that they seized the main strong point on that side of the city. The day following, both wings of the American army attacked the city.

Lieutenant Grant, sick of being stuck with mules, had managed to get back to his old Fourth Infantry Regiment, which went charging into Monterrey with fixed bayonets. Mexican soldiers fought street by street, using the adobe buildings for cover and firing their artillery straight down the long avenues from the plaza. Texans, who knew adobe, showed Taylor's

army how to deal with this; with pickaxes and guns they battered their way in through the side walls of the adobe houses, avoiding entirely the open streets with their hailstorms of bullets and shot. Young Grant's troops ran out of ammunition; he leapt on a horse and galloped back to headquarters, sliding down along the horse's side as he crossed the broad avenues where the cannons roared. Untouched, he reached headquarters and got more ammunition for his men. With the Americans closing in on the plaza, the surviving Mexicans asked for terms—and Taylor let them march out of the city, on the promise not to fight again. Of course, they did.

Taylor's campaign, with other, much smaller campaigns in California and New Mexico, had severed the north of Mexico. The Mexican government nevertheless refused to make peace, which led to the second half of the doubleheader. General Winfield Scott prepared to land at Vera Cruz and march on Mexico City, in the center of the country, to force the government to accept defeat.

To do this Scott stripped Taylor of most of his regulars, everybody figuring that the Mexicans would concentrate against the obvious threat of the invasion at Vera Cruz. Instead, the Mexican General Santa Anna attacked Taylor, camped with 4,759 men in the north at Buena Vista.

The colorful and mystifying Santa Anna marched his army across the desert to take Taylor by surprise; his huge army arrived already half-starved and exhausted, but Taylor wasn't ready for them, and the American volunteers on his left flank gave way before the first wild Mexican charge. A regiment of red-shirted Mississippi men, commanded by Colonel Jefferson Davis '28, rushed to hold the position. Mexican heavy cavalry charged them; Davis formed his men into a funnel shape, and when

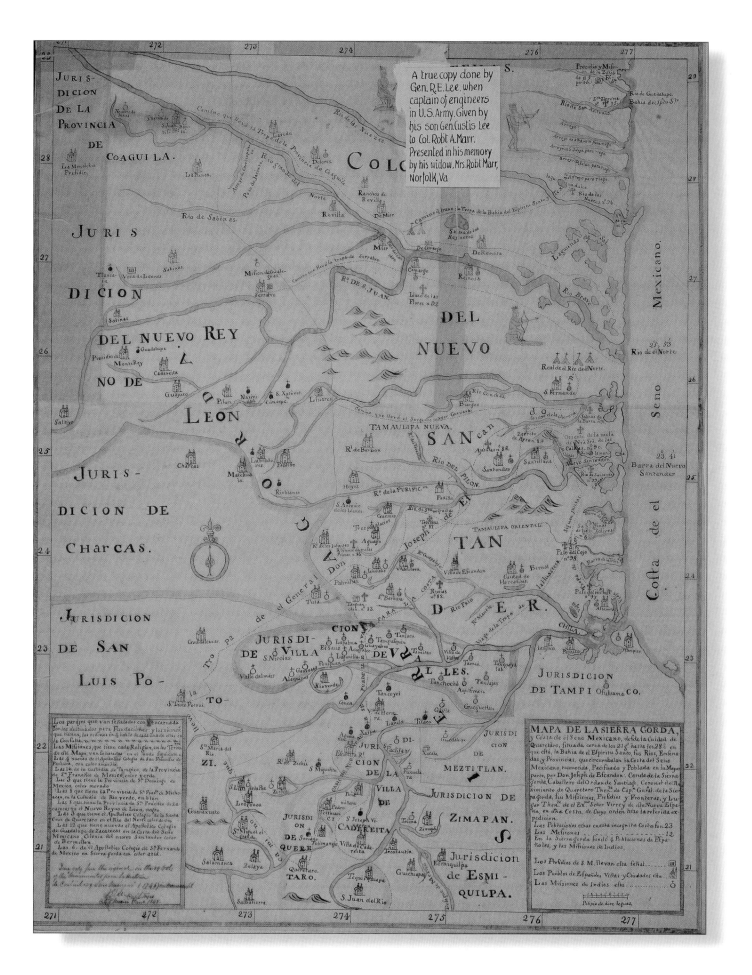

the Mexicans rode into the open end, the rifle-men opened fire from either side. Its vanguard mowed down, the Mexican assault crumpled.

Davis got no rest. Gathering his Mississippians he charged across the field to help bolster Taylor's right flank, now under infantry attack. Braxton Bragg was commanding a three gun battery, with Lieutenant George H. Thomas '40, and Thomas W. Sherman '36, manning batteries alongside him. Taylor sat calmly on his old horse Whitey and ordered, "Doubleshot your guns and give 'em hell." The guns blasted holes in the oncoming Mexican lines, but the enemy still struggled gamely forward, until Davis' Mississippi rifles opened fire and riddled them. Santa Anna's army reeled back, bloodied and dis-heartened. Taylor had lost huge numbers of men, but the Mexican general called it quits and marched his army away again.

Winfield Scott, meanwhile, was landing at Vera Cruz. He had ordered Colonel Ethan Allen Hitchcock '17, to assemble him a staff of West Point men; the only officer Scott asked for by name was the captain of engineers, Robert E. Lee, of Virginia. Hitchcock added Pierre Gustave Toutant Beauregard '38, and Lieutenant George B. McClellan '46.

Scott began by pounding Vera Cruz into sub-mission with four days of terrific bombardment. Then he pushed west, toward Mexico City, try-ing to get away from the swampy coast before the yellow fever season began. Santa Anna was ready for him at a round-topped hill called Cerro Gordo, which the Mexicans had heavily fortified. Under Scott's orders, Lee and Beauregard found a way around the hill, dragged artillery up to fire on Cerro Gordo from the side, and broke the Mexican defense. Thousands of enemy soldiers surrendered, and Santa Anna himself was nearly captured. General Scott lost

U. S. forces storm Chapultepec, September 13, 1847. The ancient seat of Aztec emperors, Chapultepec overlooked Mexico City; when the Stars and Stripes replaced the Mexican tricolor, the capitol below was doomed.

Counterclockwise, from below: Cadets drilled with artillery on the Plain. The drawing classroom's good natural lighting also permitted this early photograph. Louis Bentz, a German immigrant with the Artillery Corps, was assigned to blow all bugle calls during the day, for changes of class, church call, and so on. His dog Hans was always in attendance. Cadet quarters, sketched here, were drafty, bare, cold, and subject to frequent inspections. Cadets hid contraband food supplies up the chimney.

only sixty-three dead.

However, he promptly lost 3,000 more, volunteers who announced that their terms of enlistment were up, and they were going home, thank you. Scott had to wait until more reinforcements arrived to pick up the advance again. By that time, Santa Anna had raised another army, which was waiting for the Americans in the Valley of Mexico.

The only approaches to the capital of Mexico were along causeways above the surrounding marshes and lakes. Santa Anna had stuffed his men into strong points on these causeways, but once again, Scott called on Captain Robert E. Lee, and Lee found a way around one fortified point. Attacking from the flank, Scott's army drove the Mexicans out of their defenses in a matter of minutes.

With Mexico City only five miles away Scott faltered once more. He let Santa Anna shilly-shally around again, talking peace while raising another army. Scott ordered a division of 2,500 men to take an intervening foundry, El Molino del Rey, which turned out to be stuffed with enemy troops. In the ensuing battle only desperate heroics gave the victory to the Americans. Captain Robert Anderson '25, wounded early on, nonetheless worked his guns in the teeth of enemy fire, and then led his artillerymen into the foundry to fight hand to hand beside the infantry. The Americans took El Molino, but suffered terrific losses.

Now Scott turned to the nearby castle of Chapultepec, where about 1,600 Mexicans, including the teenaged cadets of the Mexican military academy, were dug in on a hill. Scott sent Lee to oversee the bombardment of Chapultepec, and directed the Fourth Infantry, where Lieutenant Grant was now fighting, to hold the ground on the left, where Santa Anna

had a force of some 5,000 men ready to attack when the advancing Americans exposed their flank.

Shielded behind a breastwork, a Mexican battery was pounding the causeway just ahead of them. An American gun had foundered there, falling into the ditch, its horses shot. The lieutenant who commanded it, however, was walking around beside the gun, trying to rouse his men, who had taken shelter in the ditch from the deadly barrage.

"There's no danger," this young man called, strolling around among the dead horses and the hail of shot. "See, I'm not hit." It was Thomas Jackson. One of his men finally crept out to help him and they dragged the gun back up out of the ditch and aimed it at the breastwork. Jackson began loading and firing the gun pointblank at the Mexican battery. Captain John Bankhead Magruder '30, came up to join him; together they hauled another cannon up beside the first, and the Mexican gunners lost heart and ran. The infantry stormed the breastwork and captured their guns.

At Chapultepec the main attack had reached the walls but had no ladders to scale them. When the ladders finally arrived, Lieutenant Lewis Armistead, who had not graduated with his class in 1837 but who had joined the army anyway, seized the Eighth Infantry's regimental colors and started forward. A bullet dropped him. Lieutenant James Longstreet '42, took the colors and went up the ladder. When he fell too, Lieutenant George Pickett, the flamboyant Immortal of the Class of 1846, grabbed the flag and raced up the wall, waded through the carnage inside the castle, reached the peak, pulled down the Mexican flag and raised the American colors.

Now came the assault on Mexico City itself.

Three of the most influential American teachers of the 19th century, these men, all West Point graduates, dominated the faculty of West Point for most of the 19th century. From top: Dennis Hart Mahan taught military science, William H. C. Bartlett, engineering, Albert Church, mathematics.

■ George Crook entered West Point to graduate thirty-eighth in a class of forty-three, the lowest-ranking cadet ever to rise to major general, U.S. Army. Became a noted Union commander in the Civil War and one of the most acclaimed leaders of the Indian Wars after 1865.

■ James Birdseye McPherson entered West Point where he would graduate first in his class and become one of the finest young leaders of the Civil War. A favorite of Grant and Sherman, they gave him command of the Army of the Tennessee. Killed at the Battle of Atlanta, 1864.

■ Graduates 1802–1850: 1,493; 1841–1850: 435.
■ The president of Brown University stated USMA graduates did "more to build up the system of internal improvement in the United States than [graduates of] all other colleges combined."

■ James Abbott McNeill Whistler entered as a member of the Class of 1855. A series of drawings depicting a cadet on guard duty, progressing from attentiveness to slumber, are still preserved in the USMA Library.

■ Robert E. Lee was named Superintendent of the Military Academy.

■ Philip Henry Sheridan graduated thirty-fourth of fifty-two. Sheridan took five years to complete West Point, suspended for a year for lunging at an upperclassman with a bayoneted musket; at graduation, he was only eleven demerits short of expulsion.

■ The West Point Museum founded, today recognized as housing the finest collection of military artifacts in North America.
■ James Ewell Brown "Jeb" Stuart graduated in the top third of his West Point class.

The desperate defenders forted up in the adobe buildings around the fortified San Cosme gate, sending volleys of musketry and artillery fire against anybody who tried to approach up the open streets. There were however buildings outside the gates; Lieutenant Grant and some of his men used them to cover a move well over to the left of San Cosme, dismantled a small gun, carried it up to a church belfry, and from this advantage bombarded the defenders inside the wall.

George McClellan and his engineering company, remembering the tactic from Monterrey, tunneled in through the empty houses to within close range of the gate, and climbed onto the flat roofs; from there they blasted the defenders with merciless fire. Finally, Henry J. Hunt '39, charged his artillery horses forward into the teeth of the Mexican cannon. When the horses went down Hunt and his men swung the gun around and began to fire at close range into the Mexican weapons massed behind the gate, and the defense faltered and the infantry rushed in and seized San Cosme.

At the next gate, Belen, Lieutenant Fitz-John Porter '45, single-handedly dragged an eight-inch howitzer up to the gate. When the Mexicans rushed out to capture him he sent them scuttling off with a barrage of canister, and

then began taking out the Mexican guns. One by one the Mexican batteries fell still, as the soldiers died or fled. By sundown Belen gate also was in American hands, and the guns were dropping exploding shells and canister into the central plaza of Mexico City.

During the night, Santa Anna skulked away. The next day, Winfield Scott entered Mexico City to the strains of Yankee Doodle, and the awed Mexicans came out to applaud. The Mexican War was over.

Individual Mexican soldiers were as brave and strong as their American counterparts, and far more numerous; they had the advantage of fighting on their own territory, fighting for their country and their honor. The generals on both sides made mistakes. The difference in the Mexican War was the officer corps from West Point. Their discipline, esprit de corps and training held the lines, reconnoitered the terrain, operated field artillery, and seized the strongholds, all in the face of a savage defense. They had proved their worth. West Point was safe.

The flanking movements that characterized the American assaults on Mexican positions had their origins in the classes of Dennis Hart Mahan, which all seniors took. One of Sylvanus Thayer's most momentous decisions had been to

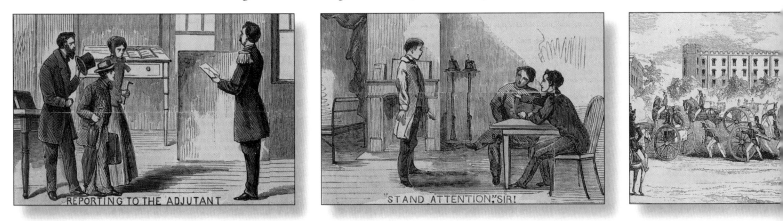

REPORTING TO THE ADJUTANT

"STAND ATTENTION, SIR!

■ In April, Colonel Robert E. Lee received orders to leave West Point and take his first field command in the West.

■ History was reintroduced to the curriculum after debate in the Academic Board.
■ Fitzhugh Lee [1835-1905], grandson of the famed Revolutionary War cavalry commander Henry "Light Horse Harry" Lee and nephew of Robert E. Lee, graduated near the bottom of his class. Later a Confederate General and successful businessman.

■ Professor of Spanish authorized.
■ Edward Porter Alexander [1835–1910] graduated third in his class. Revised "wig-wag" flag communication system and was a Confederate artillery commander.

■ The course of study was reduced to four years before being expanded again to five years in 1859 and again reduced to four years in 1861.

■ William Emory Merrill [1838–1891] graduated at the head of his class. During the Civil War, he was in charge of maintenance on 300 miles of railroad through the heart of the Confederacy that was the only line of communication to Federal forces in Tennessee and Georgia.

■ Graduates 1802–1860: 1,941; 1851–1860: 448.
■ Stephen Dodson Ramseur graduated from West Point. Attached to "Stonewall" Jackson's corps where he served with distinction at Chancellorsville and Gettysburg. Mortally wounded in 1864.

hire Mahan, the son of an Irish immigrant, right after he graduated first in his Class of 1824. The job lasted more than forty years, and began with a four year tour of France, during which Mahan visited French military academies and studied French military art, then fresh from the stunning victories and strategies of Napoleon Bonaparte.

Mahan came back from this tour steeped in French military culture. He taught at West Point until 1871, and wrote manuals and texts as well. (His son, naval historian Alfred Thayer Mahan, became president of the Naval War College in Newport, Rhode Island.) Superintendents came and went, but Mahan, and his fellow giants on the Academic Board, Bartlett and Alfred Ensign Church, who taught mathematics, were constants, and they dominated West Point's intellectual landscape.

As a student of Napoleon, Mahan believed in the decisive battle, the blow that broke an enemy and won the war in a single stroke. And he believed in attacking. "Carrying the war into the heart of the enemy's country is the surest way of making him share its burdens and foiling his plans." The cadets soaked this up as they absorbed the discipline of the parade ground and guard post. This imperative—attack, attack— would resonate up Cemetery Ridge and in the Bloody Angle, in Knoxville and Atlanta, and over the graves of thousands of Americans.

Mahan's influence extended beyond his classrooms. In 1852, he founded the Napoleon Club, in which the officers on duty at West Point met weekly in a large room of the Academic Building to study and discuss the campaigns of the French Emperor. George McClellan '46, delivered a celebrated paper to the Napoleon Club, on the War of 1812, in which he extolled the virtues of offensive warfare.

While he was at West Point, McClellan also translated a French manual on bayonets, and introduced the practical study of bayonet fighting to the officers and cadets. A few years later, while observing the Crimean War, he noticed the superior design of Hungarian cavalry saddles, and adapted it for American cavalry—the McClellan saddle, still in use.

McClellan left West Point in 1852, the same year that Robert E. Lee became superintendent of the Academy. The Superintendents who followed Thayer had less to do; the Academic Board refused anyway to deviate from Thayer's system (unless of course it was in their favor), and by the time Lee came to it, the office was mainly one of nursemaid to the cadets. Lee swiftly became one of the most popular super-

Five engravings from Cadet Life at West Point *by Theodore Davis show cadets reporting for their first day, drilling with field pieces, building field fortifications, and learning the niceties of the mortar.*

PRACTICAL MILITARY ENGINEERING

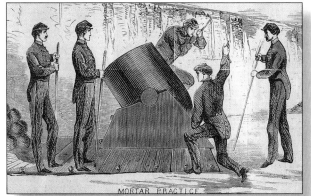

MORTAR PRACTICE

"IF SILICON WERE A GAS . . ."

In 1851, aged sixteen years and eleven months, James Abbott Whistler entered the United States Military Academy. His credentials were sterling: his appointment secured through the offices of Senator Daniel Webster, his father before him a successful and famous graduate of the Academy. But going to West Point was largely the idea of the young man's mother; she hoped to convert her dreamy, handsome, gifted son into a civil engineer as successful as his father.

George Washington Whistler, USMA 1819, had left the Army soon after graduation from West Point and gone into railroad building. Eventually he became the chief railroad engineer for the Czar of Russia. The boy James Whistler grew up largely in Saint Petersburg, where he drank up the Old World. He attended the Imperial Academy of Fine Arts; his earliest years he had loved to draw, and he immediately showed excellent promise.

Delicate of health, nearsighted, undisciplined, something of a rebel, he was, predictably, a failure at West Point. He shocked one of his professors by announcing he'd never heard of the Battle of Buena Vista. He acquired an outrageous 218 demerits in three years. Classmates remembered him falling off horses, sleeping through early morning roll calls, sneaking off to Benny Havens' Tavern for buckwheat cakes and flirtation. Only in his drawing classes did he excel, standing first in his class.

Drawings from his West Point days remain, but these disappointingly ordinary exercises hardly point to the work to come.

In his other classes he was lackluster, and Chemistry was ultimately his downfall. At an oral examination, asked to expound on the properties of silicon, he burst out, "Silicon is a gas." That was the end of his career at West Point.

Yet he was popular with his classmates, who nicknamed him Curly, for his mop of thick dark hair. In spite of his failure he loved the Academy. He thought he looked very well in the uniform, and enjoyed the aristocratic manners. Probably West Point got him away from his mother, who pelted the Superintendent with letters demanding special attention for her son.

Once dismissed, Whistler tried hard to have himself reinstated, and even in a last despairing clutch at the military life applied to the Naval Academy. Yet at West Point, clearly, he was already transforming himself from James Abbott Whistler, child of rock-ribbed and egalitarian Yankee technocrats, into James McNeill Whistler, non-conformist Bohemian dandy-cum-Russian-prince and the most important American painter of his era. Ever afterward, as he cut a romantic and fascinating figure in Europe's art scene, he referred to himself as "a West Point man." He never tired of announcing to adoring London society matrons, "If silicon were a gas, I would have been a general." The Academy had rejected James Whistler, but Whistler, all his life, prided himself on having once belonged there. —C.H.

At West Point James Whistler excelled only in his drawing classes. The postures of these two cadets, seen in early sketches, suggests his attitude toward Army discipline.

intendents in the Academy's history. Throughout his life the Virginian's character, dedication to duty, and consideration for others endeared him to everybody who had dealings with him. His tenure at West Point was no different.

His own son, George Washington Custis Lee, was a member of the Class of 1854, his nephew Fitz-Hugh Lee of the Class of 1856, and perhaps this gave him a special insight into what these young men were going through. In any case, he took a personal interest in each of his charges.

"Madam," he wrote, to a worried mother, "I regret to inform you that your son Cadet James A. Whistler is quite sick." The courtly letter that follows promises that the Academy will do everything to care for him. Typically, young Whistler, who would eventually make his mother far more famous than even she could have hoped for, was a poor student at West Point; Lee devoted much of his time to cadets in trouble. But Whistler, as it would turn out, was beyond help.

Lee coached, cajoled, and nursed along, and when he saw a boy was sure to fail, he wrote to the cadet's parents advising them to let him resign, rather than endure the humiliation of being dismissed. If anything he was too protective of the cadets, as later he would be protective of officers under his command, shielding them from the consequences of their own failings. He took their problems seriously, even trying to change the design of their helmets to make them more comfortable; the cadets admired and loved him.

But as a role model, Lee was without peer. His bearing was superb, his courtesy inexhaustible, his probity legendary: when his own nephew Fitz-Hugh got in trouble for drinking, Lee recommended his dismissal. The Secretary of War overruled him; Fitz-Hugh Lee went on to a long military career.

The Lees always had an active social life. At West Point the superintendent's house was large and had a fine garden, and Lee and his family were at home every weekend to calls from upperclassmen. On holidays they put on lavish receptions, often using George Washington's own silver service, which impressed the cadets immensely.

During long summer days, Lee rowed on the Hudson with his children, or explored the countryside on the mount he had ridden during the Mexican War, the mare Grace Darling. He and Mrs. Lee attended local concerts, entertained visiting dignitaries, supervised their enormous number of children. But the work of the Academy wore on Lee—the long hours and paperwork, the endless correspondence and the minutiae. When he was offered the colonelcy of the new 2nd Cavalry Regiment under Albert Sidney Johnston, he accepted, even though it meant posting to the remote frontier, far from his family and his beloved hilltop home at Arlington, Virginia.

In 1855, Lee left West Point for the last time, with the cadet band playing *Carry Me Back to Old Virginny*, in the rain. The wharf was crowded with officers telling him goodbye, and many of the cadets wept to see him go.

The country was sliding toward deadly partisan division. Robert E. Lee represented the ideal soldier, brave, honorable, and loyal. The crisis was coming that for many West Pointers would test the meaning of all those values, and Lee's character would set the tone for much of that as well.

Yet the noisiest struggle at West Point during these years was the endless tinkering with the curriculum. Under the direction of the Army

By 1857, as shown in this elaborate color print by Behrens and Meyer, West Point was an impressive campus, with substantial granite buildings and numerous elegant visitors. The Artillery and Sapper Depots, middle left in the print, still stand.

CADET BARRACKS.

ART'Y DEPOT.

SAPPER DEPOT.

MESS HALL.

GENERAL VIEW OF WEST POINT

ACADEMY

THE PLAIN.

HOTEL.

RIDE HALL

THE CAMP

LIBRARY.

CUSTER'S DEMERITS

Robert E. Lee is legendary for serving four years at the Academy without earning even a single demerit. At the other end of the spectrum is George Armstrong Custer, Class of 1861, who succeeded in piling up a record number of 869.

Late at parade, at tattoo, at supper, at reveille—ninety-one times in four years.

Collar unbuttoned, collar missing, wearing overcoat at dinner, etc. thirty-nine times.

Improper dressing/carrying rifle improperly twenty-one times, including "repeatedly allowing piece to rebound coming to an order arms at parade."

Clearly young Custer did not take the Academy all that seriously.

Boyish conduct at parade. Trifling in ranks, three times. Making boisterous noise in the sink. Throwing snow balls, three times. Throwing bread in the mess hall. Swinging his arms while marching. Cooking in his room. Cooking utensils in his room. Bread, butter, potatoes, knives and forks in his room.

The happy-go-lucky cadet's demerits ran in spurts. For ten days or more, he would manage to go clean, and then run up five or six in a day—twenty-three in two weeks—eighteen in one week—a mindboggling nine in one day. He clearly

did not take Army decorum seriously, and the astonishing list reveals a cadet too social for his own good.

Talking to sentinels. Talking while a sentinel. Asking for help in French. Chatting in drawing. Giving orders to a section not his own. Visiting after hours.

Custer distinguished himself not at all at the Academy, graduating last in his class in 1861. Only a few days before, he had drawn five demerits for his most serious infraction.

Gross neglect of duty, not suppressing a quarrel in the imediate [sic] vicinity of guard tent he being present.

This got him court-martialed. But the time favored Custer; with the Civil War at hand the Army was desperate for officers and Custer was allowed to graduate

Cadet George A. Custer

and enter the army. During the War Between The States, he served with courage and dash, and was brevetted a brigadier general. He is best known, however, for stumbling into the ambush that led to his death and the massacre of all 210 of his men at the Battle of the Little Big Horn, the Plains Indians' greatest victory against the Army. The demerits list was an accurate indicator of George Armstrong Custer's character, and his character was his fate.   —C.H.

Chief of Engineers and the Academic Board, Lee presided over a new structure, the Five Year Course. This was an ambitious effort to pack yet more into the cadets' education: by lengthening the tour of duty to five years, the Academy could require English grammar, history, geography and a range of classes in practical military science (such as making ammunition), and military law.

The cadets (and many of the faculty) hated the change. Although the Five Year Course reflected more liberal attitudes in several areas—assigning more leaves, overhauling the demerit system, allowing cadets to play chess, and smoke in camp—the cadets complained of having to

Cadets regularly drilled with their fire engine. The use of open fires to heat the rooms (and cook illegal snacks) often led to conflagrations.

George Ryan,
Connecticut

Charles H. Morgan,
New York

Haldemand Putnam,
New Hampshire

John C. Palfrey,
Massachusetts

In the years leading up to the Civil War, fistfights often broke out between cadets from North and South. In the years to come many on both sides would die fighting for what they believed in.

Four Northern cadets from Class of 1857

stay the extra year. Congress felt the pressure, and in 1858 the Army abruptly dropped the scheme. Within the year, the Five Year Plan's supporters were clamoring to bring it back; Congress hemmed and hawed over it until the guns at Fort Sumter drove the issue into the background.

In other ways West Point was changing with the times. In 1857, for the first time, the Academy conducted graduation ceremonies, with speeches and commemorative music and the presentation of diplomas. Around the same time, each group of graduates began to have its class photograph taken.

Slowly, as the decade wore on, the uproar and unrest of the outside world was penetrating the Academy's walls. The crisis of the Union was approaching. The powerful nationalizing influence of a school devoted to the training of officers for the United States Army could not suppress entirely the centrifugal resistance of the Southerners. At the beginning of the decade, opposites like O.O. Howard, Class of 1854, and James E.B. Stuart, nicknamed "Beauty," could be friends, but only a few years later trouble was more apparent.

Morris Schaff '58, noticed the sectional rivalry and attributed it (being himself a Ohioan) to the arrogance and willingness to fight of the Southerners. For years the Dialectical Society refused any debate on the subject of whether or not a state could legally secede, but in 1857 cadets proposed to divide the Society in two—one debating club for the South, one for the North—as if the two parts of the country had no common ground to argue on. In 1858, the superintendent refused to allow cadets to go to church in Buttermilk Falls, because the preacher was an abolitionist. The Academy did all it could to keep the lid on.

Ironically, even Jefferson Davis, then Secretary of War, praised the Academy's efforts to instill in the cadets a spirit "generalized as broad as the continent." But as the nation split in two, many a young man faced a wrenching personal decision: whether to remain at West Point, under oath to serve the United States, or go back home to make war on her. Cadet Edward Anderson of Virginia wrote to his mother that he wept over the choice. West Point was coming apart, just as the Union was coming apart.

E. Porter Alexander,
Georgia

George W. Holt,
Alabama

John S. Marmaduke,
Missouri

William P. Smith,
Virginia

Four Southern cadets from Class of 1857

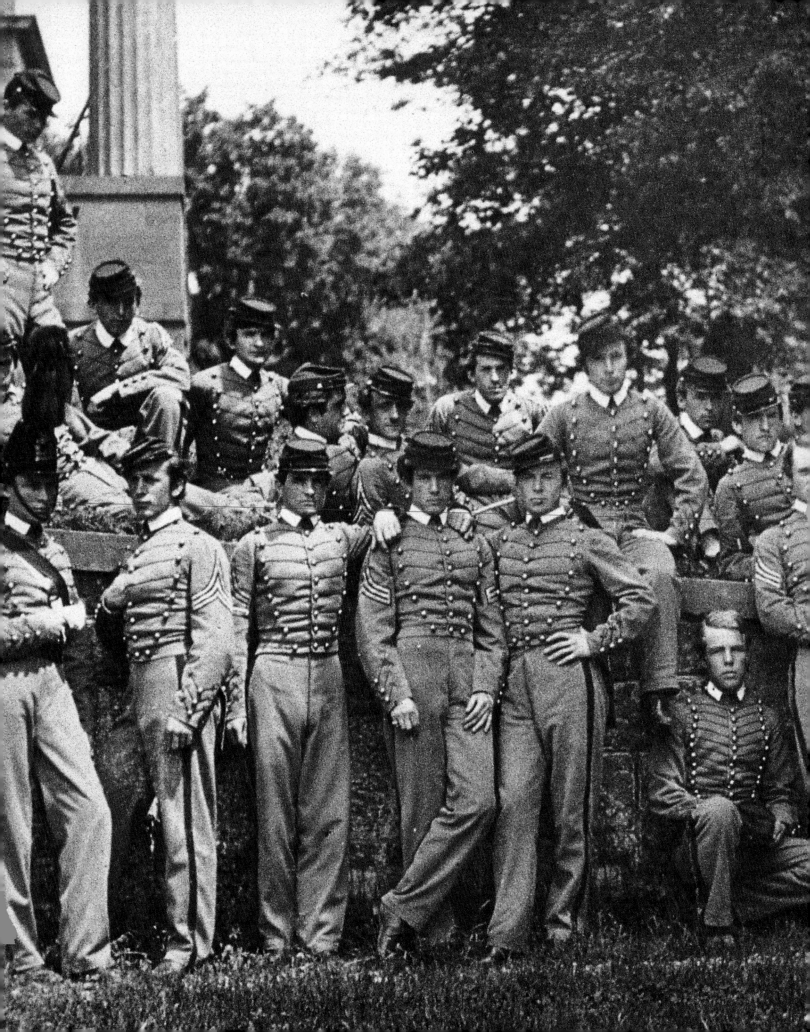

3
WEST POINT IN THE CIVIL WAR

BY STEPHEN W. SEARS

"We cannot hesitate; we must
either make up our minds to fight
under the Stars and Stripes . . . or
we must resign at once and free
ourselves from that solemn oath to
serve the United States honestly
and faithfully . . . ."

—Thomas Rowland,
Virginia, Class of 1861

■ Fitzhugh Lee [nephew of Robert E. Lee], a tactical officer at West Point, decided to go with the Confederacy. On departing West Point, he shook hands with each cadet in his company, and mounted his horse to depart. As he rode off, the Corps turned out spontaneously and saluted him.
■ First shots of the Civil War: Fort Sumter, April 4.

■ As the first step in the strategic penetration of the South, U.S. Grant captures Fort Henry on the Tennessee River and Fort Donelson on the Cumberland.
■ Lincoln visits West Point in June.
■ Battles of Shiloh, Antietam, and Fredericksburg.

In February 1861, with the nation riven by the secession crisis, the commemoration of Washington's Birthday seemed certain to assume special significance on the West Point calendar. At 6:00 a.m. on the 22nd, in place of reveille, the cadets were roused by the corps band playing national airs. This was greeted in the barracks by hisses from Southerners and by cheers from Northerners. At 11:30 a.m. all officers, faculty, and the entire corps of cadets assembled in the chapel. The uniform of the day included cross belts, sidearms, and bayonets, and the corps marched in to the accompaniment of the band. The colors were paraded to the altar. Then came the traditional reading of Washington's Farewell Address. It was soon evident that this historic plea for national unity by the Father of His Country was falling that day on deaf ears. As cadet Morris Schaff remembered it, "the very air of the room was filled with foreboding."

PRECEDING SPREAD: Left, members of the Class of 1863 posed in front of the Academic Building. All wear Union Army kepis; all would soon be off to the battlefields of the Civil War. On the right are George A. Custer '61 and his recently captured Confederate friend and West Point classmate James B. Washington, the great-grand nephew of the first president. This photo was taken just before Washington was led off to prison.

This symbolic day could hardly end without some symbolic demonstration. It occurred at tattoo. In the Cadet Barracks, over the course of recent years, Northerners had come to congregate in the east wing while Southerners tended to occupy the west and south wing. The central sally port served as a virtual Mason-Dixon Line. That evening, replacing the usual tattoo beaten by drum, the band assembled on the Plain and marched to the barracks playing martial music. By Morris Schaff's account, "every room fronting the area was aglow, every window up and filled with men." The first selection, *Washington's March*, aroused few passions. Then, approaching the sally port, the band swung into *The Star Spangled Banner*. From the east wing the response was a barrage of cheering—strictly against regulations—led by second classman George Armstrong Custer of Ohio. That ovation was promptly answered from the west wing with thunderous cries for *Dixie*, orchestrated by one of Custer's best friends, Texas's Thomas L. Rosser '61. It was apparent that West Point was not to be exempt from the deep and widening fissure between North and South.

The crisis had begun for both West Point and the country with the presidential contest of 1860. It had long been recognized that politics was a peculiar preoccupation among the Southern cadets, but in this election they raised the stakes to a new and divisive level. "At this time," wrote Peter S. Michie '63, ". . . the cadets had by some gradual process become separated into two parties, hostile in sentiment and even divided in barracks." When a straw poll conducted by Southern cadets unexpectedly produced sixty-four votes for Abraham Lincoln, the poll's distressed organizers set about identifying the "Black Republicans" in their midst. One of those who admitted his abolitionist sentiments, Tully McCrae of Ohio, soon found his life made miserable by his orderly sergeant, an Alabamian. "Politics are 'raging high' here now and we hear nothing but talk of disunion," McCrae wrote home on October 27. "Some of the cadets from the southern states had a disunion meeting last night and are going to go home if Lincoln is elected."

Lincoln became president-elect on

■ During New York draft riots, rumors of threats to burn Cold Spring Foundry and West Point caused issue of ball ammunition and establishment of picket duty for cadets.
■ The Battle of Gettysburg July 1–3, the "High Tide of the Confederacy"; Vicksburg surrenders.

■ Ulysses S. Grant was made General in Chief of the Armies of the United States.
■ Battles of the Wilderness, Spotsylvania, Petersburg, and Atlanta.

■ Lee surrenders to Grant at Appomatox Court House, VA, April 9.
■ Joseph E. Johnston '29 surrenders to William T. Sherman '40 in Durham, NC, April 26.
■ In sixty major battles, fifty-five had USMA graduates commanding on both sides; the other five had graduates commanding on one side.

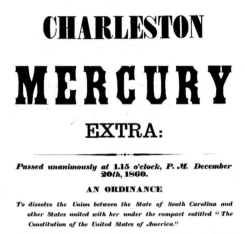

CHARLESTON

MERCURY

EXTRA:

Passed unanimously at 1.15 o'clock, P. M. December 20th, 1860.

AN ORDINANCE

To dissolve the Union between the State of South Carolina and other States united with her under the compact entitled " The Constitution of the United States of America."

We, the People of the State of South Carolina, in Convention assembled, do declare and ordain, and it is hereby declared and ordained,

That the Ordinance adopted by us in Convention, on the twenty-third day of May, in the year of our Lord one thousand seven hundred and eighty-eight, whereby the Constitution of the United States of America was ratified, and also, all Acts and parts of Acts of the General Assembly of this State, ratifying amendments of the said Constitution, are hereby repealed; and that the union now subsisting between South Carolina and other States, under the name of " The United States of America," is hereby dissolved.

THE

UNION
IS
DISSOLVED!

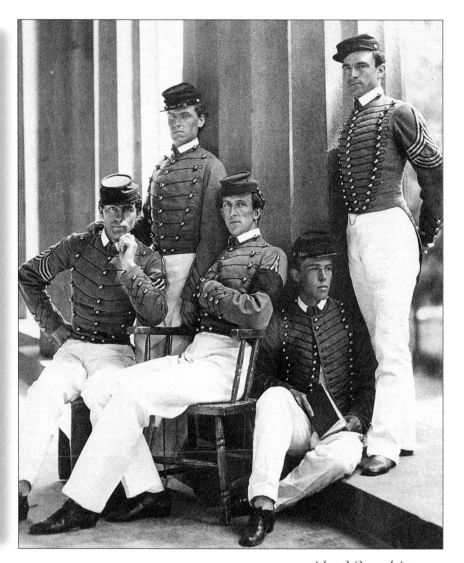

November 6, 1860, and South Carolina, having promised to secede if a Republican was elected, made good its pledge on December 20. South Carolinian Henry S. Farley, a third classman, did not wait even that long, resigning from the Military Academy on November 19. Farley led what was soon to became a steady parade of Southern cadets who declared allegiance to their respective states superior to allegiance to the nation as defined by their West Point oath. Tom Rosser's noisy barracks demonstration on Washington's Birthday proved to be the last major incident of its kind, for by the coming of spring 1861 there were too few Southerners remaining in the corps of cadets to make much noise of any kind.

For Southern underclassmen the decision to

A broadside proclaims the secession of South Carolina. Above: Cadets felt the pressure to choose sides. This group includes young men from the classes of '60 and '61. The mourning band was a common item of 19th century attire.

The Civil War began on April 12, 1861, with the bombardment of Ft. Sumter in Charleston Harbor, above, in this print by Currier and Ives.

give up their appointments was perhaps less agonizing than for many upperclassmen who could look back on four or five years of close comradeship with their fellow cadets. For plebe John W. Wofford, for example, seeking to leave the Academy immediately rather than wait upon the secretary of war's formal acceptance of his resignation, the decision was one of heartfelt but simple expediency. "There can be no doubt that my native state, South Carolina, will take her destiny in her own hands for weal or woe . . . ," he explained. "And I (being an only son) think it a most sacred duty to protect my mother in time of danger."

For other cadets the decision was neither that easy nor that quick. The painful crises of conscience generated by the rushing currents of sectionalism is exemplified by a pair of first class-

men, roommates Henry Algernon du Pont of Delaware and Llewellyn G. Hoxton of Virginia. Cadet du Pont was the son of Henry du Pont '33, head of the E.I. du Pont de Nemours Company and a fervent Republican—a party his son was opposed to "root and branch."

Initially, as the secession crisis deepened, young du Pont seemed confident of his course. "The future certainly looks very dark & threatening," he wrote, ". . . and if it is to be our lot to be employed in cutting our countrymen's throats and fighting our dearest friends and classmates, I am very sorry I ever came here." He hoped that the South's secession, if it came, would be accomplished peacefully, "so as to give a man a chance to get out of such a position by resigning as fast as he can." But gradually the belligerency of the Cotton States of the Deep

South—all of which had seceded by February 1, 1861—began to change du Pont's thinking. He concluded that Southern fire-eaters, rather than seeking peaceful compromise and separation, were actively courting war, "and I deem the sanguinary and blood-thirsty speeches these men are constantly making, perfectly revolting." When the new Confederacy initiated hostilities at Fort Sumter, it determined du Pont to graduate with his class (he finished first in class ranking) and to remain loyal to the Union.

He fully expected his roommate and close friend, Virginian Llewellyn Hoxton, to do the same. A report of Hoxton's resignation, du Pont wrote home, "is altogether without foundation. He is too sensible to do anything of the kind. He is a moderate, conservative man in his views . . . . Even should Virginia secede he will stay & graduate if he honorably can." Hoxton did indeed graduate, and even received his duty assignment, to the St. Louis Arsenal, but (as du Pont wrote) "He is in a very distressed state of mind in consequence of certain letters he has recently received from his friends who are red-hot seces-

sionists." Soon thereafter Llewellyn Hoxton saw it as his duty to go with his home state of Virginia. "I have been very much pained at the conduct of some of my best and most intimate friends of other days, but friends of mine no longer now," Henry du Pont wrote, mentioning Hoxton by name. "However, the less said about the business the better."

Cadet Hoxton's ordeal of conscience lasted some four months, for Virginia did not secede until April 1861. With South Carolina leading the march out of the Union in December 1860, her native sons at West Point endured far less suspense. Before the year was out all eight South Carolinians in the corps of cadets were gone. Then, between January 9 and February 1, six more states of the Deep South—Mississippi, Florida, Alabama, Georgia, Louisiana, and Texas—left the Union and, in Montgomery, Alabama, formed the Confederate States of America. Their native sons would leave West Point in near unanimity—thirty-eight of the thirty-nine cadets from the Deep South cast their lot with the Confederacy. Cadets from the

The Union officers at Ft. Sumter, below, left, included (seated, from left) Capt. Abner Doubleday '42, supposed inventor of baseball, Col. Robert Anderson '25, commander of the fort, Dr. Samuel Wylie Crawford, and Col. John Gray Foster '46, a fortifications specialist. From left, standing, are Truman Seymour '46, George W. Snyder, Jefferson Columbus Davis, and R.K. Meade. Below, right: P.G.T. Beauregard '38 was named Superintendent of West Point in January; four months later he commanded the attack on Fort Sumter.

McClellan won his wife Nellie away from another ardent suitor, A.P. Hill '47 (above), who became one of the Confederacy's most important generals. Hill may have taken out his disappointment in love by frustrating McClellan's plans whenever possible.

four late-comers to the Confederate nation—Virginia, Arkansas, Tennessee, and North Carolina—may have agonized longer over their decisions, but they too chose states' rights over a Union indivisible. In the end, only four Southern cadets who were at West Point during the secession crisis remained with the Union. The seventy-six others all went South.

Thomas Rowland of Virginia, first-ranked in his class, stated the case succinctly: "We cannot hesitate; we must either make up our minds to fight under the Stars and Stripes . . . or we must resign at once and free ourselves from that solemn oath to serve the United States honestly and faithfully. . . . I have been so long in suspense between Union and Secession that my mind is almost equally prepared for either event." When Virginia seceded, so did Rowland, with regrets. The mood was more cheerful among those who had no reservations about their course. "Two of the best in the second class started this afternoon," wrote Tully McCrae of Ohio. "They were accompanied to the dock by a large crowd of their friends and carried part of the way on the shoulders of the crowd of secessionists who cheered them as they left." One of the two, Charles P. Ball of Alabama, had ranked first in the class due to graduate in 1862. Ball exercised the privilege of addressing the corps after supper on the day he left. "Battalion, attention!" he cried. "Good-bye, boys! God bless you all!"

For first classman John Pelham of Alabama, destined to be one of the premier Confederate artillerists of the Civil War, the only indecision in his course was the honorable way to carry it out. "He does not intend to serve in the army," Henry du Pont wrote of Pelham, "but will resign as soon as he graduates, which is quite right under the circumstances, as he cannot be expected to fight against his home and friends."

A Surprise Visitor

IN JUNE OF 1862, with the Civil War raging, President Abraham Lincoln paid a surprise visit to West Point. He planned to consult with Professor Dennis Hart Mahan and General Winfield Scott, then in residence, on the conduct of the war, which was going badly for the Union; perhaps also he wanted to show his support for the Academy at a time when many of its graduates had joined the Confederacy.

Winfield Scott, victor of the Mexican War, was the country's senior soldier. The young and splendid George McClellan had forced him into retirement at the beginning of the war, but Scott's strategy, called the Anaconda Plan, was the only part of the Union's war that seemed to be working: blockading the South's seacoasts, seizing the Mississippi Valley, and squeezing the life out of the Confederacy. Scott (who, no West Pointer himself, nonetheless held the Academy in highest regard) met Lincoln with all the pomp expected of a man known as Old Fuss and Feathers, and escorted him to Cozzen's Hotel, in Buttermilk Falls, where the President would stay. Perhaps, during their meeting, Lincoln apologized for his part in McClellan's humiliating Scott into retirement.

After their conference the President toured the summer encampment on the Plain, went through the Academic Building, inspected the Riding Hall and the Library. In the Academic Building, he visited the room where the Napoleon Club met, and was so fascinated by the great wall map of Napoleon's campaigns that he asked for a copy—and, to the great pleasure of Professor Mahan, for a copy of *Outpost*, Mahan's legendary text on military science. Lincoln met the entire first class, and asked especially to speak to those cadets he himself had appointed.

He had offered an appointment to another young man, who would go on to become a general and father of an Academy graduate who would also become a general, but young Arthur MacArthur was so eager to get into the war that he turned down West Point and rode off with a volunteer regiment.

The President's next stop was the Foundry at Cold Spring, which was producing a steady supply of cannon; the commanding officer demonstrated the range of several of his pieces by firing them across the river at the Crow's Nest Mountain. Lincoln went back to review the cadet corps on parade, and in the evening boarded the steamer for the trip down the Hudson.

It was the first visit by a sitting president since James Monroe came up in 1817. A few months later, the Napoleon Club sent on the map, with their compliments. Meanwhile the Anaconda tightened its grip on the South, and the bloody tragic war went on, with West Point men on both sides.

—*C.H.*

Pelham determined it would be dishonorable to accept a commission from Alabama's governor while holding a U.S. government appointment, and for professional reasons he wanted to have his West Point degree. But after Fort Sumter the secretary of war ordered all Academy faculty and cadets to take an oath of allegiance. John Pelham submitted his resignation and left for Alabama.

The question of loyalty among cadets from the border states—Maryland, Delaware, Kentucky, and Missouri—proved not surprisingly to be just as tangled as it was for their home folks. West Point's cadets divided painfully but sharply on the issue—twelve from the border states went South while ten went North.

The turmoil at the Military Academy affected officers as well as cadets. On January 23, 1861, Major Pierre Gustave Toutant Beauregard '38 arrived to assume the superintendency from Major Richard Delafield. Three days later, Louisiana, Beauregard's native state, seceded. Two days after that, the secretary of war revoked Beauregard's appointment and ordered Delafield back to the superintendent's post. Beauregard protested, claiming he had no intention of going with his state unless secession finally resulted in war. The war secretary had good cause to suspect otherwise. When a cadet from Louisiana had

Simon Bolivar Buckner

Ulysses S. Grant

In the painting at right, Grant, typically on horseback, watches the siege of Fort Donelson in the winter of 1862. Simon Bolivar Buckner '44 (above left), who graduated a year after Grant, commanded the defense. In New York City, long before the War, Buckner had given the destitute and discouraged Grant money; at the humiliating surrender, Grant, embarrassed and saddened, could say nothing, but only stuffed a wad of bills into Buckner's hands and turned away.

sought Beauregard's advice on resigning, he was told, "Watch me; and when I jump, you jump." Beauregard jumped just three weeks later, and was appointed a full general in the Confederate States army.

The most popular tactical officer on the post, Virginian Fitzhugh Lee, also felt obliged to go with his state when it voted for secession—the same decision his uncle, Robert E. Lee, was then making. Tully McCrae, a member of Lieutenant Lee's company, wrote that Lee "went to every room and shook hands with every one of us, with tears in his eyes . . . . He said that he was sorry to leave, but as he belonged to the other side of the line, it was time that he was going." The next morning the company gathered in front of the barracks to see him off, waving their caps as he drove past in the omnibus. That, it was said, was a unique honor to be awarded any "Tac" officer. In due course, some in that company would again meet Fitz Lee, general of Confederate cavalry, on the battlefield.

The bombardment of Fort Sumter on April 12 galvanized the corps of cadets. (The signal gun that opened the bombardment was fired by Lieutenant Henry S. Farley of the South Carolina artillery, the first to resign from the Military Academy following Lincoln's election. It proved to be Farley's biggest moment of the war.) The talk of everyone now, Tully McCrae wrote, was "nothing but war and rumors of war. . . . Textbooks are ignored and in their stead are placed the daily New York papers. . . ." Within a week virtually all the remaining Southerners at the Academy had resigned or been dismissed for

refusing to take the newly imposed oath of allegiance. Northern cadets were inspirited by President Lincoln's call for troops to suppress the rebellion. McCrae attended a Union meeting where "such cheers were never heard before . . . . At call to quarters, when the meeting broke up, all marched out of barracks to the tune of Yankee Doodle. . . ."

Amidst the excitement generated by Fort Sumter the members of the Class of 1861, scheduled to graduate in June, got up a petition addressed to the secretary of war calling for their early graduation so as to "take our places among those who are serving their country and defending its flag." The petition was promptly approved, with May 6 set for their graduation. There was no formal commencement ceremony, only an oath-taking and the issue of diplomas, followed by rounds of cheering and speech-making in the mess hall. Nor was any leave granted.

Orders the next day sent this May 1861 class off to Washington to drill the volunteer regiments starting to flood into the capital. A party of some thirty of the newly minted second lieutenants, after stopping over in New York to buy their arms and accouterments, was arrested by police in Philadelphia on a tip that they were secession-minded rebels supplying arms to the Confederacy. Producing their War Department orders at the station house won their release and a red-faced display of "great courtesy" by their erstwhile captors. In Washington General-in-Chief Winfield Scott, with an obvious show of relief, greeted them personally.

The class scheduled to graduate in 1862 now clamored for early release—to graduate in the

The Corps of Cadets lined up in front of the barracks for this photograph, ca. 1864, the oldest of its kind. During these years the classes seldom numbered more than 280 men.

traditional four years instead of five as planned. Desperate for trained officers of any description and of any age, the War Department agreed. This decision marked the abrupt end of the five-year curriculum. Graduation was set for June 24, but the transition from second classmen to first classmen between April and June was something of a nightmare for the cadets. "This method of cramming a year's course into two months' time is rather hard on us," wrote cadet Francis H. Parker. "I never studied so hard and did so poorly as I am doing now." It happened that another Parker in the class, James P. of Missouri, in last place academically, was dismissed for leaving to

Insouciant cadets clowned around on the pleasant tree-shaded lane that was Professors Row in the mid-1860s.

John Pelham '61 was the epitome of Southern chivalry. When a shell killed him at Kelly's Ford early in 1863 the whole South mourned.

join the Confederacy. Parker's departure left his roommate, George Armstrong Custer, by himself at the foot of the class—the June 1861 Class Immortal, or "Goat." Characteristically, cadet Custer was in arrest at the time.

Overall, of the 239 cadets at West Point at the time of the secession crisis, 151 (63.2 per cent) would stand with the Union and eighty-eight (36.8 per cent) would take up the cause of the Confederacy. What became by War Department fiat two 1861 classes, May and June, would between them send seventy-one officers into the Union army and thirty-nine into the Confederate army. This double class of 1861, plus the forty-nine from the rest of the corps of cadets who pledged themselves to the Confederacy in 1861, account for exactly two-thirds of the soldiers West Point contributed from the classes of 1861-1864 to both armies during the Civil War. As it happened, these West Pointers of '61, as they may be called, produced the most generals, the most wartime casualties, and the most attention, then and since.

That attention, of course, has focused primarily on George Armstrong Custer, June 1861's Class Immortal, who as a staff officer and a cavalryman fought first to last in the battles of the Army of the Potomac. In 1863 Custer was jumped from first lieutenant to brigadier general, and by war's end, at age twenty-five, he was a major general of volunteers. Custer's arch foe in numerous battles was Tom Rosser, his old West Point friend and now a Confederate cavalry general. After the war, in the West, the two would renew their friendship. Reports of Custer in battle at the Little Big Horn in 1876 set railroad man Rosser to organizing a rescue column until word came that it was too late.

Including Custer and Rosser, the West Pointers of '61 produced eleven wartime gener-

al officers, six Union and five Confederate. Adelbert Ames of Maine would advance from the 5th U.S. Artillery to command of the famous 20th Maine regiment to command of a division that captured Fort Fisher on the North Carolina coast in 1865. Emory Upton would prove himself an innovative infantry tactician with the Army of the Potomac at Spotsylvania in 1864. Another Class of '61 Union general who gained notice, or at least notoriety, was Judson Kilpatrick, who led a bungled cavalry raid on Richmond in 1864 but went on to command a cavalry division in Sherman's march through Georgia and the Carolinas. "I know that Kilpatrick is a hell of a damned fool," said Sherman, "but I want just that sort of a man to command my cavalry on this expedition." Fighting against damned fool Kilpatrick in the Carolinas was the Confederate cavalry general Pierce Manning Butler Young of the June 1861 class. In November 1863 Young's classmate John H. Kelly of Alabama became the Confederacy's youngest brigadier general, at age twenty-three. Ten months later Kelly was mortally wounded near Franklin, Tennessee.

A goodly number of the West Pointers of '61 first served in the engineers or the artillery, where their specialized skills were prized by these early raw armies. No less than forty-three Federals from the 1861 classes, for example, were present at the war's first major action, at Bull Run on July 21. Captain Charles Griffin's West Point Battery fought at the very center of the action and was all but demolished. Just one gun and one limber of the six-gun battery were saved. Lieutenant Adelbert Ames, commanding one of the battery's two-gun sections, was badly wounded and earned a Medal of Honor for his actions that day. Ames would be the first of seven Medal of Honor winners from the West Point

classes of 1861. (At the other end of the spectrum was a single deserter, who fled to Canada after eight months' service.)

As battle followed on battle, casualties kept grim pace. Of the 159 cadets who went to war in 1861, twenty-one—eleven Confederate and ten Union—would die in action. Three of the cadets who went south in 1861 were killed at Shiloh. Antietam claimed the life of popular Henry Kingsbury of New York. Kelly's Ford on the Rappahannock, in March 1863, claimed the popular Alabamian John Pelham, commander of Jeb Stuart's horse artillery. "The noble, the chivalric, the gallant Pelham is no more," Stuart mournfully announced. Eighteen sixty-three went on to become a costly year. Chancellorsville took the lives of two Federal battery commanders from the '61 classes, Justin E. Dimick and Edmund Kirby. To assure Kirby's widowed mother an adequate pension, President Lincoln granted the lieutenant a deathbed promotion to brigadier general. Gettysburg exacted the heaviest toll of the war on the Union men of the two 1861 classes. Charles Cross of the engineers, second in standing in the May class, was killed on the Rappahannock in the opening phase of the campaign. On the second day at Gettysburg, in the struggle for Little Round Top,

Griffin's old West Point Battery, now under Lieutenant Charles Hazlett of the May class, was in the thick of the fight when Hazlett was shot through the head and killed. At about the same time, Colonel Patrick O'Rorke, first-ranked in the June class, died leading his 140th New York in a charge. Pickett's Charge, on July 3, cost the lives of two more June 1861 graduates, both artillerists. Lieutenant George A. Woodruff, commanding Battery I, 1st U.S. Artillery in place of his May classmate Edmund Kirby, killed two months earlier, was himself killed on Cemetery Ridge. And at the very objective point of Pickett's grand assault, Lieutenant Alonzo Cushing fell in legendary fashion. Badly wounded, Cushing "pushed his gun to the fence in front," it was reported, "and was killed while serving his last canister into the ranks of the advancing enemy."

General Grant's Overland Campaign against Richmond opened in May 1864, and would before it was over claim seven more lives from the ranks of the West Pointers of '61—four Confederate and three Union. A miscellany of late-war actions also took their toll. Finally, on April 6, 1865, on the road to Appomattox Court House, James Dearing, a second classman who had resigned his appointment in April 1861,

"FOR GOD'S SAKE, PULL UP YOUR BOWELS!" — by George Plimpton

Many years ago, a friend of the Kennedys, I was invited to the White House for a dance. At one point the President took me aside. He wanted to talk to me, of all things, about my grandmother. From his earliest days in politics he had been receiving letters (in which she mentioned my name) of complaint about his treatment of her father, General Adelbert Ames, in his book *Profiles in Courage*, specifically of supposed malfeasance during Ames's administration as Reconstruction Governor of Mississippi. Half-jokingly the President complained that her letters were "interfering with matters of state."

As I was mumbling some sort of apology for her persistence, he suddenly asked, "How much do you know about your great grandfather?"

I must have looked too startled to answer, because he immediately said, "Well, I'll bet you don't know his favorite epithet."

I shook my head.

"If he found a soldier not standing up straight in ranks, he'd shout at him, 'For God's sake, pull up your bowels!'"

The President gave this quite a reading, as they say, surely enough to turn heads abruptly toward the corner where we had been chatting.

I eventually discovered where the President had discovered this rather arcane bit of information about a relatively unknown Civil War general—namely in John J. Pullen's best-seller *The Twentieth Maine*. There it is in the first chapter: "For God's sake, pull up your bowels!"

My great-grandfather, Adelbert Ames '61, was the first commander of the Twentieth Maine, a stickler on discipline (obviously starting with posture!) and was considered responsible for turning a notoriously sloppy volunteer regiment into a well-organized and efficient military unit. He was twenty-six years old, fourteen months out of West Point, when he took command. Two months before at the first battle of Bull Run he had been severely wounded and for his bravery received the Congressional Medal of Honor.

After the battle of Chancellorsville, Ames left the 20th Maine, promoted to brigadier general and put in command of a brigade that had broken under Stonewall Jackson's attack, very likely to instill in it the kind of discipline that was the mark of the 20th.

At Gettysburg, under the command of Joshua L. Chamberlain, the 20th Maine is credited with holding back the Alabama 15th at Little Round Top and preventing the left flank of the Union forces from being turned—surely the most critical moment of the battle.

At the time at Gettysburg, General Ames was in command of a division of the Eleventh Corps. After the battle, when the news of the 20th's extraordinary efforts at Little Round Top spread across the battlefield, he went to compliment his former regiment. The family story is that when the soldiers spotted him riding up on his horse, they put their caps on the tips of their bayonets, pumping their rifles in the air in salute, and shouted what was called "three times three," namely "Hip Hip Hooray" three times, as well as "Ames! Ames! Ames!"

It is indeed a matter of record that when the 20th Maine received a new battle flag after Gettysburg, the old one which had been with them throughout the war, finally carried at Little Round Top, stained, tattered, riddled with bullets, was given to Ames—a symbolic gesture that surely reflected their gratitude for the leadership that prepared them for that pivotal engagement.

"The General" as he was referred to by family members lived into his ninety-eighth year. When I was six years old I was taken in to see him. I was reminded to stand ramrod straight in front of his chair. I remember he had a thin shawl over his knees. I looked into his eyes, eyes that may well have seen Pickett's charge. I didn't know enough to ask him about that, or about General George Custer, who was in his class at West Point, or about General Dan

Adelbert Ames as a cadet

Sickles whose wooden leg is in the Smithsonian, or about his father-in-law General Benjamin F. Butler who thought he could incapacitate Fort Fisher by blowing up a close-by hulk containing 500 tons of explosive (it didn't go off properly), or what Longstreet's sulking meant in terms of the battle of Gettysburg's outcome; I only knew enough to stand up straight and say in a low whisper, "Good afternoon, Sir." I don't remember what he had to say to me in reply, if anything, but I know it wasn't, "For God's sake, pull up your bowels!"

In this 1869 painting by E.B.F. Julio, Stonewall Jackson '46 confers with Lee. At Chancellorsville, May 2, 1863, Stonewall in a spectacular maneuver turned the Union flank, but his own men shot him by mistake that night.

now a brigadier general in Robert E. Lee's army, was mortally wounded in one of the war's final skirmishes. Dearing was the last general officer to die for the Confederacy. He was the last of twenty-five West Pointers of the 1861-1864 classes to die on Civil War battlefields.

Statistically, the Civil War was very much a West Point officers' war. Of the 1,033 Academy graduates of the classes of 1830 to 1860 alive in 1861, nearly 91 per cent took part in the contest. Of these 936 graduates who elected to fight in the war, 661 (70.6 per cent) took the Union side and 275 (29.4 per cent) joined the Confederacy. Adding the cadets of 1861-1864 to these totals alters the percentages only slightly— 882 (69.1 per cent) Union and 363 (30.9 per cent) Confederate. Among the ante-bellum

graduates, however, a considerably larger percentage of Southerners remained loyal to the Union (14.4 per cent) than was true among the Southern cadets at West Point in 1861-1864 (4.3 per cent). And of the West Point graduates on active duty in 1861, secession had rather less appeal than to former graduates or to cadets then at the Academy. Fully three-quarters (75.4 per cent) of those in service in 1861 remained true to their oath, while one-quarter (24.6 per cent) went with the South.

Among these regular officers with Academy backgrounds, the partings could be anguishing. In June 1861, at a post outside Los Angeles, Captain Winfield Scott Hancock, Class of 1840, was host at a farewell party for his fellow officers who had resigned to go south. These included

George Pickett

The crushing defeat of Pickett's Charge on the third day of Gettysburg doomed the Confederacy. The painting below shows the last exhausted struggle at the stone wall on top of Cemetery Hill. George Pickett '47 (left) had carried the regimental colors to

Richard Garnett

victory at Chapultepec during the Mexican War; at Gettysburg he directed the uphill charge that forever bears his name. Richard Garnett '41 (second from left) was too sick to walk and rode his horse in Pickett's Charge; thus very visible above the marching

Lewis Armistead

men, he was riddled with bullets. Lewis Armistead (third from left), another hero of the Mexican War, walked straight to the top of Cemetery Hill and seized a Union battery before he was shot. Mortally wounded, he gave his watch to Union soldiers to take to Winfield

Winfield Scott Hancock

Scott Hancock, his old friend, whose guns had mowed him down. Throughout the action Hancock, (left) called Hancock the Superb for his courage and skill, rode up and down the whole line to steady his men. He was shot, but survived.

Alonzo Cushing '61 commanded the battery that Lewis Armistead momentarily captured. He fought for over an hour while wounded, blasting the oncoming Confederates with canister; dying beside his gun, he became a national hero. He was 22. Below is the saddle of Major General John Sedgwick '37, a fine example of the harness George McClellan had developed from European models. Opposite: Sedgwick was photographed with his staff in late 1863 or early 1864. Grant said that he was worth a division to the Union. A Confederate sniper shot him down after the Battle of the Wilderness.

Albert Sidney Johnston '26, ex-commander of the Department of the Pacific; Lewis A. Armistead, a West Pointer for two years who had joined the regulars in 1839; and Richard B. Garnett '41. Mrs. Johnston sang some of the old sentimental songs, and the forced good cheer was soon overcome by the sadness of parting. "The most crushed of the party was Major Armistead," remembered Almira Hancock. With tears "which were contagious" streaming down his face, Armistead put his hands on his host's shoulders and said, "Hancock, good-bye; you can never know what this has cost me. . . ."

In less than a year, Sidney Johnston, full general in the Confederate States army, was dead at Shiloh. In two years, at Gettysburg, Brigadier Generals Garnett and Armistead, leading two of Pickett's brigades in the fabled charge, fell at the high-water mark of the assault against Major General Hancock's Second Corps. Dick Garnett's body was never found. The mortally wounded Armistead, borne to the Federal rear by his captors, encountered an officer who identified himself as a member of Hancock's staff. Was that Winfield Scott Hancock? Armistead wanted to know. Assured that it was, he asked that his personal belongings please go to his "old and valued friend." Armistead's watch and spurs and pocketbook were handed to his one-time comrade, who had himself been seriously wounded during the charge.

The higher ranks of field commands in both armies were filled almost exclusively by West Point graduates, especially in the first half of the war. But there were never enough West Pointers to go around—to fill all the field and administrative leadership posts in all the armies. And attrition, both through casualties and through the natural weeding-out process, took a heavy toll. By the time of Gettysburg, in mid-1863, there were comparatively few Academy graduates below the highest ranks of command.

Civil War generals might take valuable lessons from West Point acquaintanceships. Outside Atlanta in 1864, Sherman learned from a Southern newspaper that his new opponent, replacing Joseph E. Johnston, was John Bell Hood. What did they know about Hood's character, Sherman asked his generals. It happened that three of Sherman's generals, John M. Schofield, James B. McPherson, and Oliver Otis Howard, had been at the Academy with Hood, with Schofield and McPherson graduating with him in the Class of 1853. Schofield described Hood as being "bold even to rash-

George H. Thomas

George H. "Pap" Thomas '39 (inset) became known as the Rock of Chickamauga after the Union commander, General William Rosecrans, lost his wits or his nerve or both, gave contradictory orders, led his army into a disaster and then wandered stunned off the field. Thomas held his position, steadied other shattered units, and stood off the Confederate Army until the Unionists could withdraw in good order. George Dury painted General Thomas, a Virginian who chose to remain with the Union. Right: General James Longstreet '40 rushed his troops by rail to reinforce Braxton Bragg '37 at Chickamauga, a rare effective use of railroads by Confederate forces. But for Thomas, they would have completely overwhelmed the Union Army.

James Longstreet

Ole Peter Hansen Balling painted U.S. Grant (center), with twenty-six of his generals, including West Pointers Philip Sheridan, William Tecumseh Sherman '39, O.O. Howard '54, George Thomas '40, George A. Custer '61, Hugh Judson Kilpatrick '61, William Hemlsey Emory '31, James Birdseye McPherson '53, George Crook '52, Wesley Merrit '60, Gouvernor Kemble Warren '50, George Gordon Meade '35, John Grubb Parke '49, Ambrose Everett Brunside '47, Joseph Hooker '37, Edward Otho Cresap Ord '39, Henry Warner Slocum '52, John McAllister Slocum '52.

Left: The Union Army charges into the Confederate lines defending Atlanta, in this painting from the Atlanta Cyclorama. William Tecumseh Sherman '40 (top right) commanded the bluecoats. Midway through the summer John Bell Hood '53 (middle right) replaced Joseph Johnston '29 (bottom right) as commander of the Confederates. Sherman correctly guessed that the impetuous Hood would attack him immediately and the forewarned Union men gave the Confederates a sound drubbing. After burning Atlanta, Sherman moved off in his March to the Sea, splitting the Confederacy in half, while George Thomas finished off Hood at Nashville. Johnston would surrender to Sherman in North Carolina on April 26, 1865. The two men became good friends after war. Johnston was a pallbearer at Sherman's funeral, where he caught the cold that killed him a week later. Below is the National Color of the Second Battalion, 18th U.S. Infantry, 1866, now in the West Point museum. On its stripes are written (top to bottom) the names of the seven battles that the battalion fought.

William Tecumseh Sherman

John B. Hood

Joseph Johnston

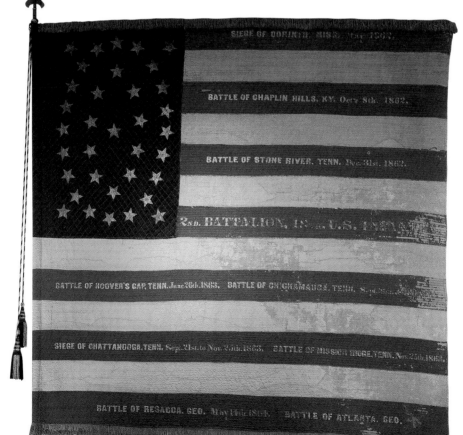

101

Members of the Class of 1864 were photographed in front of the library on a day toward the end of fall in 1863. Later in the winter and in the spring the ground would be too wet to sit on.

ness, and courageous in the extreme." He inferred from that, wrote Sherman, "that the change of commanders meant 'fight.' " He put his generals on special alert. Hood's bold and rash attacks were met and driven back and he had to give up Atlanta.

The Union generals credited with finally winning victory in the Civil War—Grant, Sherman, Sheridan, Meade—and most of their chief lieutenants had attended West Point. But so had their predecessors in the first half of the war who lost battle after battle or missed opportunity after opportunity. Critics insisted that such generals as McDowell, McClellan, Pope, Burnside, Buell, and Halleck did little credit to their Military Academy diplomas. Indeed the more vehement of these critics wanted to do away with the Academy entirely.

In the opening months of the war, perhaps not surprisingly, the critics focused on the notion of West Point as a "nursery of treason." Senator Benjamin Wade led the attack: "I cannot help thinking that there is something wrong about this whole institution. I do not believe that in the history of the world you can find as many men who have proved themselves utterly faithless to their oaths, ungrateful to the

Government that supported them, guilty of treason and a deliberate attempt to overthrow that Government which has educated them. . . ." Senator James Lane of Oregon, whose cadet son had resigned to join the Confederacy, was particularly bitter. The Union's epitaph, should it come to that, said Lane, would be "Died of West Point pro-slaveryism." Disloyalty was a complaint inevitable in a civil war. The Military Academy was by design an egalitarian institution; antebellum America was less a nation than a compact among individual states; and when eleven of those states chose to dissolve the compact, West Pointers, whether graduates or cadets, chose sides no differently than the rest of the populace.

The appropriations bills to operate the Military Academy became the occasion for renewed congressional debate over its future. By now arguments focused on the command failings of West Point-trained generals, failings which, in 1861-62, seemed all too numerous. Senator Wade argued that the war inevitably would spawn its own generals, far superior to the Academy variety. "There is no doubt, if the war continues," he insisted, "that you will have men of genius enough, educated in the field, and infinitely better educated than they possible could be in this institution." Senator Lyman Trumbull also wanted the citizen soldiers let loose, to replace the too-engineering-oriented West Pointers. "Take off your engineering restraints," Trumbull cried; dismiss "every man who knows how to build a fortification, and let the men of the North . . . move down upon the rebels. . . ." (Such arguments were not limited to the Union side. In 1861 Confederate Robert Toombs insisted that the Southern army was dying—"Set this down in your book, and set down opposite to it its epitaph, 'died of West Point.' ")

The attack on the Academy by Wade and his allies did not go unchallenged. Senator William Pitt Fessenden, for example, observed that Ben Wade "thinks commanders are born, not made. I do not. I think they are made; I think education is necessary." He was seconded by Senator James

George Custer '61 was as flamboyant as a cavalier. At the Battle of Cedar Creek, October 19, 1864, he chased down Jubal Early and captured his guns, a feat Custer celebrated by lifting diminutive Philip Sheridan clean off the ground (left). Custer and Texan Tom Rosser (bottom right) had been best friends at West Point; they chose opposite sides in the war, and encountered one another often. Coming on Rosser's command in the Shenandoah Valley in October 1864 (below), Custer rode out in clear view of the waiting Confederates, doffed his hat to Rosser, and charged. Rosser's men broke and ran; Custer chased Rosser himself for ten miles. After the war, they renewed their friendship. Hearing of Custer's desperate plight at the Little Big Horn Rosser tried to organize a rescue column but was too late to help.

Custer's trumpeter, Nathanial Sisson, blew this bugle (above) at Appomattox. Heartbroken, exhausted Confederate soldiers had to accept their bitter defeat. Right, in an 1872 painting by Richard Brooke, they fold their flag for the last time.

Nesmith. "Men do not catch the military science by inspiration," Nesmith said, "neither do they catch it as they do smallpox or the measles. They must be educated to it." In the end this view prevailed, and the Academy appropriations bills passed the Senate over the dissenters' motions. By 1863, with such Union victories as Gettysburg and Vicksburg and Chattanooga, all won by West Pointers, the critics finally fell silent.

Meanwhile, life at wartime West Point resumed its usual pace and pattern. Except for the return to a four-year curriculum, there were few changes in the cadets' routine. After the year-early graduation of the erstwhile Class of 1862, no effort was made to turn out officers either faster or with perhaps more focused military skills. Regardless of the raging conflict, West Point remained committed to producing engineers who might also command troops. News from the battlefronts was eagerly sought, with announcements of Union victories triggering the firing of "national salutes." Then there was mourning for classmates on the casualty lists.

The most noteworthy event of these years at the Military Academy was the dedication of the Battle Monument in June 1864, to honor the Civil War dead of the regular army. The dedicatory oration was delivered by Major General George B. McClellan '46, senior officer on the active list, although inactive since his dismissal by President Lincoln in October 1862. Eighteen sixty-four was an election year, the general was the all-but-certain Democratic challenger to the president, and Secretary of War Edwin Stanton grew livid at this granting of a platform to "candidate" McClellan. In short order both the wartime superintendent, Alexander Bowman, and the commandant of cadets, Henry B. Clitz, were dismissed for their part in the affair. But that was forgotten by April 1865 and the news of Appomattox, when every cannon at West Point was fired in a national salute to end all national salutes.

Back in August of 1861, when General McClellan was appointed to the command of the Army of the Potomac, his old West Point professor of military science, Dennis Hart Mahan, sent him a letter of congratulations. "I had marked a small group of you for our future generals," Mahan wrote, "and the luck has been singular that I find some of you turn up as I had hoped for." That neatly summed up West Point's credo—to produce trained and competent second lieutenants with, it was hoped, the capacity to someday be "our future generals."

Possibly Professor Mahan was disappointed

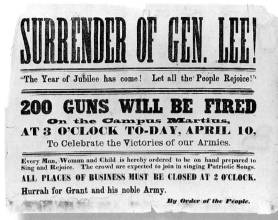

SURRENDER OF GEN. LEE!

"The Year of Jubilee has come! Let all the People Rejoice!"

200 GUNS WILL BE FIRED

On the Campus Martius,

AT 3 O'CLOCK TO-DAY, APRIL 10,

To Celebrate the Victories of our Armies.

Every Man, Woman and Child is hereby ordered to be on hand prepared to Sing and Rejoice. The crowd are expected to join in singing Patriotic Songs.

ALL PLACES OF BUSINESS MUST BE CLOSED AT 2 O'CLOCK.

Hurrah for Grant and his noble Army.

By Order of the People.

A Detroit newspaper (left) rejoiced in Lee's surrender. At the McLean House (below), in Appomattox, Lee and Grant sat side by side, surrounded by Union and Confederate officers, many of them West Pointers. Among them are George Armstrong Custer '61, Custis Lee '54, Phil Sheridan '53, Charles Griffin, Geo. G. Meade '35, and Wesley Merritt '60.

that in the end McClellan did not do better as a general, but surely he had reason to take great pride in others of his students. In June 1865 his two most distinguished graduates made a particular point of saluting their alma mater. Fresh from their war-ending victories, Lieutenant General U.S. Grant, Class of 1843, and Major General William T. Sherman, Class of 1840, arrived at West Point to review the graduating Class of 1865. It was said of both generals that their visit was an exercise in nostalgia, and no doubt it was. But it was also a highly symbolic recognition of their respect for the institution. Sherman once described West Point as "the best Military College in the civilized world," and by their visit he and Grant acknowledged that in this greatest of tests, a civil war, the Academy had passed with flying colors.

4

FROZEN INTERVAL: 1866-1915

BY CARLO W. D'ESTE

"During [its first] century, no other educational institution in the land has contributed as many names as West Point has contributed to the honor roll of the nation's greatest citizens .... None is more absolutely American."

—President Theodore Roosevelt,
Centennial Day, June 11, 1902

■ The Military Academy was placed under authority of the Secretary of War and War Department.
■ George Montague Wheeler [1842–1905] graduated West Point and in 1871 was put in charge of all surveying of the territory of the Untied States west of the 100th meridian.

■ Frederick Dent Grant [1850–1912] completed his first year at West Point, only two years after his father led Union forces to victory in the Civil War.

■ Statue commemorating Major General John Sedgwick dedicated on the Plain. The monument was cast of Confederate cannon captured by his 6th Corps.

■ Meeting held in offices of Horace Webster, Class of 1818, President of the College of the City of New York to organize the Association of Graduates of the U.S. Military Academy; it was credited with helping to bind the wounds of the North and South.

■ Graduates 1802–1870: 2,423; 1861–1870: 482.
■ Lieutenant Colonel Emory Upton '61, a tactical innovator in the Civil War, named Commandant of Cadets [until 1875].

■ George Breckenridge Davis [1847–1914] graduated. Expert on international and military law.

■ Sylvanus Thayer died on 9 September age 87. In November, his body was brought to West Point for interment. On a bitterly cold day, the entire Corps fired the final volley over his grave, the first and only such honor.

The post-Civil War years in the United States were a period of continued deep divisions; the healing of the wounds of war was painfully slow. In the immediate wake of Lee's surrender of the Confederate armies at Appomattox Court House on April 9, 1865, American disunity was never more in evidence than when John Wilkes Booth mortally wounded President Abraham Lincoln at Ford's Theatre on Good Friday.

Reconstruction has been described as "perhaps the most controversial era in American history," an epoch when citizens of both the Union and the defeated Confederacy sought to come to terms with an event that was not just devastating and divisive but that also brought about a complete reordering of the American social, economic, and political system. During Reconstruction the United States began evolving from a largely agrarian society into an industrial one. By the turn of the century the nation had begun to emerge as a new world leader.

Although the enmity between men and women of the Union and the Confederacy smoldered on, relationships between West Pointers were surprisingly cordial. The bonds of comradeship generated by their West Point experience took precedence over even the bloodiest clashes on the battlefield. For most, participation in the war meant adhering to the teachings of the institution. "Duty," "Honor," and "Country" may have guided their actions, but the fact that they were sworn enemies on the battlefield did not interfere with the bonds they had forged as cadets, friends, and later, as Army officers.

A classic example was the relationship of Grant and Longstreet. Shortly after the war Grant not only greeted his friend and former enemy but entertained him in his quarters. Grant wrote to Lincoln's successor, President Andrew Johnson, to urge that he grant amnesty to Longstreet. "I have known him well for more

than 26 years," he wrote of the brother officer who had served as a groomsman at his wedding in 1848. "I shall feel it as a personal favor to myself." Johnson was unmoved, but as president, Grant immediately appointed his old friend as New Orleans surveyor of customs.

There are other recorded examples of West Pointers reconciling their friendships but not their fundamental differences. Shortly after the war ended two former cadets who had fought on opposite sides met on a train; each greeted the other with warmth and spent the evening discussing old times. The recent Union officer, Morris Schaff, said of their meeting that, "I

PRECEDING SPREAD: Two mounted cadets, riding bareback, try to shove each other off their horses in this painting by R.F. Zogbaum. Such drills developed strength, flexibility, balance and quick thinking. Cadet John Pershing, right, First Captain of the Class of 1886, already had the look of a man at the beginning of a spectacular career.

| 1873 | 1874 | 1875 | 1876 | 1877 | 1878 | 1879 |

■ **William Murray Black** [1855–1933] entered West Point, later to become an important engineer of public works. During World War I, Black was Chief of Engineers of the U.S. Army and saw Engineer Corps expand from 2,416 to 308,318 officers and men.

■ **Marion Perry Maus** [pronounced mös] [1850–1930] graduated and moved out to fight the Indian Wars until 1890. Participated in capture of Chief Joseph and Geronimo, for which he was awarded the Medal of Honor.

■ **Tasker Howard Bliss** [1853–1930] graduated eighth in his class of forty-three. With American entry into World War I, Bliss became acting Chief of Staff of the Army.

■ **William Crozier** [1855–1942] graduated first in his class. With Adelbert Rinaldo Buffington, invented the Buffingon-Crozier disappearing gun carriage that became the standard carriage for all large-caliber coastal artillery until afer World War I.

■ **William Murray Black** [1855–1933] graduated first in his West Point class after being first for four years. One of the most prominent Army engineers in public works, he oversaw operations to raise the wreck of the battleship Maine in Havana Harbor.
■ **Henry O. Flipper** becomes first black graduate.

■ **James Franklin Bell** [1856–1919] graduated from West Point. He became known for his fearlessness, reconnoitering the Spanish fortifications in Manila by swimming into the harbor. President Roosevelt appointed him Chief of Staff of the Army in 1906.

■ **Hunter Liggett** [1857–1935] graduated. Commander of the American I Corps and later the First Army, His leadership culminated at victory in the Meuse-Argonne, 1918.

could not help wondering as he parted from me whether I could have shown so much magnanimity [in defeat] had the South conquered the North . . . I doubt it."

Two weeks after Appomattox, General Joseph E. Johnston had surrendered his Confederate army in North Carolina to another former West Pointer, William Tecumseh Sherman. In later years Johnston and his wife would occasionally travel from Richmond to Washington to dine with the Shermans, and when Sherman died in 1891, Johnston was one of his pallbearers. The cold he caught at Sherman's funeral turned into the pneumonia that killed him a week later.

The bonds forged at West Point had always been its greatest strength. From its inception, the Military Academy had introduced the Jeffersonian concept of producing disciplined professional Army officers for service to the United States through a mathematics and engineering-based curriculum. Although American educa-

tion changed dramatically during Reconstruction, West Point stuck to the traditions that, as Sherman noted, had "borne fruits of infinite value to the Democratic country, if it has not been its actual salvation." As an institution, West Point entered into a period that changed relatively little until the reforms that Douglas MacArthur attempted to institute more than fifty years later. However, West Point's prestige as a pioneer engineering school was overtaken by civilian institutions whose curriculums changed with the times.

During Reconstruction, West Point was seen as a splendid symbol of America's growing power. In 1868, an unusual meeting seemed to sum up the new feeling. It occurred when, in June, the band and the entire graduating class of the Naval Academy arrived in a small flotilla of ships that anchored at the Academy dock on the Hudson River. Created in 1845, the Naval Academy was still in its infancy, and during this period the two institutions existed in entirely separate spheres.

During West Point's graduation week, however, the midshipmen and cadets jointly participated in various activities, exhibitions, hops, and parades in which each academy marched in review and exchanged honors. Of more lasting importance were the friendships resulting from this first interchange between the two institutions. The congeniality of 1868 predated one of the greatest rivalries in all of sports.

During the period between the Civil War and World War I, the Corps of Cadets was in great demand to participate in events that showcased the institution, such as presidential inaugurations, Sherman's funeral in 1891 (held in St. Louis), the Chicago World's Fair of 1893, and the St. Louis Exposition in 1904.

One of the most powerful and effective

In 1868 U.S. Grant came up to West Point to present the diplomas to the graduating class (center). With the Civil War three years over, the country looked forward to a long interval of peace.

Frontier Guardians

In the years after the Civil War West Point graduates served on the frontier. There they took part in the merciless harrying of the Indians, but more often languished in boring duty on posts far from civilization.

Near Fort Thomas, Arizona, below left, a few officers and their ladies picnic in the shade of a saguaro cactus. The First Cavalry at Fort Keogh in Montana (right) bundle up against subzero cold and blizzard winds.

Overleaf: Frederic Remington's most famous painting, Cavalry Charge on the Southern Plains, captures a military glamour and excitement that existed mostly in the minds of civilians.

Frederic Remington
1907

The pleasure of your company
is requested at the
Farewell Hop
given to the
Graduating Class
Monday evening, June 11th 1883,
West Point.

Hop Managers.

John B. Bellinger. Samuel J. Sturgis Jr. Hugh J. Gallagher.
James K. Thompson. Irving Hale. Thomas L. Hartigan.
Waleto E. Ayer. Oscar G. Cross. James B. Hughes.

German Leaders.

Godfrey H. Macdonald.

Clarence R. Edwards.

cadets who had been expelled for drunkenness on New Year's Eve. In his day, as he observed, getting drunk to welcome in the New Year was a normal rite of passage for a cadet.

The Reconstruction years at West Point were thus a period of entrenchment during which its leadership reveled in smug self-satisfaction that an institution that had produced virtually every single important military figure of the war was hardly in need of change. The very success of West Pointers during the Civil War actually helped stifle progress in the postwar era. Although both Washington and the Board of Visitors initiated various recommendations that were thought to better the institution, most were rejected outright by an Academic Board of tenured professors who were answerable to no one.

What scant change that came about, such as minor modifications in admission standards and elimination of the stranglehold held by officers of the Corps of Engineers in the position of Superintendent, were largely so cosmetic as to be virtually insignificant.

West Point's professors were all graduates and what they taught was generally restricted to what they had learned as cadets, resulting in too much of the theoretical and too little of the practical. Teaching was by rote and there was only the approved "school solution" to a problem. Sylvanus Thayer had broadened the basis of academic diversity and instruction by recruiting professors from outside the narrow confines of the U.S. Army. During Reconstruction, however, this practice died out. Men who

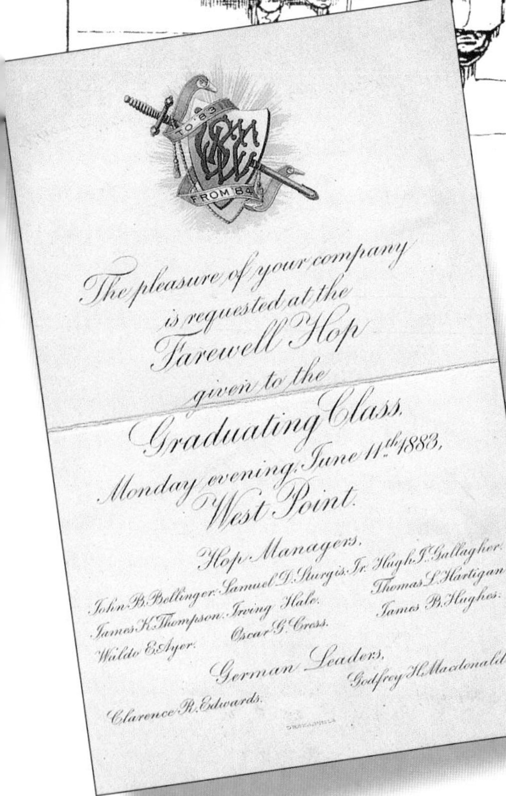

voices against change was Sherman, who argued forcefully for the status quo as he had known it in his cadet days. "Does not wisdom suggest that we leave well enough alone?" he wrote in 1879. As West Point's General-in-Chief from 1869 to 1883, Sherman enjoyed tremendous prestige and considerable influence. In return, the Corps of Cadets adored "Uncle Billy," as he was fondly nicknamed. Sherman was noted for his compassion toward wayward cadets, often using his position to overturn or reduce punishments handed down by the Superintendent for violations of Academy regulations. An example of Sherman's "boys will be boys" sentiments occurred in 1880 when he ordered the reinstatement of

roles as professional soldiers.

Meanwhile the attrition rate for what was hardly better than a second-class education was shockingly high. Only forty percent of the class of 1879, for example, actually graduated from an institution where discipline was draconian and future prospects in the U.S. Army of the Reconstruction era were dreary. Between 1870 and 1879 an average of seventy-seven percent of each class served on the frontier. During that period only eleven died in the Indian Wars, including the five who were killed on June 25, 1876 at Little Big Horn River, in Montana. For the most part, however, duty on the frontier was unerringly boring. As in other aspects of its training of cadets, West Point only marginally prepared its future officers for mounted service in the West.

had had little actual army service and lived behind West Point's stone facade imparted instruction that was not only dull and behind the times, but increasingly irrelevant. In a rapidly changing America what had once been the cutting edge of knowledge was now ancient history. Yet, a graduate of 1900 was taught using the same texts, and poor, outdated teaching methods as his counterpart of a half-century earlier. By failing to reform itself after the Civil War, the Military Academy conspicuously failed to prepare its graduates for their future

Until the turn of the century, West Point's status quo was fostered by both the faculty and Superintendents, most of whom had fought in the Civil War. Left in the backwash of change the Academy deliberately opted not to alter itself. The entire blame does not, however, rest with West Point alone. The public perception of West Point as the maker of America's great

ROBERT WEIR'S VISION

From the beginning classes in drawing were part of the Academy's curriculum, as part of the school's emphasis on engineering: men laying out forts, bridges and roads had to be able to draw plans. The first few instructors came and went, content to have the cadets copy famous works, like a Roman helmet that Jefferson Davis drew. But in 1834, Robert Weir came to teach drawing. He would stay for forty years, and under his direction the program flourished.

Weir taught his students the elements of drawing, but he expected more of them than mere copying. Cadets drew what they saw around them. A lot of student work from the time shows cadet life, including a satiric drawing by James Whistler of a guard lying down on duty, and nature, trees, and the river. In his class with Weir, Ulysses Grant produced a watercolor of Indian traders that shows a startling artistic gift. Year by year, class by class, every cadet for forty years passed through Weir's classroom,

and he taught them how to use pencil and pen and watercolor, how to observe what they saw around them, how to record what they saw on paper.

While he was teaching at West Point, Weir also worked as a painter and an illustrator, and his *Embarkation of The Pilgrims* hangs in the rotunda of the United States Capitol Building, the heart of the country. The painting is a frozen moment in time, the Pilgrims gathering for one last prayer before leaving for

Photo of Robert W. Weir from the 1865 album.

the New World, and it shows the technical mastery that served as a model for his students. *Embarkation* took him seven years to complete, and he earned $10,000 for it, which he used

to build a church in Highland Falls, near West Point.

The painting now seems dry and static, a discarded vision of the past. Most people who know of Robert Weir associate him with this painting. They should also see him all around America, in the bridges and roads and canals his students raised, using the skills he gave them, translating what they saw into plans on paper: building the country. This, surely, was also Weir's vision, and a living one.

—C.H.

West Point and its students were among Weir's favorite subjects. The heavy guns in the foreground of his view from Trophy Point (left) were used to teach siege tactics. His careful eye captured the tense concentration of a student struggling over a drawing project (right). Below, the watercolor The Snow Plow, which shows groundsmen clearing an Academy path, was a reminder of the harsh cold of an upstate winter.

1880	1881	1882	1883	1884	1885	1886

■ Graduates 1802–1880: 2,932; 1871–1880: 509.
■ Johnson C. Whittaker, a black cadet, was dismissed after a controversial court-martial.

■ The position of "Master of the Sword" was established at West Point. Title only changed to Director of Physical Education in 1974.

■ Department of Foreign Languages authorized.
■ Charles Thomas Menoher [1862–1930] entered West Point. Commander of the First World War 42nd "Rainbow" Division, so named because it was composed of troops from twenty-six states and the District of Columbia.

■ Monument to the memory of Colonel Sylvanus Thayer, the "Father of the Military Academy," dedicated.

■ First publication of the *Howitzer*, included jokes, poems, and stories and the Hundredth Night celebration.
■ Wilds Preston Richardson [1861–1929] graduated. Commander of U.S. troops in the Allied invasion of northern Russia, 1918-1919.

■ Herman J. Koehler appointed Master of the Sword. Infused new life in program of physical fitness and athletics.
■ Joseph Edward Kuhn [1864–1935] graduated first in his class. Commanded the 79th Division in the Meuse-Argonne.

■ John J. Pershing, commander of the American Expeditionary Force in World War I and the only officer ever to hold the rank of General of the Armies, graduated thirtieth out of a class of seventy-seven. Twenty-six at graduation, he was the oldest member of his class.

military leaders supported the notion that an institution of such unrivaled success should not change. Moreover, West Point's relatively modest admission standards resulted in a high percentage of admissions and an even higher attrition rate, sometimes as high as sixty percent of an incoming class. Nevertheless, West Point's attempts to raise its admission standards were rejected by Congress.

Other than a series of three-hour lectures on its campaigns by Dennis Hart Mahan, cadets barely studied the Civil War. Instead, the primary focus was on the Franco-Prussian War of 1870-71 which seemed more important. The success of Chancellor Otto von Bismarck's Prussia spawned a deep interest in German tactics and military organization. Prussia became the paradigm studied by Regular Army officers from the United States and elsewhere "who flocked to Berlin to study from the masters." The rise of Prussian military thought and efficiency resulted in a Congressional resolution that German be added to the West Point curriculum. The Superintendent balked, citing sundry reasons why introducing German would be disruptive and virtually impossible without returning the length of study to five years.

Even the great Dennis Hart Mahan was symbolic of the faculty's resistance to change. On one occasion, when a cadet who was a Civil War veteran dared to deviate from the textbook solution to explain his real-life solution of a military problem, he was sternly rebuffed. Mahan not only refused to listen to the practical explanation but bluntly said, "I don't care what you did or what you saw during the Civil War, you stick to the text." When the cadet persisted, Mahan thundered, "I want nothing further from you. Sit down, sir!"

The Board of Visitors recognized that some

change was desirable, if for no other reason than to alleviate the crushing boredom of life at an institution in an era of extended peace. Although the academic curriculum was rigid and unimaginative, there was some evolutionary change. The creation of new departments such as history and law, a fresh emphasis on the humanities, and a restructured engineering curriculum were all added by the turn of the century.

One of the few significant advances had nothing to do with academics but was nevertheless of lasting significance. In 1869, a small group of graduates intent upon healing the wounds of the war met in New York City to establish the Association of Graduates, and elected the revered figure of Sylvanus Thayer as its first president. One of Thayer's recommendations, fortunately rejected, would have given graduates an influential voice in the workings of the institution. Academy historian George S. Pappas notes that chaos would have ensued had every "DOG" ("Distinguished Old Grad," "Disgusted Old Grad," or "Damned Old Grad") been given such license.

By 1872, the Association was admitting former Confederate officers like Longstreet, not without inevitable controversy. This, too, was an affirmation of the growing rapprochement between ex-Union and Confederate graduates.

The politics of Congressional interference had always been the bane of the West Point administration and after the Civil War that did not change. Congressmen and Senators felt free to meddle at the whim of a disgruntled constituent or an expelled, or severely disciplined, cadet. Textbooks were routinely sent to Washington, where they were examined for suitability, and virtually no academy activity was immune from Congressional scrutiny and second-guessing. In the early 1870s the problem

The American Dreyfus

Henry Ossian Flipper '77 was the first black graduate of West Point.

HENRY OSSIAN FLIPPER was born in Georgia in 1856, the child of slave parents who gained their freedom in the chaos of Sherman's March and who worked hard and prospered during Reconstruction. Flipper himself won his appointment to West Point by passing a long and rigorous examination of his abilities: The Republican congressman who sponsored him knew what he would be up against and wanted to be sure his candidate had the best possible chance of succeeding.

In the years between 1870 and 1877, twenty-seven other young black men had managed to get themselves admitted to the Academy, but none had graduated. This failure stemmed less from the intellectual demands of the institution than from the unremitting hostility and brutality of the white cadets. But Henry Flipper was determined to graduate. After winning his appointment, he turned down an offer of $5,000 to hand it over to a white man's son, and in June of 1873 young Flipper arrived at West Point.

He passed the entrance examinations easily. Another, harsher test faced him over the next four years. Other black cadets had fought back against the regimen of hazing and ostracism and relentless abuse they received from the rest of the cadet corps, and had gradually been ground down and destroyed. Flipper, however, considered fighting back to be beneath him.

"To stoop to retaliation," he wrote later, "is not compatible with true dignity, nor is vindictiveness manly." The white cadets shunned him; he shunned them. He took their insults with an aloof dignity that made fools of his tormentors. He seldom left the Academy, even for holidays; he never joined the drinking and smoking and general hell-raising at the local taverns. He studied hard, and he insisted on the respect due his rank, but he met the brutal social isolation with the serenity of one who knew his enemies for lesser men. By his fourth year he had earned the grudging respect of many cadets—some of whom, while insulting him in public, told him in private they admired him.

After graduation he was posted to West Texas, where he served with distinction. But his troubles weren't over. At Fort Sill in Indian territory, he was arrested on trumped-up charges, accused of embezzlement and conduct unbecoming an officer. The embezzlement charge was quickly dropped, but he was convicted of the second. In 1882 Flipper was drummed out of the Army.

Flipper met this reversal with the same dignity and optimism with which he had handled the situation at West Point. He still had his Academy education and he made the most of it. He worked as a surveyor and engineer in mines in Mexico and the United States. He became friends with Jesse Grant, son of President Grant; he edited a newspaper; he published articles on Southwestern history. William F. Buckley, Sr., hired him as a consultant in Buckley's Venezuelan oil venture. He was a special assistant to Albert Fall, Secretary of the Interior. He wrote two volumes of his autobiography: *A Colored Cadet At West Point*—in which he recorded with poignant and affectionate accuracy the details of a community he was never really allowed to join—and *Black Frontiersman*. Throughout, he sought to clear his name and win back his rightful place in the U.S. Army.

He died in 1940. But his saga was not yet over. In 1976 after a review of his court-martial, the Department of the Army granted him an honorable discharge. The Academy named a memorial scholarship in his honor, to be granted to "the cadet who demonstrated the highest qualities of leadership, self-discipline and perseverance in the face of unusual difficulties." The first recipient was Second Lt. William Davis, a 1976 graduate of the Air Force Academy, Flipper's great-grand-nephew.

On February 19, 1999, President William Jefferson Clinton finally cleared Flipper's name with a Presidential pardon, recognizing finally that the charges against him were false. So ended the case that has led many to call him the American Dreyfus.

—*C.H.*

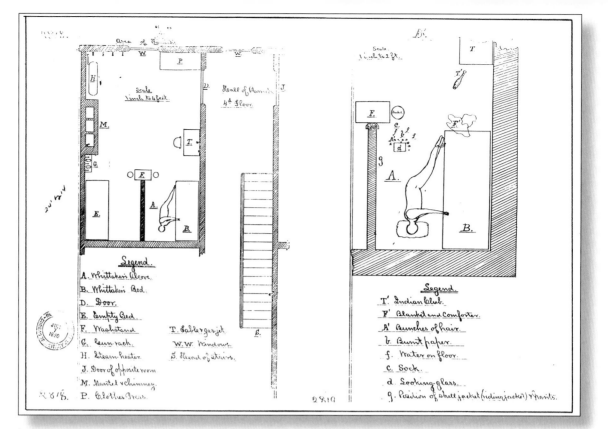

These diagrams showing how the black cadet Johnson Whittaker was found after the alleged assault indicate why suspicions grew: he could have easily tied himself up, and his head was thoughtfully cushioned on a pillow. Handwriting analysis suggested he wrote the threatening letter himself. Whittaker insisted on his innocence; the case has never been proven either way.

became so troublesome that Colonel Thomas H. Ruger, Superintendent from 1871 to 1876, was obliged to provide inane assurances that West Point was only hiring loyal Republican workers for teamster, carpentry, and other civilian jobs.

West Point's reputation was indirectly sullied by an 1870 scandal when an investigation by the House Armed Services Committee established the truth of allegations that some Congressmen were trading appointments for payoffs or favors. After a two-year investigation, and despite public criticism and cries for change, Congress predictably failed to reform its appointment procedures.

The 1870 payola scandal was soon overshadowed by an even larger controversy, revolving around the admission of the first black cadets to West Point. After 1865 it was only a matter of time before radical Republican pressure for integration would lead to the admission of the Academy's first black cadets. West Point became the obvious target and in 1870 the first black cadet, James W. Smith of South Carolina, was admitted. Smith fared badly and flunked out in his second class year. Overall, black cadets were shamefully treated at West Point, not by hazing, but by ostracism. Although the administration tried to ensure fair treatment, it could not overcome the bias that pervaded the Corps of Cadets.

The first black cadet to be commissioned in the Regular Army was Henry O. Flipper, in 1877.

Flipper's military career as a Buffalo soldier—the name given to all black soldiers on the Western frontier—ended in his court-martial and dismissal from the Army on dubious charges. Although Flipper's civilian career was extremely successful, efforts to clear his name came to nothing during his lifetime. West Point eventually honored Flipper a hundred years after his graduation with a bust in the Library; in 1999 he was granted a presidential pardon.

The next black cadet admitted to West Point was Johnson Chestnut Whittaker in 1876. Whittaker had a more difficult time than Flipper and also struggled academically. In 1879, he was expelled by the Academic Board but reprieved by the Superintendent, Major General John M. Schofield, who was sympathetic to Whittaker's plight. In April 1880, Whittaker was found severely beaten and tied to his bed; he claimed to have been assaulted by three unidentified masked intruders. The case received prominent coverage in the press and became a national cause célébre amid a storm of bad publicity for West Point. Investigation revealed that instead of a racially motivated outrage, Whittaker had faked the attack. The case was not resolved for another two years when Cadet Whittaker was found guilty of perjury and other charges. Although President Chester A. Arthur refused to approve the findings of the court of inquiry, he did authorize Whittaker's dismissal on grounds of academic failure. What had begun as a sad case of a black cadet cracking under the pressure, turned into a scandal that harmed reputations and set back attempts to integrate West Point by almost a century.

During the fifty years between 1865 and 1915, thirteen black cadets were admitted but only three managed to graduate. Although all were relegated to service with black regiments, one graduate, Charles D. Young, attained the rank of full colonel and also served as a military attaché in Haiti and Liberia. As lamentable as West Point's record, the Naval Academy failed to admit a single black during the same period.

In other respects, the make-up of the Corps of Cadets changed significantly during the postwar years. Many combat veterans of the war applied and were accepted, including a few with disabilities who were otherwise unable to meet West Point's physical standards. Although postwar classes were dominated by Northerners, by the time the Class of 1870 graduated there were already men in the Corps of Cadets who had been born in several of the Confederate states. Among them was Samuel E. Tillman of Tennessee, Class of 1869, a future Superintendent (1917-1919), whose brother had been a Confederate colonel. Graduates who had fought for the South eventually sent sons to the Military Academy. In 1880, a plebe from Texas was shocked when the band unexpectedly played *Dixie* during his first parade. "Think of it! *Dixie* in that northern state and Yankee region, only fifteen years after Lee's surrender!"

The West Point method of turning a civilian into a professional sol-

ONE-ARMED CRUSADER

West Point made soldiers of many unusual men, but none so different as J.E.B. Stuart, the fiery Virginian, and his friend O.O. Howard, the dour Maine abolitionist, both of the Class of 1854. The Virginian Stuart's meteor-like career in the Civil War was the epitome of Southern chivalry. Howard's long, often controversial, life represented the best of Northern principles.

Howard was profoundly religious, a man who saw God in every human face. This first principle of his faith put him on a common ground with all people, from the despised slave to the dreaded Apache, and gave him a moral dignity rare at a time when Henry Flipper was railroaded out of the Army because of his color.

Howard's commitment to duty was tested early. When the Civil War broke out, he was quickly promoted to brigadier general. In 1862 at the battle of Fair Oaks, two bullets shattered his right arm; what remained of the limb was amputated. Howard was back in the war within six weeks, his right sleeve pinned up neatly over the stump.

A year later, at Chancellorsville, with his 11th Corps holding the far right of the Union line, Howard watched Stonewall Jackson's troops move past him through the Wilderness and did nothing, believing (like most of the Union command) that Lee's army was retreating. When Jackson launched a flank attack, Howard's men took the brunt of it, making Howard the goat of Jackson's spectacular feat.

Yet Howard fought well for the rest of the war: on the first day of Gettysburg where he secured the critical position on Cemetery Hill, and later at Chattanooga and Atlanta. His strong anti-slavery position and his impeccable probity earned him appointment, after the war's end, as head of the Freedmen's Bureau.

Howard had known Abraham Lincoln, and under his direction the Freedmen's Bureau worked out Lincoln's vision of Reconstruction. The war had freed the slaves into a terrible limbo. The South teemed with lost, frightened, confused, uncertain black people. Howard struggled to protect them, to get them land, to set up employment and housing, and especially to provide education, the ex-

slave's surest way to justice. He helped the great University named for him, and (on leave from the Army) served as its President.

In 1872 came another test. Howard was posted to Arizona, into the middle of the long bloody war with the Chiricahua chief Cochise. Against seasoned advice, Howard went alone into the wild country to meet the formidable Apache face to face. This courage led to a treaty allowing the Chiricahua to keep their homelands in return for peace.

In 1877 Howard led the campaign in the Northwest against Chief Joseph and the Nez Perce, and put down the Bannock uprising in Idaho. He treated these Indians also with good faith and respect, and they in turn respected him. It was to Howard that Joseph offered his surrender, saying that he "knew his heart," and trusting Howard to keep his word.

In 1880, the Johnson Whittaker scandal rocked West Point, and Howard was appointed superintendent. His reputation as a champion of African-Americans helped the Academy weather the uproar of its first efforts at integration.

In a racist time he saw beyond race; the general from Maine recognized the power of education to bring true social justice; and he put not only his honor but his life on the line for what he believed in, however unpopular. Over the years West Point has produced many a man of principle. Few of those principles have worn as well as O.O. Howard's.

—C.H.

O.O. Howard struggled all his long career for justice for African-Americans, as head of the Freedmen's Bureau, as founder of Howard University, and later as Superintendent of West Point.

1912

AT MESS IN THE FIELD, WEST POINT, N. Y.

Cadets at Gymnastics, West Point, N. Y.

A Literary Fan

MARK TWAIN LOVED WEST POINT. The legendary author of *Huckleberry Finn* and *Life on the Mississippi* visited the Military Academy at least six times between 1881 and 1890, often reading from his works to appreciative audiences, and he wove affectionate references to the school into his work.

In his satiric novel *A Connecticut Yankee at King Arthur's Court*, the hero, Hank Morgan, transported back in time to medieval England, aspires to create a thoroughly modern society out of the raw material of Camelot. As part of his scheme he founds a secret military academy—which he calls West Point—to provide officers for King Arthur's army. Late in the novel there's even a competitive exam, in which a cadet named Webster shows off his knowledge of mathematics and military science before the whole court, making a fool of the noble knight opposing him, who knows nothing and is proud of it. Unfortunately King Arthur is less flexible than Hank; he staffs his army with nobles instead of the cadets.

Twain's association with West Point ran deeper even than his numerous visits. He had the first edition of *1601*, his parody of Elizabethan manners, printed at a West Point print shop; the work was a forerunner of both *The Prince and the Pauper* and *Connecticut Yankee*. Clearly, for the Missouri-born author, the Academy on the Hudson was the antithesis of the elitist and aristocratic stronghold so many of its critics considered it. He rightly saw West Point as a great leveller—keeping military careers open to talent, and thus preventing the rise of a separate military caste in the United States. For all its critics and detractors, probably most people in the United States would have agreed with him.   —C.H.

PRECEDING SPREAD: Cadet life at West Point was a constant round of drill and instruction. Five color postcards (top) show cadets fencing, firing off a battery at artillery drill, in the mess hall, eating in the open at summer camp, and doing gymnastics. In an array of photographs by William H. Stockbridge from the early 20th century, (middle, from left to right) cadets practice drawing (George S. Patton Jr. can be seen at center bending over a table), study engineering, build a bridge, and practice with the sword. The larger photographs below depict a cadet reading from a French newspaper (left) and men lined up on the parade ground (right).

dier was autocratic and had changed little since the school's birth. Plebes were assigned to four-man squads and were harassed at each and every formation by third classmen. A member of the Class of 1891 recalled hoping that, "we would fall into the hands of a big one, for the large men were always the kindest and the best drill masters. The little men, no matter what you did, would always be following you around like a little pup." For the first month plebes were taught the rudiments of military drill and ceremonies in "Plebe Camp," a nearby tent city adjacent to the Plain. Demerits were assigned for infractions of discipline and regulations, and cadets on punishment tours walked with rifle and pack. Plebes were obliged to swim for ten minutes utilizing only the approved "West Point" stroke, a form of sidestroke.

Around mid-July the new cadets were integrated into the annual summer camp with upperclassmen who eagerly awaited their arrival and warned of things to come with shouts of, "We have been waiting for you." They could expect endless harassment in the form of chores that included, according to a recent historian, "raising and lowering tent flaps; folding bedding; cleaning spurs, sabers, guns, breastplates, and shoes; sweeping the company streets; and, on hop nights, arranging clothing, putting on clean collars and cuffs, and making out the upper classman's hop cards."

Four weeks of harassment and endless drill concluded with the return of the second class from furlough and the displacement of the Corps to the barracks. At the sound of the drum, all tents were struck simultaneously, folded and piled at the end of each company street. Led by the band, the white-clad Corps marched down the road in a column of squads, made a right turn, then a left turn through the central sally port of the barracks. Dismissed, the new plebes went to their rooms to begin the task of folding each piece of their clothing and placing it on the proper shelf in the clothes press. Blouses, overcoats, and trousers were hung on hooks in the alcoves enclosing each iron bunk.

In September, the ordeal of cadet life settled into a routine that hardly ever varied. "Cadets

marched to every event: classes, athletics, meals, chapel services, and parades," the historian George Pappas noted. "Plebes were even marched to bath formations in the bathhouse across the area from their barracks . . . Life was one formation after another, from reveille at 5:30 a.m. to taps at 10:00 p.m." Sunday was the only day a plebe was granted a small measure of free time.

In 1887, *Harper's Monthly Magazine* depicted a romanticized version of West Point during one of its most tranquil eras. It spoke glowingly of the mighty Hudson and West Point with its "rock-ribbed Highlands" and the "broad, beautiful, grass-grown plain, bounded on the west by the cozy homes of the officers and professors, on the south by the stately barracks . . . Statues in bronze or marble gleam here and there amid the foliage, and tell of deeds of heroism and devotion on the part of the sons of the old academy."

Cadets hardly viewed West Point through such a rose-colored prism. Cadet rooms were utterly Spartan, devoid of any creature comforts and virtually unchanged after nearly a century. They were equipped only with iron

Furlough books were issued to Third Class cadets for their annual summer leave. The 1912 edition, above, illustrates one of the furlough's most delightful prospects: sleeping in. In the 19th century cadets going on furlough were expected to wear a modified uniform, but in the turn of the century photograph below, a group just returned shows that expectation fallen into abeyance.

Summer Camp

During Summer Camp, upperclassmen drilled the incoming class into its first semblance of military order. The new West Pointer marched everywhere and did everything in perfect order, as the engraving below of men going to the mess hall suggests, but the cadets still had their moments of high jinks (right).

The routines of Summer Camp allowed for an intense program of military instruction without the distractions of academic life. Cadets drilled in the basics they would need all through their careers. Divided into companies, plebes learned to march, to salute, to obey orders. They slept on the wooden floors of their tents, built fortifications, drilled with firearms, dug latrines, and stood guard duty, rotating as Officer of the Day. Right, from top, shows a line of tents, cadets using surveying equipment, firing rifles from a defensive square, and Company A celebrating the end of Summer Camp. Above, a crew of cadets fires a siege gun and holds dress parade at Fort Clinton.

In the gigantic riding pavilion (above), the line of mounted cadets looks insignificant. Riding was the cadets' most strenuous challenge, causing many injuries. Below, a postcard shows cadets doing a gymnastic stunt on horseback. The saber-wielding cadet (right) shows excellent jumping form.

WEST POINT. Mounted Gymnastics.

A Century of Cavalry

IN 1808, CONGRESS SUPPLIED West Point with the money and orders to set up the study of cavalry practice and tactics. For some years, this discipline did not entail actually getting up on the backs of horses, but by 1839 the Academy had acquired forty-two mounts and an instructor, and the riding program was under way. In 1855, while Robert E. Lee was superintendent, he supervised the building of a riding hall, at the impressive cost of $22,000, which, when seen from passing boats on the Hudson River, reminded some of the great castles along the rivers of Europe.

The young men rode with and without saddles, drilling, and studying the tactics of charge and retreat, sword and rifle work while in the saddle, and jumping. Legend has it that as a cadet, Ulysses S. Grant set a high jump record that stood for more than a quarter of a century on a horse no one else dared ride.

By the end of the century sixty-eight enlisted soldiers were serving as instructors. During summer training each cadet class went on a cavalry hike, which specialized in teaching the young men how to care for a horse on the march, as well as the usual field work and survival and reconnaissance training. The most accomplished of the cadets joined the Riding Club, which competed as a team in horse shows and at universities. The Riding Club survived the disbanding of the Cavalry Detachment in 1946; but the field expedition of today's cadet finds him in a deuce-and-a-half, not a saddle.

The USMA Detachment of Cavalry was reorganized in 1907, and staffed with men from the Ninth Cavalry, the unit that galloped up San Juan Hill behind Teddy Roosevelt. It was an all-black unit, and the reorganization followed the social custom of the time by separating these men from the rest of the Academy. They had their own barracks, mess, barber shops, and platoon rooms, their own athletic teams, including a tug o' war team. Best of all, they had their own polo team, which routinely whipped every team that came against it—mostly the cadet teams. Superb horsemen, dedicated instructors, the Detachment of Cavalry served flawlessly for more than forty years. Many of the men are now buried in the West Point Cemetery.

—*C.H.*

bedsteads, mattresses made of hair, one blanket and pillow per cadet, a chair and table, individual metal wash basins, soap, towels and a crude clothes press. Not only were the living conditions wretched but the academics difficult. Yet such sparse conditions were deemed to "toughen" future officers for garrison duty in America's outposts.

Although horsemanship and cavalry drills were an essential part of West Point training, as Dwight D. Eisenhower, a member of the Class of 1915 would later attest, this activity was exceedingly hazardous. It was equine drills, rather than an earlier football injury to his knee, that not only ended his budding football career, but very nearly cost Eisenhower his commission.

Equitation was the most difficult physical requirement a cadet had to successfully pass. Most of the horses were former army polo ponies with nasty temperaments. One in particular was so notoriously evil-natured that it not only threw its riders, but delighted in kicking them in the face. Once, during Eisenhower's tenure, three cadets were in the infirmary with broken jaws from the same animal.

The senior riding instructor was an eccentric Army major nicknamed "The Squire," who made horsemanship deliberately difficult. Cadets were obliged to ride with only a saddle pad and a surcingle (a makeshift girth to hold the pad in place). One of Eisenhower's classmates recalled that "Some of us fell off our horses so frequently that we could almost tell what part of the riding hall we had fallen by the taste of the tanbark." As the cadets went through the prescribed drills, the Squire would shriek, "That's terrible [Mr. So-and-so]! Oh, my God, how I suffer! What would the people in Virginia say?" His orderly was a

The Department of Tactics, photographed above in 1883, suggests in their helmets and moustaches the decidedly Germanic influence that the Franco-Prussian War had on American military thinking and garb.

black enlisted man named Hazel, "who was always armed with notebook and pencil. In the midst of his agony at our antics the 'Squire' would yell, 'Report him! Hazel, report that man!' and another 'skin' would go down in Hazel's little black book."

A lesser-known but mandatory part of a cadet's training to become an officer and a gen-

tleman was dancing instruction. During summer camp plebes received an unexpected but welcome break from the harassment and military routine in the form of daily hour-long dancing classes. Dancing instructors were brought to West Point to conduct classes which usually featured roommates as partners, although from time to time some young ladies would also par-

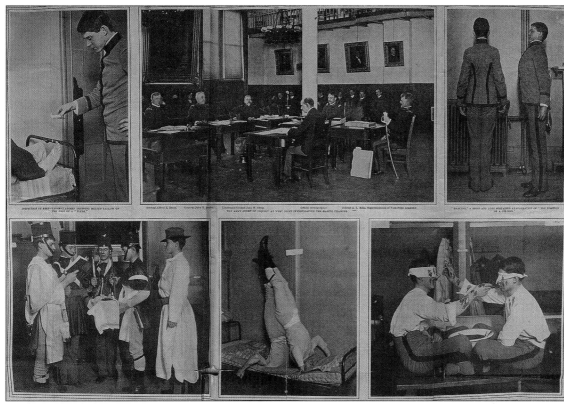

Hazing of plebes developed into a real problem after the Civil War, as the 1900 cartoon "Target Practice at West Point" (above left) suggests. Cadet Oscar Booz died some months after leaving West Point, perhaps from the effects of being forced to drink pints of tabasco sauce. The cartoon from the Summer Camp- book of 1909 depicts hazing as indistinguishable from torture. Photographs, left, depict hazing tech- niques, such as bracing— an extreme posture of attention—and forcing cadets to stand on their heads for hours.

ticipate. As cadet Henry Holt, who entered with the Class of 1891, later wrote, "It was here and only here during the entire 'Plebe Camp' that we had any fun."

West Point has been described as "a military monastery in which the cadets were isolated from the outside diseases of commercialism and money-grubbing, and the officer corps approved of this sequestration." Douglas MacArthur likened it to a provincial reformatory based on fear. Four years at West Point were their own form of penal servitude, eased only by a two-month leave the summer after the second class year and a Christmas leave or two for those in high academic standing.

Discipline verged on the Draconian and was ruthlessly enforced in the form of demerits for any infraction of the regulations. The list of do's

Fighting Man

"FIGHTING JOE" WHEELER, USMA 1859, lived up to his name all his life. Only five feet five inches tall, he acquired the nickname while wearing the blue uniform of the United States Army, defending a wagon train from Indians, shortly after his graduation.

When the Civil War began he entered the Confederate Army and served as commander of cavalry in the Army of the Mississippi. After the surrender, he went back home to Georgia, where he was elected to Congress and served for seventeen years, but his love was the Army, and eventually he re-enlisted. During the Spanish-American War, he served as a Major General, becoming one of two men (the other being Fitz-Hugh Lee '56) to command a corps in both the Confederate and the U.S. Armies.

Shortly after his arrival in Cuba, Wheeler on his own initiative attacked a Spanish position in the village of Las Guasimas. As the Spanish soldiers took to their heels, he is alleged to have shouted, "Give it to them, lads. We got the damn Yankees on the run!" He may have been slightly confused but he was always ready to fight. During the advance on Santiago, he came down with a bad case of malaria, but took the saddle to lead his men across the San Juan River through a hail of enemy fire.

He went on to serve in the Philippines. When he died in 1906, he was buried in uniform—his U.S. Army uniform. An old Confederate soldier who came to see him lying in state was taken aback. "Jeesus, General, I hate to think of what old Stonewall's going to say when he sees you in that uniform." But clearly the uniform mattered less to Joe Wheeler than the good fight itself.　—*C.H.*

and don'ts filled an entire book. Excessive demerits earned the offender punishment tours marched with military precision twice weekly with rifle and pack for two hours. Serious offenses required a personal explanation to the commandant of cadets of which approximately 90 per cent were rejected. "It hardly seems possible," reflected Joseph T. Haw, Class of 1915, "that a grown man was actually reported for touching a lady's arm." Yet, the Tactical Department was so zealous in its guardianship of cadet morals that a cadet was once "skinned" for assisting his own mother across the street.

The honor system in place today existed in a slightly different format after the Civil War. Sylvanus Thayer had first laid down the canon that a West Point cadet's word was his bond and that he was expected to act accordingly. Although accepted as a standard of conduct for the Corps of Cadets, it was never codified until the reforms instituted when Douglas MacArthur served as Superintendent from 1919 to 1922. Although there was no Honor Committee or formal mechanism for dealing with violations, the cadets themselves occasionally took action on their own initiative. In 1871, when some first classmen discovered that two plebes had lied to the commandant, they escorted the offenders from West Point with orders never to return.

One of the few new customs introduced in the post-Civil War era was the celebration of what was then called "100 days until graduation" (later the Hundredth Night Show), a dinner and satiric parodies held by the First Class, sometimes livened by forbidden alcoholic spirits. A form of release from nearly four years of enforced monasticism, the Hundredth Night was epitomized one year with the words:

The reason why we're all so happy now
For it's one hundred days, one hundred days,
It's just one hundred days till June.

The Hundredth Night for Dwight Eisenhower's Class of 1915 achieved a small measure of retribution when its participants lampooned "The Squire" and Hazel. Two appropriately

dressed impersonators appeared on stage and gave remarkably authentic imitations by crooning a song:

For I'm a nut, a nutty nut,
A Hazel nut perhaps.
I'm always fixin' little things
From reveille till taps.

Before the Civil War the practice of hazing was relatively innocuous. After the war, partly to offset the paucity of recreational activities, and with the tacit approval of both graduates and faculty members, hazing intensified and became an integral part of the daily life of a plebe at West Point. "Bracing," petty harassment at meals, on the parade ground, in quarters, and in the quadrangle soon became a part of West Point tradition. The excesses, however, included strenuous physical, and often dangerously harmful, exercise, which included eating soap, administering liberal doses of Tabasco sauce in a plebe's food, and conducting elaborate funeral ceremonies for dead rats. Hazing produced a code of silence on the part of the hapless plebes and it became a matter of dishonor to expose the upperclassmen who perpetrated such mischief. Hazing was even more abusive if one's father possessed a famous name.

In defense of hazing, its legion of advocates argued that it instilled pride and discipline, but the truth was that despite repeated attempts by various Superintendents to stamp out the practice, hazing continued: Those who had endured it believed all plebes should do likewise. Sherman's earlier fondness for remitting cadet punishments also extended to those disciplined for hazing violations. Like most other old grads, he deemed hazing an essential part of the West Point experience and saw no reason upperclassmen should be punished for carrying on the tra-

A BIGGER JOB THAN HE THOUGHT FOR.
Uncle Sam: Behave You Fool! Durn Me, If I Ain't Most Sorry I Undertook To Rescue You.

dition. Not all cadets endorsed hazing, but to oppose it openly led to retaliation, often in the form of "silencing" whereby classmates would refuse to acknowledge or speak to the victim.

By 1895, hazing had become so pervasive that dismissal had become the rule rather than the exception, with the biggest change the fact that political pressures for reinstatement were successfully resisted. Nevertheless, the practice continued virtually unabated. Among the worst examples of hazing run amok occurred in 1899 when plebe Douglas MacArthur, the son of a noted army officer and Medal of Honor winner, was hazed unmercifully because of his father's

The Spanish-American War found the Army unprepared and out of date. A Kurz & Allison lithograph (above right) shows Pershing's black cavalry at Quasimas, Cuba, June 24, 1898. After wresting the Philippines from Spain, Uncle Sam (cartoon) sinks into the sanguinary quagmire of the Philippine Insurrection. Referring to the standard rifle of the time a couplet went, "Beneath the starry flag, We will civilize them with a Krag."

1887

■ Cadet Dining Hall officially named Grant Hall in honor of the gift of the portrait of U.S. Grant by George W. Childs.

1888

■ Peyton Conway March [1864–1955] graduated. In 1918 he became Chief of Staff of the Army and oversaw the doubling in strength of the Army and the increase of the troops in France from only a quarter of a million men to over two million in eight months.

While visiting West Point during the Centennial celebration in 1902, President Theodore Roosevelt (above) pinned the Medal of Honor on Cadet Calvin P. Titus, a trumpeter in the China Relief Expedition who was first over the wall at the siege of Peking during the Boxer Rebellion in 1900. Titus went on to become a cadet, the only man to win the award while at West Point. Right: On June 9, 1902, former Union and Confederate officers sat together on the Cullum Hall stage, signifying the healing of the wounds of the Civil War.

reputation. Indeed, the level of hazing of a son seemed to be in direct proportion to the fame of the father. Among the numerous indignities he faced, MacArthur was forced to lie face down on a hard, wooden floor and pump up and down with his elbows for nearly two hours. As his tormentors taunted him to give up, MacArthur refused; finally it was the upperclassmen who called off the ordeal. MacArthur went into convulsions and might well have died.

Another ugly incident occurred a year earlier, in 1898, when a plebe named Oscar L.

Booz was repeatedly tormented by being forced to drink such copious quantities of Tabasco sauce at meals that he resigned and died in 1900 from tuberculosis in his larynx. Although the TB was not caused by hazing, the resulting public scandal led to a congressional investigation and a demand by President William McKinley that West Point reform itself. Cadet MacArthur narrowly averted dismissal after refusing to reveal to a court of inquiry the names of the cadets who had hazed him in 1899. MacArthur was later called to testify before Congress, but down-played his hazing, and again refused to reveal the names of the culprits, although he did admit under intense questioning that the practice of hazing was not essential to the training of an officer.

Bad publicity notwithstanding, hazing remained part of the fabric of West Point. The primary difference after 1900 was that hazing had evolved from a de facto traditional right to the less harmful harassments that characterize modern-day plebe training. MacArthur, for one, never forgot his ordeal and would later achieve his own form of vindication through the reforms he initiated as Superintendent after World War I.

West Pointers joyously welcomed the Spanish-American War in 1898 as both a welcome diversion and a test of their training. The class of 1898 was graduated early to enable its participation in John Hay's mischaracterized "splendid little war"—that was further mythologized by Theodore Roosevelt's Rough Riders'—successful but foolhardy charge on foot up San Juan Hill. The war with Spain was anything but splendid. Relatively few combat deaths were offset by more than 5,000 fatalities from disease. Incompetence, lack of essential supplies and equipment, squalid conditions, and scandal were its real hallmarks. Among the few West Pointers

■ William George Haan [1863–1924], the son of German immigrants, graduated. He received the Silver Star for action during the attack on Manila in 1898 and was later selected as a member of the original General Staff Corps in 1903.

■ First Army-Navy football game was played on November 29: Navy won 24-0. Navy had been playing for several years, Army never.

■ Second Army-Navy football game was played at Annapolis. A cadet sent telegrams to West Point after each touchdown, but because of his excitement, the final score was not announced until after the evening meal: "Final score, Army 32, Navy 16."

■ Charles Pelot Summerall [1867–1955] was First Captain of the class of 1892. A divisional and corps commander in World War I, he became Chief of Staff of the Army in 1926.

■ Lincoln Clark Andrews [1867–1950] graduated from West Point after completing three years at Cornell. He served in the Spanish-American War and taught physics at West Point before being transferred to the Philippines where he was governor of Leyte.

■ Fox Conner [1874–1951] graduated high in his class. His meticulous attention to detail in planning AEF operations set high standards for the American staff and impressed the French; he influenced almost every major American action in the war. Between the wars he groomed Dwight D. Eisenhower as a future wartime leader.

■ Gothic-style West Academic Building completed: designed by architect Richard M. Hunt.

killed during the war was one of the Academy's most famous football players, Denis Mahan Michie, for whom the football stadium was named after its construction in 1924. Michie was killed in action at the Bloody Bend of the San Juan River before Roosevelt's assault on the Hill. The U.S. cavalry was commanded by Fighting Joe Wheeler, class of 1859, who had risen to the rank of lieutenant general as one of the Confederacy's most able and dashing cavalrymen. During the battle for San Juan Hill on July 1, 1898, Wheeler was sitting on his horse in the middle of a stream, unruffled and exposed as fire erupted around him. Moments before, an 1886 graduate, First Lieutenant John J. Pershing, had stopped to salute him when a shell landed so close it soaked both officers. As the Spanish were routed by the Rough Riders and Pershing's all-black 10th Cavalry, Wheeler shouted the now famous (and hilarious) remark, "We've got the damn Yankees on the run!"

Pershing emerged from the war with a reputation for bravery for his role in organizing and leading his black troops in the charge up Kettle Hill and San Juan Hill. Pershing, who has been described as "cool as a bowl of cracked ice," earned lesser distinction as a tac officer while assigned to West Point the year before. Unbending by nature, so sternly and rigidly had Pershing enforced discipline that he became the most unpopular tac at West Point. The cadets began snidely referring to the former First Captain of the Corps as "Nigger Jack," an overtly racist reference to his assignment to the black 10th Cav-

In this summer camp photo, Douglas MacArthur is the cadet standing farthest right.

The USMA was often called on to perform at ceremonial events. Here, the West Point Band (right) leads the Corps of Cadets down Pennsylvania Avenue toward the White House at President William Howard Taft's inauguration parade in 1909.

alry Regiment. The denunciation eventually evolved into "Black Jack," the nickname by which Pershing was referred for the remainder of his life.

Pershing's reputation as the Army's sternest disciplinarian is in marked contrast to his struggles with French, an average academic record, and his own indifference to discipline as a cadet. During his four years at West Point, Cadet Pershing racked up over two hundred demerits, mostly for tardiness—none of which prevented him from being elected class president and, in his First Class year, appointment as Senior (First) Captain of the Corps. Nevertheless, his future conduct was predictable as a cadet. Pershing's "undoubting certainty of duty combined with a glacial self-possession," notes his biographer Frank Vandiver, tended "to irritate some of his fellow cadets," as did his reputation as a "spoony man" with "an impressive variety of girls." As acting Senior First Sergeant in charge of plebe training in 1883, Pershing "tolerated no slovenliness or sloth in his camp," and hazed his charges "with gusto." Among those put off by Pershing's aloofness was Robert Lee Bullard (Class of 1885), who would command the Second Army in the AEF under Pershing.

The other half of the war against Spain

occurred in the Philippines where Commodore George Dewey led an American fleet in the rout of the Spanish in Manila Bay in May 1898. After purchasing the Philippines for $20 million from Spain the following year, the United States began to learn the price of being a colonial power was far more costly. The first warfare of the new century to involve large numbers of West Pointers was the Philippine Insurrection. Between 1899 and 1902, the U.S. Army fought its first guerilla war, an ugly conflict with Philippine rebels led by Emilio Aguinaldo, who had helped Dewey capture Manila. In the jungles of Luzon and Mindanao, West Pointers fought for the first time in a jungle war; sixteen graduates died.

A sizeable number saw service in both Cuba and the Philippines. Philippine service also enhanced a number of reputations of men destined for later high command. Of the many West Pointers who served in the Philippines, Pershing's achievements as a soldier-diplomat were unrivaled. A number of other graduates who were future Army chiefs of staff also solidified their reputations, including Peyton C. March, John L. Hines, and Charles P. Summerall. Both wars brought what historian Pappas calls, "Media

Until the admission of women in 1976 West Point saw young ladies primarily as recreation and ornament. Left: Two cadets engage in competitive spooning with a girl sitting on the monument at Trophy Point. A cadet and his girl stroll along Flirtation Walk on the postcard, inset. Bottom, Joseph Stilwell '04, left center, is pictured with his sisters, Mary Augusta Stilwell and Alice Stilwell, among a group of friends on the steps of Cullum Hall.

Flirtation Walk,
West Point, N. Y.

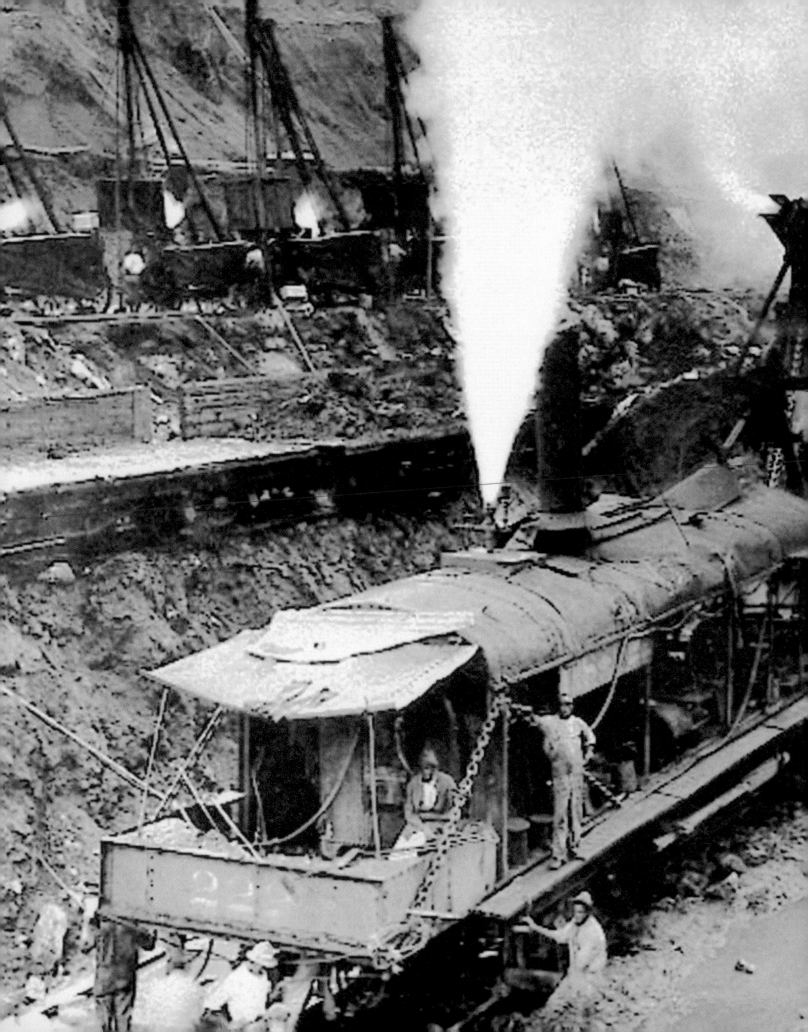

Intersection between lower and middle locks, Gatun, Panama Canal.

The Panama Canal was the largest engineering project ever undertaken. Two hundred sixty-two million cubic yards of earth came out of the Big Ditch. Inset: Men trained at West Point designed and built the enormous locks at Gatun, which have worked flawlessly ever since.

THE CZAR OF THE ZONE

At the Isthmus of Panama, the world's two great oceans are fifty miles apart, and at least since the Spanish Conquest the idea of cutting a seaway between them has been an irresistible dream. For more than 300 years it was an impossible dream. Late in the nineteenth century, fresh from the triumph of Suez, the French tried and failed, at an immeasurable cost in money and lives. When Teddy Roosevelt organized an American assault on the problem in 1903, that too seemed at first destined to fail, overwhelmed by the steaming impenetrable jungles, the ferocious heat and deluges of rain, the snakes and mosquitoes, the yellow fever and malaria and pneumonia and plague.

In fact Roosevelt's first attempt to organize the Canal project collapsed in a panicky flight as disease swept the workforce. The President tried again, with a new chief engineer, John Stevens, who for the first time managed to bring some order to the chaotic mess in Panama, compounded of the French and now the American failure.

Then, with the project starting to move forward, Stevens, abruptly, mysteriously, quit. Furious, Roosevelt declared he would give the work to "men who will stay on the job until I get tired of having them there, or till I say they may abandon it. I shall turn it over to the Army."

What he meant was, he was giving it to the Army's best engineer, Colonel George Washington Goethals, '80.

Goethals was the son of Flemish immigrants. He had grown up in poverty and made his way on hard work and sheer intelligence, graduating second in his class from West Point. He went into the Corps of Engineers and worked on rivers and harbors from the Cumberland to Nantucket; at Muscle Shoals he built a lock on the canal with a record rise of twenty-six feet. He was a correct, dignified, introverted man, supremely self-confident, whose life was his work. He was utterly honest. His imperturbable persistence would become legendary.

Roosevelt, in giving him the assignment, had put him in an astonishing position. The President had decided that the only way to get the canal built was to find the right man and give him total control; he had ordered the committee that officially oversaw the project to agree with Goethals in all things or resign. Goethals was responsible to no one. He ruled the Canal Zone absolutely, and every man and woman in it, all coupled to the single purpose of dividing it neatly in half.

Goethals came into a taut situation, with nearly everybody on the job loyal to the man he replaced and resentful of the newcomer's power. That he was an officer in the Army did not help much. Goethals didn't bother trying to warm things up. From the beginning he made it clear that he was boss. There was no negotiating. When a high-ranking engineer threatened to resign over an order, Goethals accepted the resignation immediately and would not consider retracting it even when the startled engineer backpedaled. Throughout the following seven years his personal relations with many of the higher level staff were very prickly. Yet everybody did his job; Goethals focused himself and everybody else on the matter at hand, and the work got done.

As it got done, as it became evident that they were succeeding in this—

Between them, Theodore Roosevelt and Goethals split the Isthmus on this three-cent stamp commemorating the Canal's 25th anniversary in 1939.

the greatest engineering project of all time, the Big Job—a sense of pride lit up the whole workforce, and they transferred that glow to their boss.

Goethals worked harder than anybody, ten hours a day, seven days a week. He had a special railroad car made, self-propelled, bright yellow, and went up and down the line from site to site, personally supervising the whole extraordinary work. The workmen knew when that distinctive car—they called it the Yellow Peril—barreled into sight around a curve that they had better be working at top speed and peak efficiency; "the Colonel" missed nothing.

He listened to everybody. Every Sunday morning, like a medieval king, he held a court: in the whole 40,000 person workforce anybody with a grievance could come and tell him. These Sundays drew upwards of a hundred people a day, wives griping about husbands, men with ideas about the work, workers accusing unjust foremen, even, once, a request that a certain steamshovel driver be transferred to another sector, whose baseball team needed a pitcher. Goethals listened to everybody, a mix, as one man said, "of father confessor and Day of Judgment." The baseball team got its man.

The Big Job itself exhausts superlatives; the amount of dirt excavated, the tonnage of dynamite, the ingenious machinery, the staggering cost. What now seems even more amazing than the actual building of the Canal was the transformation of the Canal Zone.

The key to completion was to create livable conditions for the thousands upon thousands of people who worked on it. Goethals and his men took a mountainous tropical jungle so hot, rainy, and dense with inimical lifeforms that the first few explorers got lost and went mad within a few miles of their starting points. In the space of a few years they turned it into a ten-mile-wide strip of ersatz New Jersey, complete with bowling alleys, baseball teams, movie theaters, and Masonic Halls. If the people living in this utopia seemed suspiciously very much alike, even robotic, that was the flip side of their success: they were engaged in a great work, and they loved what they were doing, unified and upbeat as only a winning army can be.

Besides George Washington Goethals, several other West Point men served in the Canal Zone. William Sibert '84 headed the Atlantic Division, where the great Gatun dam and locks were built; Major David Du Bose Gailliard '84 was in charge of the Central Division, the famous Culebra Cut through the mountain spine. To head his design staff, Goethals brought in Lt. Colonel Harry Foote Hodges, '81, who designed mechanisms nobody had ever tried to make before, and which have worked flawlessly since the 1914 opening of the Canal. These men, with Goethals, took up Teddy Roosevelt's challenge and delivered. He gave it to the Army, and the Army did the job.   —*C.H.*

1896
■ *Howitzer*, first published in 1884, changed format to combine with cadet album and become a yearbook. The book was omitted by some classes and until 1904 was published without official sanction.

1897
■ Battle Monument was dedicated on Trophy Point May 31. Designed by Stanford White, it honors the Regular Army casualties of the Civil War. The metal came from fifty bronze guns captured from the Confederates. The shaft of the monument is the largest piece of turned granite in the Western Hemisphere.

1898
■ Cullum Memorial Hall completed. Designed by McKim, Meade, and White in Classical Revival style. Named after Major General George W. Cullum, USMA 1833, Superintendent 1864-1866.

1899
■ Cadet Douglas MacArthur reported to USMA as a plebe in the Class of 1903.
■ The Academy adopted black, gold, and gray as its colors and the mule as its mascot. Tradition holds that the cadets took an oversized white mule to the Navy game and that when the Navy goat charged it, the mule "hoisted it into the blue stands."

1900
■ The reservoir south of Fort Putnam officially named Lusk Reservoir in honor of LTC James L. Lusk, USMA 1878, West Point's former Constructing Engineer.
■ Chapel of the Roman Catholic Most Holy Trinity completed.

1901
■ In West Point's first century, 238 graduates were killed in battle.
■ Congress prescribed examination of appointees requiring them 'to be well versed in such subjects as [the Secretary of War] may from time to time prescribe.'

1902
■ At Centennial celebration, Medal of Honor presented to Cadet Calvin P. Titus [fourth classman] for "gallantry at Peking, China, August 14, 1900, while a soldier of the Fourteenth United States Infantry."
■ June: Congress approves $5.5 million expansion of West Point.
■ In first century of existence: 4,121 graduates; appropriations for century $22,259,274.55.

coverage . . . ostentatious in its praise of West Point and the education given its cadets."

The Spanish-American War was also significant in that four former graduates who had served the Confederacy as generals were recommissioned as generals in the U.S. Army. In addition to Joseph Wheeler, they were: Matthew Calbraith Butler, Fitzhugh Lee, and Thomas Lafayette Rosser, George A. Custer's great friend. It was yet another positive sign that the wounds of the Civil War were nearly healed.

In 1867, Charles Dickens had described West Point as "the fairest among the fair . . . with memories of Washington, and events of the Revolutionary War, is the Military School of America." It was with this attitude that West Point began its second century of existence, which except for the advent of hazing and intercollegiate sports, had changed little since the Civil War at what was now a venerable but still academically stagnant institution.

The centennial celebration in 1902 drew President Theodore Roosevelt, Secretary of War Elihu Root, and a host of other dignitaries to West Point during June graduation week, highlighted by parades, ceremonies, and lavish ora-

In the building boom of the early 1900s, West Point held a design competition, which was won by Cram, Goodhue and Ferguson of Boston. The firm was responsible for the predominantly Gothic style of USMA architecture, like the Chapel, below, completed in 1910.

Thirty-six percent of the graduates of the Class of 1915 (below) would go on to become generals, making this "The Class the Stars Fell On." Among these shining lights were (above, left to right) Dwight D. Eisenhower, Omar N. Bradley, and James A. Van Fleet.

tions. Roosevelt proclaimed that during its first century, "no other educational institution in the land has contributed as many names as West Point has contributed to the honor role of the nation's great citizens." Moreover, "taken as a whole, the average graduate of West Point during this hundred years has given a greater sum of service to the country through his life than has the average graduate of any other institution in this broad land."

More importantly, the centennial marked the final healing of the wounds of the Civil War. Although the new Cullum Hall, named in honor of former superintendent George Washington Cullum, was officially opened in 1898, it was the centerpiece of the centennial celebrations. Though the building was dedicated to West Point's graduates, in his bequest, Cullum had stipulated that no Confederate alumni were to be honored. However, by 1902 Cullum's

■ Cadet Douglas MacArthur graduated with the highest scholastic record attained by any cadet in twenty-five years.

■ Class of 1904 applied for official permission to publish the *Howitzer*, and Superintendent, General Albert L. Mills granted it, making it the first officially sanctioned edition of the yearbook.

■ The Model 1903 bolt-action rifle was issued to replace the .30 caliber Krag-Jorgensen. Called the "Springfield" or the "03," it would remain the cadet weapon until 1940, when the M-1 semi-automatic Garand replaced it.

■ One morning the hands on the clock tower of what is today Eisenhower Barracks were missing, full moons painted over both clock faces, with the inscription "100 days Till June." The following day, a package arrived for Col. Robert L. Howze, the commandant, containing the hands.

■ *Bugle Notes*, the handbook for cadets containing useful information as well as detailed trivia and nonsense to be memorized by Plebes for questioning by upper classmen, first published.

■ Edmund Louis "Snitz" Gruber [USMA 1904] composed the *Caisson Song* on a guitar, while on duty in the Philippines. The song was soon adopted as the official song of the Field Artillery and later as the official song of the U.S. Army.

■ George S. Patton, Jr., graduated after being set back one year for deficiency in mathematics. He became first American to compete in the Modern Pentathlon— an event stressing horsemanship, running, swimming, and marksmanship—at the 1912 Olympics.

views were not only outdated, but no longer represented the widespread feeling that enough was enough. On Alumni Day, June 9, the principal speaker was a former Confederate General, E. Porter Alexander, Class of 1857, Longstreet's chief of artillery, who praised the valor of both the Union and the Confederacy. Afterwards, the band not only played the *Star-Spangled Banner* but also *Dixie*, as many of the assembled alumni on the stage of Cullum Hall,

former foes, tearfully embraced.

West Point's infrastructure was literally falling down around itself. It was time to rebuild and between 1903 and 1913, a massive construction program was funded by Congress. The result was that virtually all of West Point was either rebuilt or expanded, with the addition of new buildings such as the imposing cadet chapel which dominates the West Point skyline.

One of West Point's most famous sons,

■ Cadet Chapel completed. The stained glass window over the altar has twenty-seven panels, each depicting a militant Biblical character. The Chapel Organ is the largest in the Western Hemisphere. The chapel seats 1,500.

■ Paul S. Reinecke graduated, composer of West Point Alma Mater. According to tradition, Reinecke composed the song while walking punishment tours in the fall of 1908.

■ The Department of mathematics made an instructor available during cadet recreation hours to give extra instruction to cadets who requested it.

■ East Academic Building [later renamed Bartlett Hall] completed as part of the Centennial rebuilding program in "Military Gothic" style.

■ Herman Koehler completed and published the "Koehler Manual" [*Physical Training With and Without Special Equipment*], which became the basis for physical training throughout the Army during World War I. Koehler became known as the "Father of Army Physical Training."

■ Dwight David Eisenhower never held a rank higher than color sergeant. He graduated near the middle of his class, with one hundred demerits his first year. Other 1915 graduates: Omar N. Bradley and James A. Van Fleet.

Dwight D. Eisenhower, arrived in 1911 as a cocky plebe in what would later be renowned as "the class the stars fell on." The Class of 1915 would become the most celebrated in West Point history. No class ever produced more successful generals. In addition to Eisenhower and Omar N. Bradley who attained the five-star rank of General of the Army, fifty-nine members (36 per cent of the class) later became general officers. They were a virtual "who's who" of World War II, including Joseph McNarney, George Stratemeyer, and Joseph Swing. Those who commanded divisions in the European Theater of Operations under Eisenhower were: Charles W. Ryder, Le Roy Irwin, Roscoe Woodruff, Leland Hobbs, John W. Leonard, Leroy Watson and James Van Fleet, who later attained four-star rank as the commanding general of the Eighth Army in Korea. At his death in 1992 at the age of a hundred, Van Fleet was the last surviving member of the Class of 1915.

For a headstrong, poor boy from rural Kansas desperate to attain a free education, Eisenhower did not always take West Point seriously. During his four years his laid-back attitude toward discipline and the Academy's stern rules might well have resulted in expulsion had he been caught for some of his antics. As it was, Eisenhower's disciplinary record reflects copious demerits and a not inconsiderable time spent pounding the quadrangle pavement walking punishment tours.

Eisenhower's knee was badly injured during a football game against Tufts in 1912. After examining his swollen knee his doctors prescribed only rest until the swelling disappeared, leaving Eisenhower convinced he had recovered. Then disaster struck. "The doctors didn't warn me I had a permanently weakened knee. So I went riding," doing a voluntary "monkey-drill team"

performance which required dismounting and remounting a horse at the gallop, often while facing to the rear. The first time Eisenhower tried it, "I just crashed myself all to pieces."

Eisenhower spent four agonizing days in the infirmary where the injury was pronounced permanent. "So I had to give that [athletics] up." His leg was immobilized in a cast, his days as an athlete at an inglorious end; "it was just too hard for me to accept for a while," he once remarked.

In the spring of 1915, Eisenhower's unresolved knee injury was deemed sufficiently serious that the Army planned to deny him a commission. Had it not been for the timely intervention of the academy surgeon, Lieutenant Colonel Henry A. Shaw, Cadet Eisenhower would not have been commissioned in June 1915. Fortunately, Shaw was a pragmatist who believed neither Eisenhower nor the army would benefit. He lobbied members of the Tactical Department and the Academic Board to support Eisenhower. Shaw's efforts paid off when the decision was reversed and the War Department agreed to Eisenhower's commissioning.

Eisenhower graduated with a rather cynical disdain of ever returning to West Point in an official capacity during his future army service. Nevertheless, West Point fulfilled its mission by imbuing the youthful Kansan with a strong sense of duty and honor that grew as the years passed. Joseph Haw may well have spoken for the class of 1915 when he noted that "the historic traditions of West Point were rarely discussed yet somehow the part the Academy had played in the history of our country was unconsciously absorbed by the most thoughtless cadet ... There was no flag-waving but there grew up within us a deep pride in our school and our army and a feeling that we must live up to the

STAR OF STARS

—by Stephen E. Ambrose

Dwight David Eisenhower of Abilene, Kansas, was one of 164 graduates in the Class of 1915, one of the most famous of all West Point's classes—the class the stars fell on. Fifty-nine of them rose to the rank of brigadier general or higher, three to the rank of full general, two to the rank of general of the army. Members included Vernon Prichard, George Stratemeyer, Charles Ryder, Stafford Irwin, Joseph McNarney, James Van Fleet, Hubert Harmon, and Omar Bradley. Eisenhower was not one of the top graduates, either in scholarship or discipline. Indeed he stood 125th in discipline. Cigarette smoking was strictly forbidden, for example. "So," Eisenhower remarked laconically, "I started smoking cigarettes." But these and other infractions hardly bothered him. He later admitted that he "looked with distaste on classmates whose days and nights were haunted by fear of demerits and low grades." During World War II, he expressed astonishment that one of his classmates had made general officer rank. "Christ," he said, "he's always been afraid to break a regulation."

His own favorite story about a cadet prank centered on the sometimes absurd literalness of the regulations and orders. Eisenhower and another plebe, named Atkins, were guilty of an infraction. The cadet corporal who caught them, named Adler, ordered them to report to his room after tattoo in "full-dress coats," meaning a complete dress uniform. The two plebes decided to do exactly as ordered and that night reported to Adler wearing their coats and not another stitch of clothing.

Adler roared in anger. He ordered them to return after tattoo "in complete uniform including rifles and cross belts and if you miss a single item, I'll have you down here every night for a week." They did as ordered and suffered through a long session of bracing and lecturing, but

the laughs they and their fellow plebes got from Adler's discomfort made the prank worthwhile.

Hazing had little appeal to Eisenhower. In his third-class year, a plebe, dashing down the street to carry out an order, ran into him and tumbled to the ground. Reacting with a "bellow of astonishment and mock indignation," Eisenhower scornfully demanded, "Mr. Durngard, what is your P.C.S. [Previous Condition of Servitude]?", adding sarcastically, "You look like a barber."

The plebe pulled himself together and replied softly, "I was a barber, sir."

Eisenhower turned red with embarrassment. Without a word, he returned to his room where he told his roommate, P.A. Hodgson, "I'm never going to crawl [haze] another plebe as long as I live. As a matter of fact, they'll have to run over and knock me out of the company street before I'll make any attempt again. I've just done something that was stupid

and unforgivable. I managed to make a man ashamed of the work he did to earn a living."

In 1964, Eisenhower was with Walter Cronkite during the filming of a documentary entitled "D-Day Plus Twenty Years." They were sitting on a stone wall overlooking Omaha Beach on one site, the cemetery on the other. Cronkite asked him what he thought of when he returned to this sacred soil. Had he asked that question of Bernard Law Montgomery, Monty would have spoken of how good the plan was, how the Allies had fooled the Germans, about the excellence of his staff. Had he asked Omar Bradley, Brad would have responded about how well-trained the troops were, what a grand job they did. George S. Patton would have replied about how many Germans the Allies had killed.

Eisenhower lettered in football until a severe knee injury cut short his sports career.

Eisenhower's response was, "You know, Walter, Mamie and I get our greatest pleasure from our grandchildren. When I look at all these graves, I think of the parents back in the States whose only son is buried here. Because of their sacrifice, they don't have the pleasure of grandchildren. Because of their sacrifice, my grandchildren are growing up in freedom."

These anecdotes, separated by a full half-century, speak eloquently to the kind of man he was. And to the kind of man West Point could turn out.

great tradition we had inherited."

In 1911, the entire Corps consisted of 650 young men and was organized as "The Battalion," consisting of six companies, A through F. Of the 287 cadets who constituted the Class of 1915 (at the time, West Point's largest ever plebe class), only 164 actually graduated—an attrition rate of forty-four per cent. The class was hardly a representative cross-section of young American men. Most were predominantly Protestants of Anglo-Saxon, Irish, English, Scottish, or German origin. Other than its larger numbers, this class hardly differed in makeup from previous classes in the half century that followed the Civil War.

Some, like George S. Patton '09, attended West Point out of a desire to become Army offi-

cers, but a great many others, like Eisenhower and his classmate from Missouri, Omar Bradley, attended West Point primarily because it offered them the free education they could not otherwise afford. Omar Bradley called his four years at West Point, "the most rewarding of my life." Unlike Eisenhower, Bradley "loved every minute of it," in no small part because of his passion for athletics, particularly baseball, at which he excelled.

Until the advent of World War I, West Point's existence continued in the same timeless fashion that characterized the half century since the end the Civil War. By 1914, however, the calm was about to be shattered by the most catastrophic war in history. Its impact on West Point and its graduates would be profound.

5

THE GREAT WAR AND AFTER

BY ROBERT COWLEY

"The standards for the American Army will be those of West Point. The rigid attention, the upright bearing, attention to detail, uncomplaining obedience to instruction required of the cadet will be required of every officer and soldier of our armies in France."

—John J. Pershing,
Commander of the A.E.F., 1917

■ Washington Monument completed. Gift of an anonymous donor, it is a replica of the monument in Union Square, New York City. Originally located at the corner of Thayer and Cullum Roads, it now stands in front of Washington Hall, the Cadet Mess Hall.

■ 267 cadets began as what would become the Class of 1919. They graduated November 1, 1918, toured the battlefields of Europe and were recalled as "graduated cadets" or "student officers," uniformed in olive drab and gold bars on December 3. They graduated a second time on June 11, 1919.

■ At the end of World War I West Point graduates held almost all positions of responsibility in the army.
■ The year of Chateau-Thierry, Soissons, St. Mihiel, and the Meuse-Argonne.

■ Douglas MacArthur became Superintendent for three years. His tenure was marked by the reestablishment of the Honor System; upgrading of faculty qualifications; and the establishment of a system of intramural competition by cadets in all major sports.

■ Graduates 1802–1920: 6,810; 1910–1920: 1,875.
■ Major Robert M. Danford, Commandant of Cadets, introduced a course on leadership based on the pioneering work of Lincoln C. Andrews, USMA 1893.

■ *West Point Songs* saw print, the first collection ever published. The authors were Philip Egner, the Academy bandmaster, and Frederick C. Mayer, the organist and choirmaster.

■ Maxwell Davenport Taylor [1901–1987] graduated from the Military Academy, First Captain and fourth in the Class of 1922. Following the Second World War, Taylor became superintendent of the USMA, where he significantly revised and updated the curriculum. President Eisenhower named Taylor Army Chief of Staff.

A t West Point, World War I is a war without monuments. There is almost no visible trace of a conflict that will soon have not a single survivor of the four million Americans who served, eight decades ago, a conflict that was known in its time as the Great War, until a greater one came along. In Cullum Hall, if you wander down from the old ballroom that is now given over to wrestling, you may spot at the foot of those broad stairs a few inconspicuous bronze plaques with Distinguished Service Crosses in tarnished relief. All memorialize graduates killed in action in 1918: Robert Jayne Maxey '98, Cantigny, May 28 . . . Arthur Edward Bouton '08, near Soissons, July 18 . . . Hamilton Allen Smith '93, also near Soissons, July 22 . . . James Andrew Shannon '03, Châtel-Chéhéry in the Argonne, October 8. Their names are almost lost among the bigger and more conspicuous plaques that line the staircase, like the one listing the West Point Congressional Medal of Honor winners. By way of comparison, there are eight names for the Second World War but only one for the First. Who remembers Emory Jenison Pike '01?

PRECEDING SPREAD: *In the spring of 1917, the French General Joseph Joffre, center, the Hero of the Marne, reviews the Corps during a visit to West Point. The U.S. had just declared war on Germany, and Joffre had come to plead for immediate and massive American aid. Right: Douglas MacArthur '03 was one of the genuine American heroes of World War I, whose achievement under fire marked him for greatness.*

The general American disregard for World War I should come as no surprise. We were in serious combat for just five and a half months. Compared with the combined fatalities of France and the British Empire, over two million men, the 50,000 American battle deaths seem insignificant—though an average of almost 10,000 dead per month can hardly be dismissed as the loose change of mortality. Thirty-two West Pointers died in combat, though their battle death rate was slightly higher than that of the entire American officer corps. (The death rate among middle-rank commanders—majors, captains, and first lieutenants—was dramatically higher: twenty-two per thousand for all officers of those grades compared to forty-two per thousand for West Pointers.) It's also worth noting that graduates won no less than sixty-odd Distinguished Service Crosses, the nation's second highest award for bravery. But casualty figures aren't a fair measure of the importance of our first European military venture. Our partic-

ipation literally tilted the balance in favor of the Allies at a time when it seemed that Germany was about to redeem the opportunities squandered in 1914. Those few months of battle, as well as the effort required to raise a huge army from scratch and ship it across the Atlantic, established the United States as a major power in the world, *the* coming great power, even if we rushed to deny our pre-eminence the moment the war ended. West Point, too, would share in that abdication of responsibility. And once again, as it had done in the past, the Academy would be forced to redeem itself.

The Class of 1915 graduated on June 12, and after a three-months-long summer furlough, the new second lieutenants scattered to army bases all over the continent. The U.S. Army then numbered about 100,000 men, all professionals, but was mainly a constabulary force. That it could play a significant role in the year-old European war seemed out of the question—though when a German U-boat torpedoed the British liner *Lusi-*

■ First publication of *The Pointer*, a cadet semi-monthly publication of humor and comment. Its immediate predecessor as a cadet journalistic endeavor was *The Bray*, which had appeared in November 1919.

■ Michie Stadium completed. Named for Lieutenant Dennis Mahan Michie, USMA 1892, founder of the first West Point football team, killed in action at San Juan, Cuba, July 1, 1898.

■ Department of Practical Military Engineering abolished, its functions having been assumed by the Department of Civil and Military engineering.

■ United States Hotel Thayer completed at Highland Falls entrance. In the Tudor style, it accommodates 500 guests.

■ Garrison Holt Davidson [1904–1992] graduated high in his class. General Davidson was one of the youngest generals in World War II. He received his first star from General George S. Patton at the age of thirty-nine in Sicily, where he was chief engineer for Patton's First Armored Corps.

■ James Elbert Briggs [1906–1979] graduated from West Point and entered primary flying school before transferring to the Air Corps from the Field Artillery. He became the second superintendent of the Air Force Academy.

■ Lt. Gen. James A. Gavin graduates. Led daring airborne attacks in Europe during World War II, and served twice as ambassador to France under President John F. Kennedy. He wore the two stars of a major general at age thirty-seven, one of the youngest men ever to hold that rank.

tania in May, with the loss of 128 American lives, sentiment began to swing in favor of the Allies and there was talk of inevitable involvement.

Some of those 1915 graduates got an early (but in view of the European fracas, irrelevant) taste of campaigning after raiders, led by the Mexican bandit Francisco "Pancho" Villa, killed seventeen Americans at Columbus, New Mexico, the following March. A punitive expedition led by Brigadier General John J. Pershing '86 penetrated four hundred miles into Mexico but did precious little punishing. Villa and his main force eluded Pershing, and his goose chase nearly provoked a war with Mexico. For the officers, the expedition must have been a clubby affair: almost all were West Pointers. One who earned headlines, as well as a long deferred promotion to first lieutenant, was twenty-nine-year-old George S. Patton '12, who served as an aide to Pershing. While heading a party of foragers in automobiles, Patton encountered three armed Villistas on horseback. Shots were exchanged. The Americans cut down the Mexicans and then drove back to Pershing's headquarters with the corpses tied like dead deer to the car hoods. It was Patton's first firefight—and also, in the words of his biographer, Martin Blumenson, "the first time in U.S. Army history that a unit had motored to battle."

In the meantime West Point went on as it always had, isolated from, and seemingly impervious to, the mounting pressures for preparedness and President Woodrow Wilson's frantic efforts to remain neutral. "He kept us out of war" became the most memorable slogan of the election campaign of 1916; as events would soon prove, he didn't. Cadets neither had the time to read the newspapers, nor were they encouraged to do so. According to a local newspaper on September 19, 1914:

The officers, cadets, enlisted men, and civilian employees at West Point have been forbidden to discuss the present European War. This order follows the line of the president's neutrality proclamation. It is said that it was caused by several soldiers getting into a hot argument over the war recently and almost coming to blows.

Aside from instilling leadership qualities in cadets, the endless marching and drilling and polishing had no relation to war as it was being fought in the trenches of the Western Front. That would all change on April 6, 1917, Good Friday, when Wilson signed a declaration of war. Two weeks later, the Class of 1917 would be graduated early and rushed into service.

West Pointers would largely run the military side of the war, to an extent even greater than they had done in the Civil War. Of the general officers in the American army, some three-quarters, or 366, were West Point graduates, including two Chiefs of Staff, Tasker H. Bliss and, later, Peyton C. March, and the Commander of the American Expeditionary Force, Pershing. Thirty-four of the thirty-eight corps and division commanders on the Western Front were West Pointers. Under the pressures of time and the demands of the manpower-starved Allied commanders, Pershing had to forego the luxury of leadership experimentation: he turned to West Point classmates or people he had admired during his cadet days or his brief tenure as a tactical officer. Some of those he would find wanting and would summarily fire them "without application"—meaning that once an officer was relieved of command, he could not appeal; his career in the Army was in effect over.

Pershing, the man at the head of the largest American military force ever assembled, and on foreign soil to boot, was practically everyone's first choice to lead the A.E.F. Though admired by many, as it has been often said, this frigidly laconic general was loved by few (and most of those were women). He was a fanatical disciplinarian. He was inflexible to a fault—something the Allied leadership soon learned when it attempted to "amalgamate" American troops into their divisions under French and British commanders. Pershing would have none of it: He insisted on a separate American army. (To his credit, he did willingly lend divisions when they were needed in the crisis of the spring and summer of 1918.) "The standards for the American Army will be those of West Point," he proclaimed in October 1917. "The rigid attention, the upright bearing, attention to detail, uncomplaining obedience to instruction required of the cadet will be required of every officer and soldier of our armies in France."

The 1st Division, supposedly a regular outfit but padded out with new recruits, was the first American unit to reach France. It was hardly in the West Point mold. The 1st arrived at the end of June, two weeks after Pershing and his 191-man staff had been pelted with flowers as they drove to the Hotel Crillon in Paris. A battalion marched in a specially organized Fourth of July parade in the French capital. Pershing remarked that "the untrained, awkward appearance of the unit, which was regarded by the French officers as representing our Regular Army, could not have escaped their critical observation." Patton, who accompanied Pershing to an inspection of a training depot as his aide-de-camp, found the just-arrived troops sloppy, their officers lazy, and the field exercises listless. At the end of the year Patton left to head a school for the new Tank Corps at Langres. (His first memo as commander emphasized those West Point virtues, personal appearance and proper saluting.) For three

months his men had to train without actual tanks; gunnery practice had to be conducted from wooden tank mock-ups on rockers to simulate firing while moving over rough ground.

It was October before a few battalions of the 1st Division showed up in a quiet section of the line east of Nancy. Though many of the commanders were West Pointers, French officers kept the new arrivals under tight rein. The Americans suffered their first casualties. They took part in raids and were in turn raided. On the night of February 26, 1918, Colonel Douglas MacArthur, Chief of Staff for the 42nd (Rainbow) Division, went out with a party of French poilus. He reappeared in the early hours of the morning, prodding a captured German colonel through a gap in the wire with the riding crop he always affected. But the seat of his breeches had been somehow ripped out along the way. The exploit earned him a Silver Star. By the end of March, when the Germans launched the first of a series of great offensives that nearly turned the war around, Americans held just seventeen of the 468 miles of the Western Front and could muster a combat strength of 162,000, drops as yet inconsiderable in the Allied manpower bucket.

Not until May 28, almost a year after Pershing's arrival, would the A.E.F. encounter its first real test. It came at Cantigny, a hamlet in southern Picardy that had been swallowed by the German March offensive. Cantigny had no special value or operational significance other than the fact that it faced a stretch of line held by the 1st Division. As Western Front operations went, the attack on Cantigny was tiny, a single-division affair, little more than a glorified raid. It nearly didn't come off. The day before the German Seventh Army had poured over the ridges above the Aisne River plain and had advanced as much as ten miles in a single day. Ferdinand Foch, the new

Allied Generalissimo, needed a victory, even a small one. Cantigny would demonstrate to a war-weary and now frightened French public that the Americans were at long last ready to fight.

The Cantigny operations, the A.E.F.'s first offensive action in the war, had West Point written all over it. The new 1st Division commander, Robert Lee Bullard, was a West Pointer, as were most of the brigade, regimental, and even battalion commanders. The main burden of the attack was shouldered by Hanson E. Ely's 28th Infantry Regiment. Ely was a former Academy football player, noted for his raspy voice and bushy eyebrows. At 6:45 a.m., some three thousand of his men set out across a plateau, gently sloping upward, passed through the village, stopping long enough to root Germans out of cellars and trenches with grenades, bayonets, and flame-throwers, and passed into the fields beyond. In

less than an hour Ely's men had secured their objectives and had begun to dig in and string wire. That turned out to be the easy part. The Germans retaliated with an unrelenting artillery barrage. When Ely asked for counterbattery fire, he got almost no help. The French had already withdrawn the big guns that had given such support that morning, as well as tanks and planes, all of them needed on the Aisne front, where the Allied retreat had turned into a rout. Ely's casualties mounted. One of them, the first of those names set in bronze by the Cullum Hall stairway, was Lieutenant Colonel Robert J. Maxey '98, nicknamed "Moxie" by his troops. Maxey, the energetic commander of B Battalion, was hit by a shell fragment but (the words are those of his DSC citation) "caused himself to be carried to his regimental commander [Ely] and delivered important information before he died." Ely

Black Jack Pershing '86 (seen above leading his cavalrymen across the Rio Grande) spent much of 1916 and 1917 chasing the bandit chieftain Pancho Villa around northern Mexico. Pershing never caught Villa but he emerged even so with his reputation enhanced.

In 1916 the thunder of howitzers like the one above was still far over the horizon for the cadet and his girl in Howard Chandler Christy's drawing, right, both from the Cadet yearbook.

and his men held on for three days before they were relieved. The Germans never did retake Cantigny. But the operation had cost the 1st Division more than a thousand casualties, most of them from Ely's regiment.

Meanwhile, on the Aisne front the German southward sweep continued. In little more than a week, they reached the Marne at Chateau-Thierry, in places pushing the Allies back more than thirty miles, the sort of gain that had, until the spring, been unthought of on the Western Front. In the crisis, Pershing threw in American troops, who fought side by side with the French. Marine brigades of the 2nd Division counterattacked at nearby Belleau Wood, taking nearly a month and unnecessarily high casualties to clear the enemy from half a square mile of blasted trees, but giving the desperate Allies a needed lift. People in Paris, just forty-odd miles away, could see the ominous throbbing glow of battle in the night sky. It was clear that the German march on the French capital would soon continue.

The story of West Point in the Great War is a story of command, as it was supposed to be. It is also a story of bravery, and not infrequently, a mixture of both. Ely at Cantigny was a model of gruff grace under pressure. So was Ulysses Grant MacAlexander '87 on the Marne. A stocky, fifty-four-year-old Kansan, MacAlexander was the colonel in command of the 38th Regiment of the 3rd Division. He was a man who took chances, who thought nothing of walking into the open as he inspected the ground he was to defend, who went on sniping expeditions with his Springfield .30 caliber rifle. MacAlexander

(with another West Pointer, "Billy" Butts, the commander of the 30th Regiment on his left) was about to make one of the notable defensive stands of American history. It would take place on the south bank of the Marne, a few miles east of Chateau-Thierry, on July 15, 1918. That was the day the Germans made what would prove to be their last bid to win the war, an attempt to encircle the city of Reims and to drive beyond the Marne ridges to the open plains where they could wheel on Paris.

MacAlexander's regiment defended the valley of the river Surmelin, a creek really, that ran into the Marne. Ridges four to five hundred feet high rose from both sides of the valley. One he shared with Butts's 30th Regiment, the other with a French division. On the summit of the latter ridge, he took the precaution of digging U-shaped trenches around the ruins of a mill. The German attack began just after midnight on the 15th. "The hills north of the river broke out into a procession of brilliant flashes," wrote First Lieutenant Donovan Swanton, a recent graduate who commanded a machine gun position. After a two-hour pounding, the Germans began to cross the Marne in boats and on pontoon bridges. Some got across and established beachheads, others were forced back across the river. In places, the American riflemen and gunners hiding in the underbrush along the riverbank were wiped out. "But," Swanton wrote, "the circle of German dead bore eloquent testimony to the tenacity of the defense."

MacAlexander, someone noted, was "everywhere." The French division pulled out, leaving his right flank exposed. Now his foresight paid off. He placed men in the trenches around the ruins, and they held out. Others of his badly depleted regiment retreated to the opposite ridge. The Germans, driving down the

Surmelin, were suddenly menaced from both sides, as American artillery poured round after round into the valley. "By noon the following day," wrote the Commander of the 3rd Division, Joseph Dickman (another West Pointer), "there were no Germans in the foreground of the Third Division Sector except the dead."

The Allies struck back three days later, hitting the western flank of the Aisne-Marne pocket in an attack that caught the Germans by surprise. On that day, July 18, the balance of the war shifted. French and American divisions cut the main road leading from the city of Soissons to Chateau-Thierry, and it was only a matter of time before the Germans would be forced to evacuate the entire salient. From that moment on, they would never again take the offensive.

In this landscape broken by abrupt wooded ravines, where the Germans had turned farms and villages into fortresses, we encounter two more of the names on the Cullum Hall plaques. Major Arthur Bouton '08 was the man whose planning had been responsible for the final capture of Vaux, the village next to Belleau Wood. Now, as he led his battalion across a sodden wheat field, a shell fragment struck and killed him. Then there was Colonel Hamilton A. Smith '93, the commander of the 1st Division's 26th Regiment, an exceptional officer who had served in Cuba and the Philippines. He was forty-five, a decade older than the 1st Division's bright young Chief of Staff, and a close friend, George C. Marshall (a graduate of VMI, not of West Point). One night in July, Marshall was told

The West Point Class of 1917 was so eager to get into the fight that it asked to graduate two months early, on the heels of the war declaration. Above, Woodrow Wilson's Secretary of War Newton D. Baker hands out a diploma at that April graduation. The Class of 1918 would graduate in August, almost a year ahead of time.

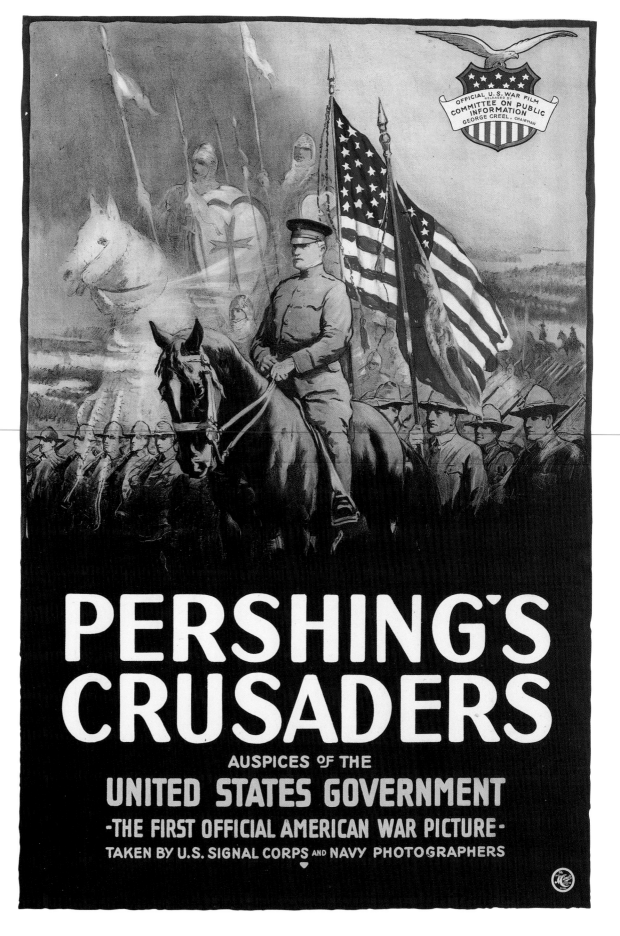

Pershing led the American Expeditionary Force into the War in France. The 1917 poster (left) is evidence of the romantic aura still clinging to combat even in the ugliest of wars.

to report to Chaumont, where he would join Pershing's General Staff. About midnight, Smith stopped by Marshall's room to say good-bye. The two men sat on the edge of Marshall's bed and chatted for an hour. An aide interrupted their conversation: Orders had come for the 1st Division to pack up and get ready to move. Neither expected an attack so soon, and there was obviously nothing final in their leave-taking.

Two weeks later, Smith's regiment, by now badly depleted, was astride the road from Soissons to Chateau-Thierry, that was its principal objective; all of his officers had been killed or wounded, and Smith was forced to act as a small-unit leader. Relief was at hand. Smith was showing officers of a Scottish division around his front-line positions when a German machine gun began firing in his direction. As he directed his men to take it out, he was cut down and killed instantly, the highest-ranking American officer killed in the Soissons operation.

It was in these days that Douglas MacArthur began to create his military legend. Thirty-eight years old, the Chief of Staff of the 42nd Division became, at the end of June, a brigadier general, the youngest in the Army. Already he was beginning to pick up press clippings. After the Soissons attack, the Germans started to evacuate the Marne pocket; Allied divisions, including the 42nd, followed close behind the still-dangerous enemy. MacArthur was never far from the front, working as a Chief of Staff during the night, leading men in battle during the day, a

military Frank Merriwell. He would accompany his men in attack, crawling Indian-fashion, or urging them up steep river banks under mortar and machine gun fire, or would race from regiment to regiment, pleading for them not to let up. Heedless of his own safety, he never wore a helmet, refused to carry a gas mask. Ordinarily, generals let other men do the fighting. Before the war was over, he would win seven Silver Stars, and two Distinguished Service Crosses.

Not until September, long after the Aisne front had quieted, did Pershing's Americans fight as a separate army. His object was the St. Mihiel salient, a cone-shaped excrescence (Foch called it a "hernia") that threatened Verdun from the south and blocked the way to Metz and the iron mines of Briey: It was both the oldest and the last German salient on the Western Front. MacArthur, as usual, was in the thick of the

Used in action in October 1917, the French 75mm gun, below, is now in the West Point Museum. Most of the weapons the AEF used were borrowed from our French and British allies.

Under the pressure of
WWI the old-fashioned
U.S. Army caught up in
a hurry. Right, George
Patton '09 stands in front
of a French light tank.
In the recruiting poster for
the Tank Corps, far right,
the stately knight in
armor has turned into a
screeching wildcat, all
claws and teeth.

attack, even though recovering from the flu. At 5:00 a.m. on the morning of September 12, he led his 84th Brigade over the top, wearing an enlisted man's clothing and carrying a rifle, to make himself less conspicuous (a protective expedient picked up from the British). George Patton and thirty of his little Renault tanks advanced with the 42nd Rainbow Division. Sometime during the morning he encountered MacArthur. "I walked along the firing line of one Brigade," Patton wrote. "They were all in shell holes except the general, who was standing on a little hill. I joined him and the creeping barrage came along toward us, but it was very thin and not dangerous. I think each one wanted to leave but each hated to say so, so we let it come over us." It was clear that the two men did little more than pass the time of day. "One properly placed German shell at this moment of World War I," a military historian recently noted, "would have eliminated two major inspiring and controversial figures of World War II."

The new American First Army pinched off the St. Mihiel salient in four days. It hit just as the enemy was about to pull out—leading a British historian to dismiss the operation as "one where the Americans relieved the Germans." In the First World War, 7,000 casualties constituted a walk-over. Some divisions, especially the greenest ones, suffered extensively. Consider the experience of Lieutenant Colonel Emory Pike, the 82nd Division's machine gun officer, who became West Point's only World War I Medal of Honor winner. Pike, a forty-one-year-old Iowan, who missed being the "goat" of the Class of 1901 by one place, was memorialized in the West Point Annual Report of June 1921, as being "genial, sympathetic, tolerant, improvident"—whatever that means—"but a good soldier." Pike was cited for his role on September 15 in pulling together "advance infantry units" which had become disorganized during a heavy artillery shelling. "Though badly wounded, Colonel Pike continued in command, still retaining his jovial manner of encouragement, directing the reorganization until the position

Lt. General Hunter Liggett '79 (above) took over command of the First Army in France from Pershing. In mid-October Liggett was handed a demoralized and disorganized force, which he turned into a victorious one. Below, in the Argonne forest, Americans of the 1st Division await the order to go over the top.

could be held." What the citation doesn't mention is the chaos that occurred when German artillery on the flank of the American attack had in a few minutes caused almost three hundred casualties in a battalion attacking a village called Vandières. Pike kept the survivors from bolting—"stragglers" had become an increasing problem in those final months—and helped them to secure the place. He died of shock the following day, to become just another bronze name in Cullum Hall.

St. Mihiel was a relatively easy mark, but its reduction gave no indication of what was to come. For allowing Pershing's mainly American army to conduct its first separate operation, Foch had exacted a harsh *quid pro quo*: to join his great offensive from the North Sea to Verdun, and in less than two weeks. The new area of American responsibility was the twenty-mile stretch known as the Meuse-Argonne sector. Pershing rushed already tired divisions fifty-odd miles to their new jumping-off place. A combination of deep hilly woods crisscrossed by ravines and hardscrabble valleys, it was one of the wildest areas of France, and one of the poorest. In four years of stalemate, the Germans had used the time to turn the Meuse-Argonne into

a wide complex of machine gun nests, pillboxes, and interlocking trench systems. Major General Hunter Liggett '79, Commander of I Corps, described the Argonne Forest itself as "a natural fortress beside which the Wilderness in which Grant fought Lee was a park."

The Meuse-Argonne offensive began in the misty dawn of September 26, 1918; it would last forty-seven days, involve a million men and twenty-one divisions (eight times the size of Grant's army in 1864), and cost Pershing 122,000 casualties, of which 26,277 died. An average day's human wastage was 2,500. It was the largest battle in American history until that time—in fact, one of the largest, period. The current fashion of military historiography is to portray Pershing's opening moves as a disaster. Many of the troops were undertrained, control from above was alternately too tight and too loose. Traffic jams were like nothing ever witnessed before on earth, too many divisions were packed too tightly and a couple fell apart and had to be pulled out of the line, and Pershing relied too much on straight-ahead wave attacks, the like of which an incredulous enemy had not witnessed since the prodigal days of 1914 or 1915. "*Tout le monde à la bataille!*" Foch pro-

claimed, but there was nothing like this terrain anywhere else along his 250-mile line of attack. The towns of Sedan and Mexières, the objectives of Pershing's push, moreover, controlled Germany's principal east-west rail system on the Western Front, and clearly would be held at all costs. It took Pershing until the middle of October to reach his first day's objective.

Lieutenant-Colonel Patton was wounded at a hamlet called Cheppy that first morning while trying to round up stragglers and force them to help extricate tanks stuck in a ditch. (When one man refused to follow his orders, he hit him over the head with a shovel.) Patton won a Distinguished Service Cross. The number of DSCs handed out to West Point graduates in the next month and a half (just under thirty) is a measure of the desperate character of the Meuse-Argonne fighting. To pick citations at random: "Always on the firing line, he led four attacks under heavy fire from artillery, machine guns, and snipers on the hill east of St. Juvin, the fourth of which was successful." (Colonel Walter M. Whitman, '91; Fléville and St. Juvin,

The American Expeditionary Force under Pershing entered the war at the very end, and endured five months of non-stop fighting. The drawing by Sergeant James Scott depicts the AEF slogging toward the St. Mihiel front through mud and rain, a trademark of that war. Inset, left: the men embark at Southhampton, England, for France. Right: doughboys hold trenches in a landscape blasted by artillery during the Second Battle of the Marne.

October 11–12.) "He led his battalion in an attack, although exposed to machine-gun fire from both flanks and front, steadying his men by his fearless example. He was instantly killed while directing the reduction of a strongly entrenched machine-gun position." (Major Fred A. Cook, '06; St.-Étienne-à-Arras, October 9.) "Having been wounded in the side by shrapnel while caring for wounded men of his platoon, Lieut. Long refused to be evacuated. . . . While withdrawing his platoon . . . he was instantly killed by shellfire." (First Lieutenant Frank S. Long, '17; Fléville, October 5, 1918.)

Some of the losses deprived the army of leaders who might have shone later on. Take the case of MacArthur's classmate, a tall, handsome Minnesotan named James A. Shannon, another of those names in Cullum Hall. He had fought in the Philippine Insurrection and had accompanied Pershing on his punitive expedition to Mexico. He had also briefly directed the Harvard R.O.T.C. program in 1917. "Few leaders have endeared themselves more to the men serving under him," recalled the Harvard *Nineteen Nineteen Class Album*. In France, Shannon served on Pershing's staff and was another close friend of George Marshall. He asked for a transfer to a combat unit and was leading a regiment when he was mortally wounded at a single-street village called Châtel-Chéhéry. He died on October 8, the same day and the same place that Sergeant Alvin C. York bagged his legendary horde of Germans. At the end of the month, Marshall visited the spot where Jimmy Shannon had been hit during the attack he led. "I don't recall any tragedy of the war that so distressed me," Marshall wrote, and then added a bit of soldierly fatalism: "After I sensed the effect of his death on the Army in general, it seemed to me that in no other way could his rare qualities and shining example have been so forcibly impressed on a large number of people."

Somehow Shannon's classmate, Douglas MacArthur, survived. He seemed to be, and his men believed it, "bulletproof." For all the controversy that his later career would arouse, there is one fact about his life that is indisputable: He was one of the genuine heroes of World War I. That Pershing was able to crack the final German defensive line and claim some measure of success in his stalled offensive was largely owing to MacArthur and the 42nd Division. A key to that line—known as the Kriemhilde Stellung for the Nibelungenlied heroine—were two heights rising out of barren wheatfields, Hill 288 and the Côte de Châtillon. Charles P. Summerall, a former West Point First Captain, visited MacArthur in his farmhouse headquarters. "Give me Châtillon," he demanded, "or a list of five thousand casualties."

"If this brigade"—MacArthur's 84th—"does not capture Châtillon," the young brigadier answered, "you can publish a casualty list of the entire brigade with the brigade commander's name at the top."

On October 14, the 84th stormed Hill 288 in a wave and pushed the Germans off; but the same costly frontal attack only left the Americans with a slight purchase on the Châtillon—which they lost in a counterattack the next day. Summerall repeated his demand; MacArthur repeated his answer. That night he reconnoitered the line and noted a place where the barbed wire was not deep. All the men who accompanied him were killed; but he thought he had found what amounted to a half-open door. The next morning MacArthur led most of his men against one flank of the Châtillon, pinning the Germans down while sending a battalion of Iowans through the thinly-wired gap on the other. They worked their way around the back of the hill and struck from the rear; by the end of the day the Châtillon was in American hands. The exploit cost the 42nd Division more than 4,000 casualties. Summerall recommended MacArthur for a Medal of Honor and a promotion to Major General. Pershing would give him the latter—but only a DSC, his second. (MacArthur didn't get his Medal of Honor until 1942, for his defense of Bataan and Corregidor, an award that was far less deserved.)

Not only were the American divisions showing strain. So was Pershing. Allied politicians were maneuvering for his removal. There are hints that, in mid-October, he suffered a near-breakdown. He had tried to take on too much, and even he, for all his self-assurance, seemed to recognize that he was not at his best as an operational leader. He relinquished command of the First Army and turned it over to Major General Hunter Liggett, his most steady, imperturbable, and imaginative subordinate. Liggett would orchestrate a turnaround of a demoralized army the like of which we had not seen since George Thomas at Chickamauga and would not see again until another

Cadets, below, do calisthenics in the 1920s. "Over there," MacArthur wrote, "I became convinced that the men who had taken part in organized sports made the best soldiers."

The Hundredth Night

FOR FIRST CLASSMEN, the one hundredth day before graduation tends to fall in late February, when the harsh dark winter is beginning to lift. In the 19th century, both the prospect of spring and the realization that their West Point days were nearly over gave the moment particular significance, and, cadets were pleased to discover that on the one hundredth day the sun reached above the eastern mountains just as they were marching back from breakfast, a sign of good things to come. That night in the mess hall a celebratory mood took hold. Plebes and upperclassmen exchanged places and the plebes got a chance to get back for months of torment. Upperclassmen waited on tables, while plebes ordered them around as mercilessly as the higher orders

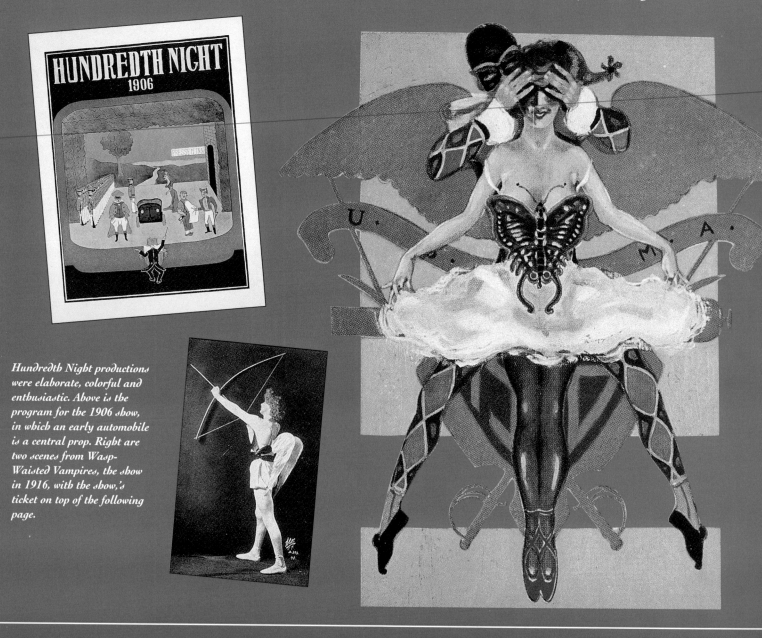

Hundredth Night productions were elaborate, colorful and enthusiastic. Above is the program for the 1906 show, in which an early automobile is a central prop. Right are two scenes from Wasp-Waisted Vampires, the show in 1916, with the show's ticket on top of the following page.

THE WASP-WAISTED VAMPIRES
100TH NIGHT
A MUSICAL COMEDY IN TWO ACTS

had done the beasts, piling on the indignities. In time, the boisterous event began to include the presentation of skits and other entertainment, and eventually these festivities crowded out the role reversal games. By the end of the century the Hundred Night Show was an expected high point of the Academy year. Much of this entertainment, like Shakespearean comedy, derived its amusement value from dressing men up as women. Since West Point went co-ed, real women are available for these parts, and the show is by reports much toned down. Still, Hundredth Night is a vital part of the West Point year, a harbinger of spring, a glimpse of light at the end of the tunnel, and a reaffirmation that, in spite of privileges of rank, cadets are all in this together. —*C.H.*

Hundredth Night shows often featured men dressed comically as women, as in this early 1900s tableau, above. The scene right is from 1940s The Show Goes On.

INTIMATE GLIMPSES IN THE LIFE OF CADET JOSEPH X. FUNNEL, VII

Here is the end.—the faux pas ne plus ultra; eagles scream, stars fall from the flag, strong men faint bells are rung, cathedrals crumble, children are born, Generals crane their necks, even the Secretary of War looks askance. Joe, the little beggar, receives his last skin—with A MISSING BUTTON!!!

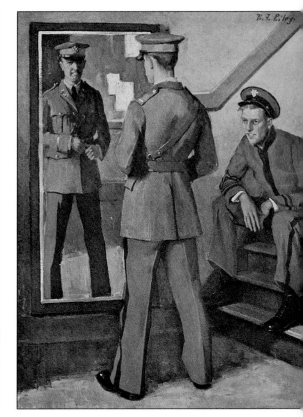

Between the wars the Academy's punctilio became legendary. In this cartoon (from the Howitzer, *the West Point yearbook), a mythical cadet suffers humiliation at graduation over a missing button. Right is another* Howitzer *illustration of cadet fashion; under the amused gaze of a comrade a young soon-to-be graduate tries on his new second lieutenant's uniform.*

West Pointer, Matthew Ridgway, rallied the Eighth Army in Korea in 1951.

Liggett was sixty-one and a graduate of the Class of 1879, who had served in the barren outposts of the West, and in Cuba and the Philippines. He had been head of the Army War College. He was a devotee of maps and military history, who calmed himself by playing double solitaire as he waited for the results of an attack to come in. He was, to put it kindly, stout, and his physique had originally prejudiced a weight-conscious Pershing against him. "Unquestionably there is such a thing not only as being too old to fight but too fat," Liggett said. "That disqualification is the more serious if the fat is above the collar." In his case, there was none.

Except for local attacks, Liggett put the offensive on hold for two weeks while he "tightened up" his army. He saw to it that the deplorable roads were mended, brought up stockpiles of supplies, pulled out depleted and, in cases, broken divisions, and replaced them with fresh and experienced units. He had his military police round up stragglers, that sure symptom of a wrecked army, returning them to their divisions, sometimes with the sign, "Straggler from the Front Line" attached to their backs. Liggett estimated that there were 100,000 of them, a tenth of his army. By Novem-

ber 1, when the offensive resumed, straggling was no longer a major problem.

In just two days Liggett's army shattered the German line and was wheeling to the northeast, the sort of maneuver that this time did not invite confusion. Preparation had proved its own reward. In places trucks were used to carry infantry, but even they could not keep up with the retreating enemy. Lieutenant Colonel Courtney H. Hodges, who had flunked out of West Point in 1905 and re-enlisted as a private, led a company of the 5th Division across the Meuse and managed to hold on for forty hours until help arrived; soon American troops were pouring across the river. Hodges would command the First Army in France and Germany in 1944–45. The final days became a race. The French wanted to capture Sedan and wipe out the disgrace of their defeat there in 1870. Pershing wanted it for the Americans. In a rush to reach the town first, units of the 1st Division, known as "Pershing's Pets," moved across the front of the 42nd Division; on the night of November 6, a patrol captured the 42nd's new commander, Douglas MacArthur, at gunpoint. They mistook his deliberately sloppy garrison cap for the headgear of a German officer. They soon released MacArthur, but for one of the few

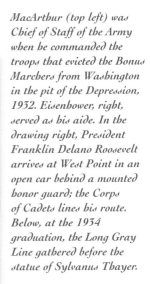

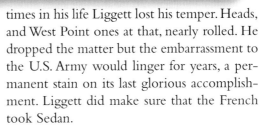

MacArthur (top left) was Chief of Staff of the Army when he commanded the troops that evicted the Bonus Marchers from Washington in the pit of the Depression, 1932. Eisenhower, right, served as his aide. In the drawing right, President Franklin Delano Roosevelt arrives at West Point in an open car behind a mounted honor guard; the Corps of Cadets lines his route. Below, at the 1934 graduation, the Long Gray Line gathered before the statue of Sylvanus Thayer.

times in his life Liggett lost his temper. Heads, and West Point ones at that, nearly rolled. He dropped the matter but the embarrassment to the U.S. Army would linger for years, a permanent stain on its last glorious accomplishment. Liggett did make sure that the French took Sedan.

Then, abruptly, the war was over.

West Point, meanwhile, was plummeting into chaos. The process started reasonably enough when the Class of 1917 demanded an early graduation. Granting its wish, the War Department moved the event forward to April, just two weeks after the declaration of war. Then the War Department sanctioned a more drastic speed-up. The next class was graduated at the end of August, after little more than three years. (Twenty-one members of those two classes died in France; others were maimed so badly that their careers were cut short.) The class that should have been the Class of 1919 also graduated a year early, in June 1918; a three-year system seemed to be in effect for the duration. Worse was to come. As officer losses mounted, the War Depart-

In June 1936 the National Geographic *did a feature on West Point, focusing on placid non-military pursuits like summer sunbathing, spooning, and getting married. In the background the impeccably turned out cadets line up for Dress Parade.*

A new arrival at West Point is "braced" by an upperclassman. The harsh discipline and demanding life led to a high attrition rate among cadets but for the majority who remained, lifelong pride in having stuck it out.

ment now panicked. On October 1, 1918, the Cadet Adjutant stood up in the dining hall to read the order, to cheers, that all classes except the plebe would be graduated in one month, and would immediately board troopships for France. West Point was fast losing its status as a military college and was becoming just another officers' training school; even intercollegiate sports had been cut out. On November 1, the two classes of cadets, 511 strong, were graduated as second lieutenants, and within days had been replaced by two other groups of short-timers. In two years, 1917 and 1918, five classes had been graduated.

The Armistice of November 11 only made a confused situation more confused. The two recently-graduated classes were recalled for an

extra six months of training. Since they had already received their commissions, their status was hazy. Though the West Point administration continued to treat them as cadets, the other cadets had to salute the new Second Lieutenants, causing no little resentment. Even uniforms were different. The plebe class that had entered in June 1918—which included a future head of the Joint Chiefs of Staff, Lyman L. Lemnitzer, and the future football coach, Earl Blaik—wore the usual cadet gray. A member of the Class of 1920, Lemnitzer and Blaik's class, described the mess formation as the "weirdest thing that was ever seen." First would come a battalion of second lieutenants five hundred strong dressed in olive drab, then the second contingent in traditional gray, and finally the most recent arrivals—who, because of the wartime cloth shortage, were dressed in salvaged privates' uniforms with canvas leggings and campaign hats circled by orange bands. They were promptly referred to as "the orioles" (one of whom was a future Superintendent, Maxwell D. Taylor). The full four-year course of study would not be reinstituted until 1919, with the Class of 1923—a change that was formalized by Congress in March 1920.

Without a war to distract him, and with the Army downsizing with unseemly haste, the skinny bearded Army Chief of Staff, Payton C. March '88, could turn to the problems of the military academy, which he had in large part created. In May 1919, he summoned a young officer just off the boat from France, Brigadier General Douglas MacArthur—whose promotion to Major General had been cancelled by the end of the war. "West Point is forty years behind the times," March said. He then offered MacArthur the job of Superintendent. His mission would be "to revitalize and revamp the

The West Point Had Its Goats

UNDER THE GENERAL ORDER OF MERIT, men received their diplomas from the USMA according to their class rank. Throughout the early years of the Academy, the lower-ranking members were known as the Immortals. But in 1886, the Spanish instructor who taught the cadets with the lower standing had a remarkable goatee, and the name of his beard transferred itself somehow to his charges, thereafter known as the Goats.

Many men graduated at the bottom of their classes and went on to distinguished (or at least notable) careers. Rene Derussy, Class of 1812, became superintendent of the Academy after Thayer resigned. George Pickett '46, flamboyant CSA general and fashion-plate, was last in his class primarily because of his insistence on being out of uniform—i.e., wearing the flowing cravats he loved so much. George A. Custer was the last man in the Class of 1861. Powhatan H. Clarke, tail end of the Class of 1884, won the Medal of Honor in the Indian Wars. And Emory Pike, West Point's only Medal of Honor winner in World War I, missed being the goat of 1901 by one place.

Traditionally, the goat was roundly applauded as he approached the podium to receive the degree he had just barely managed to earn. For some years, in addition, he received a dollar from everybody else in his class, at least guaranteeing a good party. But in 1977, the General Order of Merit was abolished. —*C.H.*

academy." With reluctance—he protested that he was a field officer and not an administrator—MacArthur accepted.

A month later the thirty-nine-year-old Brigadier General moved into the Superintendent's house with his mother. He was, after Sylvanus Thayer, the third youngest man ever to hold the position. (The second youngest was a Civil War hero, Colonel Thomas H. Ruger, who had been appointed in 1871, aged thirty-eight.) West Point had never seen MacArthur's like. He dressed much as he had done in the trenches—already unorthodox enough—in battered leather puttees, a short coat and a grommetless cap. He went everywhere with a riding crop tucked under his left arm, lifting it to the bill of his cap to acknowledge a cadet's rigid salute. "He was just neat enough to pass inspection," commented the Post Adjutant, Colonel William A. Ganoe. In the administrative offices (where he spent as little time as possible), he was remembered as a relentless pacer, who perched on subordinates' desks or put his stockinged feet up on his own, as he scrawled answers to letters on the backs of envelopes—which he then handed off to be typed. Once when he was sick, MacArthur phoned a junior officer to let him see the mail.

"Bring over the papers that are going to win or lose the next war. You sign the others." Those years resounded with the interjection, "Bon!"—his favorite—or the phrases, "Go to it!" or "Hop to it, my boy!" And yet, for all his familiarity, his genial touches on elbows or shoulders, MacArthur was curiously remote. As he put it to one aide, "When you get to be general, you haven't any friends."

On his arrival, MacArthur found West Point "in a state of disorder and confusion," a place "cloistered almost to a monastic extent." He resolved immediately to make changes big and small. His most immediate goal, as he wrote, was to foster "a progressive increase of cadet responsibility tending to develop initiative and force of character rather than automatic performance of stereotype functions." He outlawed the hazing that had almost killed him as a cadet. Though plebes still braced at attention, chins thrust into their sternums, and addressed upperclassmen as "sir," humiliation or violence, such as doing splits over a bayonet, would not be tolerated. He moved to get rid of Beast Barracks. He expanded privileges to allow First Classmen to have pocket money—$5 per month. (Until then the prevailing belief had been that the wealthier

HONOR: CODE AND SYSTEM

No aspect of West Point is more misunderstood by outsiders than the honor code and its 20th Century descendant, the honor system. The honor code is as old as the military academy. From the days of Superintendents Alden Patridge and Sylvanus Thayer, it was assumed that cadets, as men of honor, would not lie, cheat or steal. This noble ideal did not prevent rambunctious characters from sidling off the post for a midnight snort at Benny Havens or otherwise fracturing regulations by smuggling food and occasionally women into their rooms. The goal of the honor code was not the production of plaster saints. As long as a cadet did not lie while breaking a regulation, his honor remained intact.

The honor system began surreptitiously in 1897, as a cadet-organized "Vigilance Committee" which sat as a clandestine court judging those who failed to meet the highest standards of the honor code. When General Douglas MacArthur became superintendent after World War I, he discovered the existence of this committee and decided to recognize it as a formal body, with the power to enforce honor in the most uncompromising way. Those found guilty were expelled from the academy. The honor system was succinctly summarized for incoming cadets: "A cadet will not lie, cheat or steal, nor tolerate those who do." The no-toleration clause was at the heart of the honor system—and it soon became its most controversial feature. Not a few cadets and even more civilians found it hard to understand or forgive cadets who turned in fellow cadets for honor violations. The idea seemed to threaten the brotherhood of the corps, the essence of the Long Gray Line.

Meanwhile, the academy's administration began mixing honor with the regulations in ways that further circumscribed cadets' already limited freedoms. This in turn caused a substantial minority of the cadet corps to grow cynical about honor. In the 1970s, some "cadet Nazis" who served on the honor committee and enthusiastically backed its sentence of expulsion were booed by their classmates when they received their diplomas.

The administration compounded this error by giving different sections of the corps the same examination at different times on the same day on the assumption that honor would forbid anyone from revealing the questions to the not-yet-examined. "If we have to arrange everything so there's no test on the Honor System, there's no point in having it at all," one faculty member said. The result was a series of cheating scandals in which cadets were expelled in wholesale lots.

Another unforseen problem was scrupulosity. Some cadets became so obsessed with the minutiae of honor that they confessed trifling offenses. One morning a cadet told a tactical officer that he had shaved when in fact he had skipped it. His beard was nonexistent and he got away with it. He turned himself in to the honor committee—which promptly expelled him.

Even more bizarre was the idea, articulated by the faculty and at least one superintendent, that the cadets "own" the honor system and no senior member of the academy can have anything to do with how it operates. A 1976 investigatory commission headed by astronaut Frank Borman condemned this notion as "simply not true." But over the years this erroneous idea had led to an abdication of officer involvement in the system.

Even more dismaying to the academy was the discovery that the American people did not support this ferocious emphasis on honor. Cadets who have contested the honor system and in some cases sought recourse in the courts have won widespread public sympathy. Even the Army Times, an unofficial but widely read service newspaper, condemned the "Chicken Cadets" who wanted to expel a man for a single mistake.

West Point has tried to respond to these critical voices by simplifying the regulations and disentangling them from the honor system. The superintendent is now the final judge of a cadet's punishment for an honor violation. Not all violators are dismissed. Some are turned back to the next class. Others are sent into the enlisted ranks with the promise that they can reapply to the academy in a year or two if they prove themselves. Others undergo "honor mentoring," an intense one-on-one series of meetings with a senior faculty member. These reforms have met stiff opposition from many graduates and not a few cadets, who want to stick with the one-mistake-and-out system.

None of these changes intimate an abandonment of the honor system. The contemporary academy insists that cadets must still learn to choose " the harder right rather than the easier wrong." West Point argues character is essential in the army, where the lives of men and women may depend on an officer's honesty. At the same time, a growing number of faculty maintain cadets need to know more than the rights and wrongs of honor as it it practiced at West Point. In the real world of the army, choices are seldom simple and some sort of compromise may be the best solution. As the Long Gray Line begins its third century, the honor system still sparks vigorous debate.

—Thomas Fleming

cadets would abuse the drawing of money for personal use.) He granted six-hour leaves on weekends. (How far could you stray in that amount of time?) He required every cadet to read a newspaper every morning and be prepared to comment on it in English class. He strengthened the student honor code, turning *ad hoc* vigilance committees into a formal Honor Committee. After observing cadets parading in their nineteenth-century uniforms at summer encampment, he commented to Ganoe, "How long are we going on preparing for the War of 1812?" The next summer MacArthur sent the First and Third classes to Camp Dix in New Jersey to rub shoulders with the Army regulars they would soon command and to get some exposure to combat training.

What may be his most permanent legacy was his emphasis on athletics. "Over there," MacArthur said, "I became convinced that the men who had taken part in organized sports made the best soldiers." He also felt—something

■ Graduates 1802–1930: 9,026; 1920–1930: 2,216.
■ Lauris Norstad [1907–1988] graduated in the middle of his West Point class, destined to become the youngest Air Force officer to attain four-star rank.

■ Grant Hall completed, Thayer Road directly across from the Administration Building, (now Taylor Hall). It is the cadet reception hall.

■ Mathematics Department obtained permission to send selected instructors to civilian institutions to pursue courses in advanced mathematics.

■ Bachelor of Science degree authorized for award to graduates of the Military Academy.

■ T. Bentley Mott, USMA 1886, criticized West Point in an article in Harpers Magazine. Although firmly believing in "the essential excellence" of West Point and its training, he felt that it gave preparation for life in the Army.

■ Benjamin O. Davis, Jr. was the first black to graduate from West Point in the 20th century. For much of his career in the Army Air Forces during World War II, he commanded the only all-black squadron, and then group, in North Africa and Italy. He retired as a three-star Air Force general in 1970.

■ William Childs Westmoreland graduated as First Captain of the West Point class of 1936. Superintendent of West Point from 1960 to 1963, he won President Kennedy's commitment to double the size of the Corps of Cadets. Selected as commander of American forces in South Vietnam, he became associated with the policies that will be long debated in that war.

Hunter Liggett might have taken exception to—that too many officers in France had been woefully out of shape. In place of three competitive sports, there would now be seventeen. He required every cadet to participate in an intramural sport or on a varsity team. Instead of the dreary inactivity of enforced blue-law Sunday afternoons, cadets were encouraged to compete on athletic fields. Afternoons he would appear on the sidelines of the football field and on occasion suggested plays. He once tried to show a favorite student athlete, the future football coach of the Black Knights, Earl Blaik, how to hit a curve ball. He tried, but failed, to attract a young football coach named Knute Rockne from Notre Dame. He wanted to build a 50,000-seat stadium with railroad yards for special trains; Congress would have none of it, though it did vote the money for the 16,000-seat Michie Stadium (named for Army's first football captain), completed in 1924, two years after MacArthur had gone.

But MacArthur would suffer a loss that proved fatal when he attempted to expand and otherwise modernize the curriculum. The trouble was that he had but one vote on the twelve-man Academic Board, and only a couple of allies. Many of the department heads arrayed against the Superintendent had been on the faculty since the turn of the century, if not before it, and refused to give in to what they viewed as the necessary traditions of the academy, ones directed at producing "mental discipline." At one particularly testy meeting, the Superintendent came out for a strengthened English department. Soldiers should learn to use weapons, not words, an elderly colonel replied—and then kept interrupting as MacArthur tried to reason with him. Finally, MacArthur slammed his fist on the table. "Sit down, sir!" he said. "I am the

superintendent." Increasingly, compromises became impossible. MacArthur secured such victories as the introduction of the slide rule and the study of economics and the internal combustion engine; World War I tactics were substituted for those of the Civil War.

Meanwhile, his adversaries had mounted a campaign to remove MacArthur. They enlisted the backing of influential DOGs (Disgruntled Old Grads, as Ganoe called them). "Graduates," he recalled, "came and pounded on my desk. My office got letters denouncing the supe as the wrecker of West Point." Then, in March 1921, the Republican administration of Warren G. Harding took over. Pershing replaced MacArthur's chief supporter, March, as Army Chief of Staff. Pershing was no fan of MacArthur—and, like William Tecumseh Sherman after the Civil War, felt that there was risk in meddling with tradition. He was clearly, if tacitly, on the side of the DOGs. "The longer I live . . . the more I reverence the things that inspire the heart and soul of young men at West Point," he said.

A woman seems to have been MacArthur's final undoing, though his biographers have argued the role she played. Louise Cromwell Brooks was one of the richest women in America, a thirty-something divorcée who had briefly been Pershing's mistress. Later, in Washington, she often acted as his official hostess. He looked on benignly as his handsome polo-playing aide, Colonel John G. Quekemeyer, became unofficially engaged to her. In the fall of 1921, at a dinner party in Tuxedo, New York, MacArthur and Mrs. Brooks met. The attraction was immediate; a few weeks later, at the Army–Yale game, MacArthur proposed. Army lost; she accepted. They announced their engagement in January. Pershing was apparently furious—as much because of the jilting of his favorite aide as any-

■ Delafield Pond reconstructed as an outdoor swimming pool and named after Major General Richard Delafield, USMA 1818, Superintendent 1838–1845 and 1856–1861.

■ Colonel Fulgencio Batista, chief of the Cuban Army and his entourage inspected the U.S. Military Academy as guests of Brigadier General Jay L. Benedict. Officially only a colonel in the Cuban Army, Batista had led Cuba since the revolution of September 4, 1933.

■ Baseball field between Thayer and Cullum Roads renamed Doubleday Field in honor of Major General Abner Doubleday, USMA 1842, who was said to have laid out the first modern baseball diamond.

■ Graduates 1802–1940: 12,239; 1930–1940: 3,213.
■ Henry O. Flipper, the first black graduate of the U.S. Military Academy, died at age eighty-four.

■ Coach Earl H. Blaik introduced the gold composite football helmet to replace the leather type, at once lighter and more protective.
■ Stewart Field near Newburgh placed under jurisdiction of Superintendent, USMA.
■ Pearl Harbor attacked, December 7.

thing else. On January 30, 1922, Pershing sent MacArthur a letter out of the blue: He was to be transferred to the Philippines at the end of the school year. The pretext for his removal was that MacArthur had testified before a House budget committee without the permission of the War Department. MacArthur protested in vain. He and Louise Brooks were married on Valentine's Day, in Palm Beach. On June 30 he vacated the Superintendent's house for good.

Brigadier General Fred W. Sladen '90, the man who replaced MacArthur as Superintendent, comes across as a bit of a heavy but in fact was a soldier with an enviable record, who had won a Distinguished Service Cross in the Meuse-Argonne. A War Department insider, he was clearly the choice of the rebellious Academic Board. He did what was expected of him. Sladen promptly revoked weekend leaves and pocket money. He restored Beast Barracks and brought the summer camp back to West Point, in all its Napoleonic splendor. As he said, tactical training was not "intended to produce glorified drill sergeants." His announced rationale was that the War Department was phasing out Camp Dix and West Point could not afford to send cadets farther afield. The parsimonious years of the Coolidge Administration would neither be good for the Army nor for the military academy. Of the MacArthur reforms, only the Honor Committee and the expanded athletics system remained. Every officer would still be an athlete.

It was almost as if MacArthur had never been Superintendent and the clock had been turned back to 1915. You still woke to the bugle call of 5:50 a.m. reveille, still marched to mess hall twenty-one times a week, still were expected to recite in every class six days a week, still formed up in companies chosen by height, still had to climb stairs two steps at a time or stare at the table in mess hall and not look around (if you were a plebe), still tried to catnap for ten or fifteen minutes between classes in your monastic rooms (since your mattress was folded up during the day, you threw a blanket on the bedsprings), and still did not get an extended leave until the summer between your second and third years. Your greatest release was football, when the entire 1,374-man student body would entrain for Boston or New Haven or the Army–Navy game, which might be held as far away as Chicago. Harvard and Yale were still major football powers in those days. The Corps of Cadets would march as a body several miles from the train station to the football stadium and back. William H. Baumer, Jr. '33 remembered that "It was always a difficult matter to march from Boston Common to Harvard Stadium and then when you got to the stadium to find no facilities for relieving oneself. . . . About all we could figure out was to form little squares and relieve ourselves. This is one of the unbelievable difficulties that never appears in print." As much as ever, West Point was still "Hell on the Hudson."

There were changes that seemed more cosmetic than anything. Washington Hall, the cadet dining hall with a seating capacity of 2,500 (the chairs would not be filled until 1942) was completed in 1929. Lieutenant Colonel Herman Beukema, the most famous West Point teacher of his era, inaugurated a course in strategic raw materials in 1931, the same year that the Department of Ordnance and Gunnery started automotive instruction. (It was Beukema who announced to his instructors: "Gentlemen, there is a war coming.") Courses in ancient and medieval history were dropped in favor of what seemed more important as the 1930s advanced: modern European and Far Eastern history. Many of the instructors of this period, World War I

West Point graduates like Maxwell Taylor and Alfred M. Gruenther, future generals, seemed frozen in permanent lieutenancy. In 1935 the corps was expanded to 1,960, and in 1939—the same year that 500 co-eds from Stephens College in Missouri were bused in for a weekend—television was first demonstrated. In the summer, cadets could take dates swimming at the New Delafield Pond, and now on hop weekends you might find gym rooms covered with mattresses.

Meanwhile, the horse maintained its immemorial ascendancy. Not until 1928 did cadets receive their first exposure to the tank. On the morning of June 29, a visiting trainload of First Classmen arrived at the Tank Center at Fort Leonard Wood; they were back on board at 1300 hours. That same year, however, the number of hours for equitation instruction for the First Class was doubled. Six years later, mechanized vehicles made their first appearance at summer camp, but it was only a token one. As late as 1939, according to the Annual Report of the Board of Visitors, the military academy owned 243 cavalry horses, 108 artillery horses, and four mules.

The horse was just one of many backward-looking manifestations that would meet their match in Robert L. Eichelberger, the Superintendent who took over in November 1940. His

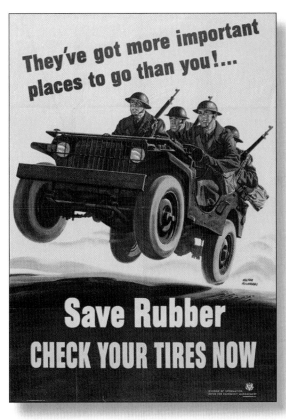

They've got more important places to go than you!...

Save Rubber
CHECK YOUR TIRES NOW

On the eve of World War II West Point cadets were still studying horsemanship. Cadets on the far left select riding boots. The training picture top shows more modern armored cavalry. The legendary Jeep, which was just being introduced in the early 1940s, makes an appearance (middle), and below, Robert L. Eichelberger, the Superintendent (1940-42) responsible for great and lasting changes at the Academy, relaxes in the field during the New Guinea campaign.

term was short—in the summer of 1942 he left West Point to join MacArthur in the Pacific—but his influence was lasting. He arrived with a mandate: to prepare for the war that now seemed inevitable. He downgraded equitation (as it had been known since 1829). He emphasized physical training and military instruction, bringing in regulars to assist in infantry training.

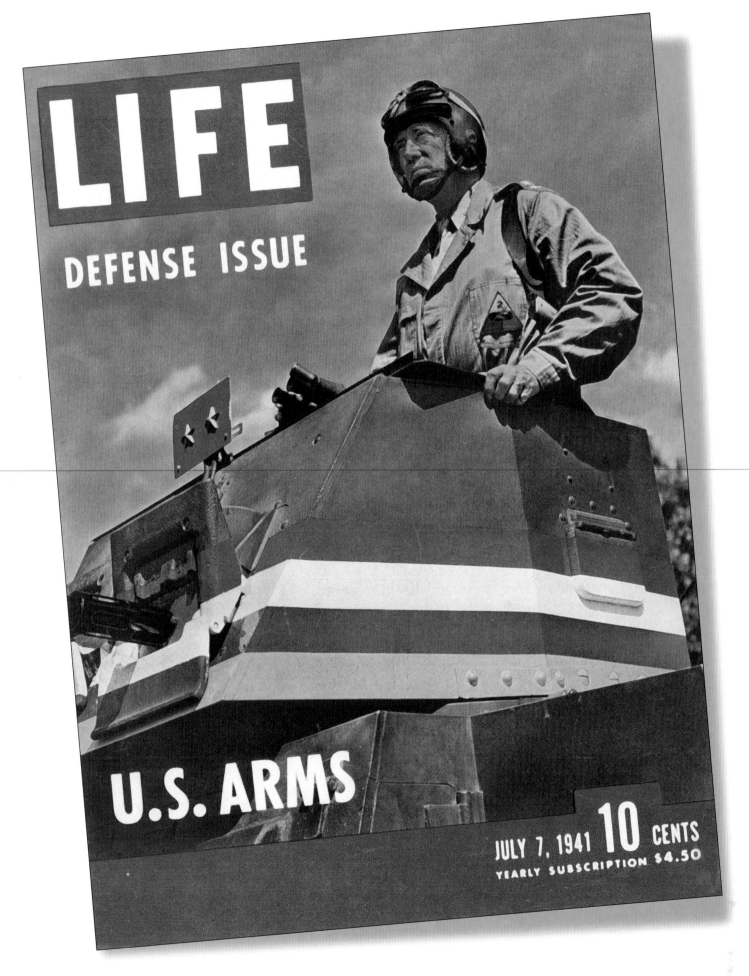

He made large land purchases, including Stewart Field, where he inaugurated an air cadet program. And, tired of losing football teams, he imported from Dartmouth a former Army football star, Earl "Red" Blaik, as coach.

The following August, Eichelberger looked on as forces designated Red and Blue began their annual tactical maneuvers in nearby Orange County, New York, countryside that surrounded the base. Fourteen hundred men took part in the week-long exercise, and already the evidences of change were plentiful. Low-flying planes "spewed a simulated machine-gun fire down on the roadways"—the words were those of the local Newburgh *News*—"forcing the troops to take cover in ditches, while anti-aircraft units mounted on armored cars fought off the assailants." Searchlights probed the night skies, sometimes catching "little gray mothlike planes." Cadets in washbasin-shaped World War I-style helmets practiced amphibious warfare in "the latest-type landing boats" (which looked suspiciously like motorized lifeboats), crossing a lake in three waves behind a smokescreen. The *News* published a photo of a "Jeep," a vehicle it described as a "little wonder." Whether the Red or the Blue won is not recorded, but the maneuvers were evidently regarded as a success.

That fall of 1941, selected cadets of the First Class served as instructors in order to release officers for emergency assignments. One of those thirty-six student instructors, who taught French to plebes, was Elliot Cutler '42. (In future years he would be head of the Department of Electrical Engineering, retiring with the rank of Brigadier General.) It was an enviable assignment. Distinguished by the special broad black bands they wore on their gray sleeves, they lived in separate barracks, walked to the mess hall, went to the movies, and could

...we here highly resolve that these dead shall not have died in vain...

REMEMBER DEC. 7th!

keep cars in Highland Falls (all unheard-of privileges); as Cutler remembered, "We were treated like Third Lieutenants." On a late fall Sunday, Cutler and a group of friends drove to the Polo Grounds in New York, to watch a professional football game between the New York Giants and the Brooklyn Dodgers, an NFL team in 1941. Midway through the game, they heard a public-address announcement: "Will Colonel Donovan please call Washington." One of Cutler's West Point friends turned to him and remarked, "Sounds like the Germans have invaded another Balkan country."

The game went on; the Giants lost 21 to 7. As the West Pointers were leaving the stadium, they saw news vendors holding up special editions. The Japanese had bombed Pearl Harbor.

George S. Patton, seen left on a Life cover in the summer of 1941, was the epitome of the tank commander, seemingly ready for anything. But the nation wasn't ready for the Japanese attack on Pearl Harbor. Above, a poster proclaims the country's grief, shock, and outrage.

6 THE ACADEMY GOES TO WAR AGAIN

BY TOM WICKER

"Never tell people how to
do things. Tell them what to
do and they will surprise
you with their ingenuity."

—George S. Patton

■ Stewart Field, where West Point air cadets trained, expanded from 221 acres to over 1,000 acres.
■ Department of Natural and Experimental Philosophy renamed Department of Mechanics.
■ Fall of the Philippines, Midway, Guadalcanal, and Invasion of North Africa.

■ 330 tons of antique cannons at West Point melted for scrap metal in war drive.
■ January 19, 1943 graduated three-year class.
■ Victory in North Africa, Invasion of Sicily and Italy.

When the Japanese bombed Pearl Harbor on December 7, 1941, the United States Military Academy at West Point was much like the Army of which it was a proud part—outmoded and inadequate. The fancily uniformed Corps of Cadets still trained on horseback three times a week and had to learn how to load a 75-millimeter howitzer pack on mules. Riding breeches still were a part of required dress, not to be discontinued until November 1942. Even football, one of the Academy's most prized traditions, had fallen on lean times—seven losses in 1940, including a 49-0 shellacking by Penn, and defeats by Navy in 1940 and 1941.

Fortunately, the newly appointed Superintendent, Brigadier General Robert L. Eichelberger '09, was determined to change a lot of things—and ultimately did—including both the Academy's gridiron fortunes and its treasured but antiquated equine tradition (U. S. Grant '43 had established a high-jump record that lasted more than a quarter-century; George S. Patton '09, made a riding crop as much his World War II trademark as his pearl-handled pistols).

When Eichelberger took over in 1940, the Academy continued in many ways to exhibit the often-stultifying weight of tradition—even after numerous far-reaching reforms by a predecessor, Douglas MacArthur. The new "Supe" felt it necessary to add course-hours in physical training and military instruction; and for the class due to graduate in June 1941, Eichelberger ordered academic work suspended in April, and intensified military training for the remaining weeks—with motorized vehicles and weapons substituted, for the first time and to the extent possible, for the long-familiar horse-drawn equipment. That was not a great extent, since the entire Army of 1941 was mostly organized, trained and equipped only as it had been for the previous twenty years.

Eichelberger brought Regular Army soldiers to the Academy to assist in the modernized training. He also took the even more historic step of making an airport, Stewart Field in nearby Newburgh, N.Y., an integral part of the Academy. Until 1936, despite World War I experience and the publicized rearmament of Germany—particularly the development of the Luftwaffe—West Point had offered those cadets interested in what still was the Army Air Corps only a series of lectures. They also could receive twenty hours of something called "air experience"—tactics and organization, but probably not even including an actual "ascension" in a Loening Amphibian airplane kept by the Air Corps on the Hudson River for survey and map-making purposes.

In 1942, however, the War Department authorized the Academy to commission up to 60 percent of its graduates in the Army Air Corps—those who opted at the beginning of their second class year (called "yearlings" at West Point, sophomores elsewhere) to become "air cadets." The acquisition of Stewart Field enabled that authorization to become a reality. For air cadets, actual flight training—twelve hours of it—began in July 1942. At first, those in flight training had to commute between the Academy and the airport; but air cadets of the Class of 1944 were moved into barracks at Stewart Field—though they still were governed by West Point rules and regulations. To help integrate flight training with the Academy's basic curricu-

PRECEDING SPREAD: As sailors on the battleship Missouri *look on, General Douglas MacArthur (seen leaning over the table, center) accepts Japan's unconditional surrender in Tokyo Bay, September 2, 1945. Right: Dwight David Eisenhower led the Allies into Europe on D-Day and presided over the victory that re-establishes democracy in Western Europe.*

■ May 30 dedication of
the Air Cadet Memorial in
honor of cadets killed while
training as aviators.
■ Deficiency in physical
education established as
sufficient reason for discharge.
■ D-Day, capture of Rome,
Battle of the Bulge,
MacArthur returns to
Philippines.

■ Tactical Training and
Firing Center used for
summer cadet training
named Camp Buckner in
honor of Lieutenant General
Simon Bolivar Buckner, Jr.,
USMA 1908, killed at
Okinawa June 18, 1945, the
highest ranking officer to
die in WWII.
■ Germany and Japan
surrender.

*Bayonet practice replaced
fencing class as combat
training at West Point took
a new and more realistic
turn.*

lum, the airfield's commanding officer then became a member of the Academic Board.

A wartime class that graduated in January of 1943 was the first whose air cadets qualified for "wings" at commissioning. Fifty years later, members of that class published a sort of alumni yearbook relating the classmates' careers, in which it was recalled that, as air cadets in primary flight training, they had flown open-cockpit Stearman PT-17s, Fairchild PT-19s, and Ryan PT-21s. The weather in the mountainous area around West Point, however, did not pro-

vide good flying conditions, one reason why the air cadet program lasted only four years. The last cadets to receive their "wings" were commissioned in 1946, before an independent Air Force shifted training to other facilities. All told, West Point in the war years and immediately after graduated 1,033 "air cadets" into the Air Corps.

Nine more died in training accidents at Stewart Field. Four other West Point cadets had died in Air Corps flight training in the years before the Stewart Field acquisition—two at Spence Field, Georgia, and two at Curtis Field, Texas.

Under Superintendent Robert C. Eichelberger, West Point expanded its land holding by 10,000 acres, most of which was used for expanded training facilities. These photos show cadets learning the tricks of the trade. Above, a crew float a Jeep across Lake Popolopen on a makeshift raft. From a barricade, right, cadets in full pack sling grenades. At the end of the war Camp Popolopen was renamed Camp Buckner, for Simon Bolivar Buckner '08, killed at Okinawa.

On the new training course, cadets could even practice house-to-house fighting in an imitation village.

Some changes are best not made and in the World War II years, at least one near-disastrous mistake of the past was mostly avoided. A quarter-century earlier, World War I had seen a chaotic attempt to speed up cadets' terms at West Point, in order to feed officers quickly into the vast civilian army then being raised. But suddenly, before those in authority had expected it, Germany surrendered and an armistice was signed on Nov. 11, 1918 (as in the between-war years every schoolchild learned, owing to the moment of silence observed in classrooms at 11 a.m. on the eleventh day of every eleventh month—"Armistice Day").

The end of that war made the graduation speed-up unnecessary. But despite this unpromising history, after Pearl Harbor the War Depart-

ment again considered calling the Corps of Cadets immediately into the expanded World War II Army, converting the Academy into an emergency officers' training school. But Superintendent Francis B. Kilby, West Point '05—successor to Eichelberger, who had requested and been given a transfer to the South Pacific command of General Douglas MacArthur—brought in an experienced Regular-Army training officer, Colonel P. E. Gallagher, as Commandant of Cadets, with orders to bring military instruction up to date. Gallagher turned the plebe year into a basic infantryman's program, shipped the whole Corps to a brief training session with the Fourth Armored Division, and took First Classmen (seniors) on educational tours of Forts Benning (infantry), Sill (artillery) and Knox (armor).

These innovations, together with a condensed three-year course of study Superintendent Wilby had ordered to be devised, mostly saved the Academy from the ill-fated speedups of World War I. In October 1942, President Franklin Roosevelt confirmed the switch to the new three-year course (partially to avoid the appearance that West Point provided a "refuge" for draft-age young men), with two exceptions—the original Class of 1943 was to be graduated six months early, in January 1943 rather than June, and what had been the Class of 1944 was restyled as another Class of 1943, to be commissioned a year ahead of time, in June 1943.

Not until September 1945 was the traditional four-year course resumed; half the cadets who had entered the Academy in 1944 were designated the Class of 1947 and continued in the wartime three-year course; the other half was called the Class of 1948, and assigned to the restored four-year curriculum. FDR also had ordered, ostensibly for morale reasons, that intercollegiate football at the Academy was to be continued, despite the war.

Thus, West Point, like most higher educational institutions, remained fully functioning during the war; in fact, the Academy expanded physically, primarily with the purchase in late 1942 of 10,300 nearby acres—sixteen square miles. The purchase had been authorized (actually to consist of more than 15,000 acres) by Congress in 1931; but as was typical of those pre-war, Depression years, by 1939 only 528 acres had been added to Academy holdings.

The huge 1942 purchase permitted the establishment of "Camp Popolopen," named for a lake on the site, with twenty-four target ranges, two moving target ranges, an amphibious-training area, a 200-yard assault course (cadets carrying a nine-pound rifle, two hand grenades and a nine-pound combat pack had to complete it in four minutes), pillboxes, a model village for urban combat training, and even a mechanical freight train—facilities far superior to anything the supposed "military academy" had enjoyed in the past.

Authorized additions to the gym and the mess hall, however, were not completed until 1946—victims of wartime conditions. These long overdue additions had been sorely missed for years, because Congress in 1942 had ordered the Corps expanded by more than 25 percent—from 1,960 to 2,496 cadets. The roster was to be filled as follows.

8 appointments each for 48 states (384)
4 per Congressional district (1,740)
4 per territory (Alaska, Hawaii)
6 for the District of Columbia
4 for Puerto Rico
2 for Panama
172 for U.S. at large
180 from regular Army, Navy, National Guard

As West Point in the war years reformed itself into an institution to produce officers sufficiently acquainted with modern warfare to lead mass armies of once-and-future civilians, the institution had more nearly to reflect the nation's everyday life. The public impression of an elite school for a military caste had to be countered. Inevitably, the cadets' overly formal, "foreign-looking" dress and appearance were changed to make them look more like millions of draftees. A khaki drill uniform and sun helmets for summer were introduced, as were "new pattern" steel helmets, a gray garrison cap, and combat boots to replace old-Army leggings. Not only were riding breeches abandoned in 1942

(though some officers, like the stubborn General Patton, continued to affect them); so was the old lace-up field boot and the Model 1903 rifle—replaced by the M-1 in 1940.

Other wartime innovations in a tradition-wrapped institution included substituting First Classmen teaching halftime for a number of regular-officer instructors; retired officers and civilians ultimately were added to the faculty, too. The new three-year curriculum caused a number of courses to be dropped, but some, of necessity, were added—notably language classes in German and Portuguese (in honor of a wartime ally, Brazil; but even today a Brazilian officer comes to West Point each year to teach the course in Portuguese). Instruction in Russian was somewhat belatedly started in 1945.

"Walking guard," a traditional West Point punishment for rules infractions, became armed patrol, with gas masks at the ready. The traditional march cadence, 128 steps a minute, was reduced to 120—to make it easier for marching formations to keep step and maintain discipline. "Dog tags," like those for "GIs," were issued to cadets. An obstacle course—with ladders, swings, tunnels, fences to be climbed—appeared on "the Plain," which always had been the Academy's parade ground. In 1943, with Blaik's revised physical standards in place and more appointments available, the biggest plebe class in history—1,075—entered "the Point" and took its place in "Beast Barracks." The latter was one thing that hadn't changed: six weeks of hazing and misery at the hands of upper classmen who, as plebes, had endured the same time-honored "welcome" to the Academy.

The Department of Drawing—George Patton was to complain in 1945 that "nothing I learned [in Drawing] . . . in any way contributed to my military career"—was redesignated the Department of Military Topography and Graphics. With computers far in the future, a course in slide-rule instruction was transferred from the Department of Physics to the Department of Mathematics. Mass calisthenics and intramural athletics became required; training films were adopted; a brief course in "Rules of Land Warfare" was inaugurated; a Radar Laboratory was built; and fencing was eliminated from the physical education program, while skiing equipment was made available for 600 cadets.

One member of the wartime Class of 1944 had an experience probably not duplicated before and certainly not since. That class was graduated and commissioned on June 6, 1944—D-Day on the beaches of France. As First Class-

men formed up that morning to march to their last West Point breakfast, the battalion commander turned to Sergeant Major John S. D. Eisenhower, and remarked: "You heard, of course, that the Allies landed in Europe this morning."

That was the first news Cadet Eisenhower had had of the gigantic invasion launched by forces commanded by his father, Dwight D. Eisenhower '15. John Eisenhower's graduation day, consequently, also would be his introduction to "big-time publicity." In his memoir, *Strictly Personal*, he wrote that he and his mother soon "found ourselves facing a bank of something like forty photographers, bulbs flashing unmercifully . . . " Cadet Eisenhower—about to become a second lieutenant—resented such attention mainly because he was "singled out conspicuously from those whose comradeship I valued—my classmates."

Late in 1945, the training facilities built early in the war at Camp Popolopen were renamed "Camp Buckner," honoring General Simon Bolivar Buckner '08, who had been killed on Okinawa in June in the last weeks of the war. General Buckner was a descendent and namesake of a Confederate general, West Point 1844, who in 1862 had surrendered Fort Donelson to forces commanded by a West Point acquaintance, U. S. Grant, 1842. On Oct. 2 of that year, not long after Hiroshima and Nagasaki, Colonel B. W. Bartlett delivered the Academy's first lec-

Sick, starved, and almost out of ammunition, on April 9, 1942, the men on Bataan in the Philippines reluctantly obeyed an order to surrender. Many West Pointers were in the emaciated column, above, and many would die in captivity. On Corregidor, General Jonathan M. Wainwright '06 held out a a month longer but also surrendered (left), the lowest point in the war for the United States. Alexander "Sandy" Nininger '41 was the first West Pointer to win the Medal of Honor in the war. Barely six months out of West Point, he volunteered to help a beleaguered company, and although wounded three times, repeatedly attacked Japanese positions, destroying foxholes and taking out snipers before he was killed.

General Joseph Stilwell '04 served in China as commander of the China-Burma-India Theater. Sent with a Chinese army to defend against an attack up the Burma Road early in 1942, Stilwell was driven back by the rampaging Japanese and retreated to India. Offered a plane ride out, he refused, and instead walked out with his men. "I claim we got a hell of a beating," he said. Right, Stilwell sits somewhere on the Burma Road, cleaning his tommy gun, a world away from the happy moment on the steps of Cullum Hall in the photograph on page 137. Below, his hat and shoes from that long march are in the West Point Museum.

ture on "The Theory of the Atomic Bomb."

More drastic change, however, always was resisted at West Point, and the remaining few of its precious horses—at one time about 400 of them, some named Grant, Lee, Sherman, Sheridan and McClellan—were among the wartime untouchables. Not until 1947 was "horsemanship" eliminated altogether from the Academy curriculum, and all horses withdrawn from the post.

Even in wartime, cadet life remained largely unchanged by the war—as was student life at many civilian universities. Still a yearly feature, for instance, was the "Hundredth Night" show—a West Point tradition since 1896, a theatrical written, directed, produced and acted by cadets on the hundredth night before graduation. On March 8, 1941—after 17 months of war in Europe, with Pearl Harbor only nine months in the future—the Class of '41 (soon to go from the Plain directly into combat) put on the 45th annual Hundredth Night, cryptically entitled *Malim in Se*, a musical comedy set on the mythical island of "Malihony" (where "every man's a pagan suckled in a creed outworn").

A sort of parody of West Point itself, the show was written by four First Classmen and enlivened—as all Hundredth Nights used to be—by cross-dressing cadets impersonating women. Its business manager was Cadet Jack Norton (later to command the First Air Cavalry Division in Vietnam). The program, reflecting the times, featured Petty Girls (leggy beauties drawn by an artist named Petty, usually for *Esquire* Magazine) and mentioned the famous columnist and broadcaster Walter Winchell, the sarong-clad movie actress Dorothy Lamour, the author Eugene O'Neill, a current movie named *Hurricane*, and used one phrase, innocent then,

that would be highly suggestive today—"gay playwrights."

The Class of 1942 staged *Yea Furlo*, another musical comedy, this one featuring a song called *Deep Night and You* with such lame lyrics as "Oh dearest hold me tight in the soft moonlight." But the dances must have been of unusual quality; they were staged by Nelson Barclift, a serviceman who had been drafted into the Army in 1941 out of Broadway's *Lady in the Dark*, then sent to West Point on detached service.

The Class of 1943, its graduation date moved up to January of that year, was not on hand to produce a "hundredth night" for the spring. In 1944, the show was resumed but was upstaged by the appearance at West Point of someone definitely not a cadet in woman's dress—a real Conover model named Mary Hyatt, who had been voted "Miss Hundredth Night."

Academy discipline remained tough and demanding. The Class of 1943, however, remembered years later a notable breakdown. The authors of its 50-year book recalled the entire Corps of Cadets being caught in a thunderstorm while marching to camp: When the "Firsties" broke ranks to run, the whole corps followed, running en masse across the Plain to the shelter of tents.

West Point weekends, to which fortunate cadets could invite "drags"—as dates are unappealingly called—also continued during the war (as the attraction of the sexes does in any climate). A booklet (published in 1948 but appropriate for the war years, too) offered some advice—"pretty well molded by custom and tradition"—to prospective drags, including instructions to travel by the now long-vanished West Shore line, which then made a regular stop at West Point. "Young lady guests" could be quartered in a dormitory at the Hotel Thayer

Air power emerged as a major factor in WWII, as the poster far right suggests. West Point led the way with its flying school at Stewart Field in nearby Newburgh, NY. Benjamin Davis '36 (right) masterminded the creation of the Tuskegee Airmen, the first all-black fighter group. Seen above being congratulated by his sponsor, Congressman Oscar de Priest of Illinois, Davis commanded the 332nd Fighter Group in Italy and went on to become the first black Air Force general.

for $1 a night; they needed a formal dress for "hops" (dances) but gloves were "a matter of choice" and gum chewing was precluded by Academy formality. Hats were "always worn to chapel." If Sunday lunch was to be enjoyed at the Thayer, most drags—long before the age of feminism—had to pay the check, because only First Classmen could carry cash on the post; most cadets were allowed real pocket money only when on leave and had to turn it in when they came back.

Blind dates were then, as now and always, problematical. "Steve was the marter (cq) of the evening," wrote Cadet Robert W. Parks '44, to an acquaintance after one such weekend. "A boy came up to Steve . . . and asked him to drag the girl friend of his OAO ["one and only"]. Well, of course, she was so 'D' [apparently unpresentable] that she could barely pass through the gates, since all animals are barred from the post. Anyway, he utterly refused to drag this girl today for his ol pal . . . the guy said I don't blame you but thanks."

Drags could be just as unsparing. Cadet Channing Wallace Gibson '44, got a "Dear John" letter from "Mary Jo," who told him straight out: "If you have any of the qualities of a gentleman, you will rip it up." Gibson had better luck after the Army-Notre Dame tie game in New York City in 1941: he took a drag dressed in "knockout" red and white to a place called the "Queen Mary" on East 58th Street, then to the Astor Ball. Afterwards, he boasted in a letter, she returned with him—but only "as far as Weehawken."

As in all institutions, food at West Point was a matter of constant discussion, usually not complimentary. "Had a bad meal" on Jan. 23, 1941, a plebe confided to his diary. "That comes every year, they say. Don't know whether it was meat or not. Many boys cast their dinners up and out. Guess I have a cast-iron stomach."

Wartime restrictions could not always be avoided. The *Monitor*, a "yearling"-produced photographic record of the Corps at summer training camp appeared in 1944 with board covers and in

yearbook size. In 1945 and 1946, the *Monitor* was reduced—no doubt by paper shortages—to notebook-sized editions, paperbound.

Entertainment usually was available—and not just the Hundredth Night shows. In the spring of 1941, the entire Broadway production and cast of *Arsenic and Old Lace* was imported to West Point, where one cadet observed that the star—the one-time Frankenstein's monster of the movies, Boris Karloff—proved to be "a very refined sensitive person," about whom "the only frightening thing" was his "deep-set, penetrating eyes."

On January 24, 1943, cadets heard the svelte opera star Lily Pons in concert at the Academy. In March, for classical music lovers, the Juilliard Symphony played on the post; a famous actress of the day, Cornelia Otis Skinner, appeared on April 4. That year, the *Pointer*, a cadet magazine, recommended a list of Broadway plays for weekend leaves. It included *Something for the Boys*, a popular musical featuring the brassy voice of Ethel Merman, later to be the star of *Annie Get Your Gun*; and also touted Elizabeth Bergner, another famous actress, in the drama, *The Two Mrs. Carrolls*. But probably the most enticing recommendation was for the renowned stripper, Gypsy Rose Lee, in *Star and Garter* at the Music Box.

The back cover of the *Pointer*, for the January 7, 1944 issue, consisted of something no longer seen these days—a four-color ad for Chesterfields, "the cigarette that satisfies." Even non-smokers of the time, if any, probably studied the ad for its glamorous photo of Betty

In a wartime photo, air cadets wave to a flight of trainers that have just taken off from Stewart Field, in Newburgh.

Grable, a sexpot blonde then starring in the movie *Pin-up Girl*.

During the war years at West Point, cadet pay was the grand sum of $65 a month—even so, a vast improvement on the well-known "twenty-one dollars a day, once a month" then earned by privates in the ranks. From the $65, a cadet was docked $14 a month for a fund from which he was to buy uniforms and equipment after being commissioned. A cadet also was allowed 85 cents a day for rations. And by "exercising proper care" of the textbooks he bought he probably could sell them for $35 upon graduation. He also was

required to deposit at least $300 upon entrance to the Academy.

"Fixed expenses" included three-year contributions of $7.50 to the "cadet hostess establishment," which chaperoned weekend drags, and $36 for "football trips." Optional expenditures usually included an average per cadet of 40 to 55 cents for movie admissions to the War Department theater (to see such films as *Liliom* with Tyrone Power); cadets wishing to join the Debating Society (of which U. S. Grant once had been president) paid average dues of 25 cents a month.

In Dwight Shepler's painting of the landing at Fox Green Beach on the Normandy coast, it is June 7, 1944— D-Day plus one. But landing craft still had to run a gauntlet of German fire.

Then, too, there was football—in most of the war years, the best college football in the country, many would say in the sport's history. Had Superintendent Eichelberger stayed longer at West Point, he would have seen that his wishes after the devastating 49-0 Penn victory in 1940 had come to fruition beyond his dreams.

After watching the cadets cheering the "brave old Army team" right to the bitter end of that embarrassing defeat, Eichelberger had told his associates: "It looks as if we are developing the finest bunch of losers in the world. By the Gods, I believe the cadets deserve a football team that will teach them how to be good winners!"

He proceeded to do something about it, spurning the tradition of active-duty Army officers serving as football coaches and setting out to hire Earl "Red" Blaik away from Dartmouth

College. Blaik, West Point '22, once an Academy athletic star and a former assistant coach, had resigned from the Army and gone into professional coaching. But after seven seasons of success at Dartmouth, Blaik would consent to return to West Point only if the Academy's restrictive height-weight limits were raised. They were, so that a six-footer could weigh 201 and an applicant who was 6-foot-four was permitted to weigh 226. Blaik decided he could find good football material within those restrictions (academic standards, as at most schools, also could be slightly eased so that players he wanted could be admitted). So he consented to return, with his entire coaching staff, to "the Point."

The "Black Knight" era of three national championships, 1944-46, ultimately followed. It took Blaik—owing partly to those relaxed physical standards—only a few years to build a football empire: in 1941, five wins, three losses

The headline below trumpeted the D-Day return of the Allies to the European continent. West Pointers played key roles in planning and commanding the operation.

The Washington Post

CARRIER DELIVERY

The Weather
Today—Fair and warmer. Yesterday—
High, 72; low, 58. (Details on Page
6-B.)

WASHINGTON: TUESDAY, JUNE 6, 1944

NO. 24,827   Entered As Second Class Matter, Postoffice, Washington, D. C.   Copyright, 1944, By The Washington Post

ALLIES LAND IN FRANCE, WIPE OUT BIG AIR BASES

Nazis Admit First

Bulletin
London, June 6 (Tuesday) (AP)—An

Roosevelt

Allies Chase

1st Atlantic Flattop Loss
U. S. Escort Carrier Is Sunk;

Brigadier General Anthony McAuliffe (Class of November 1918), above, was in the thick of the wintry fighting at the Battle of the Bulge, right, where, as acting commander of the 101st Airborne Division, he found himself surrounded at Bastogne, Belgium. McAuliffe's reply to a formal German demand to surrender — "Nuts!" — may be the most famous quote of WWII.

(one, unhappily to Navy) and a tie with Notre Dame; in 1942, a 6-3 season but losses to Notre Dame and again to Navy. (That year, tackle Robin Olds, who was to command the Eighth Tactical Fighter Wing in Vietnam in 1966-67, made All-America; in 1985, he was elected to the College Football Hall of Fame.)

In 1943, Blaik shifted Army's attack to the new-fangled T-formation, ideal for the speedy halfback, Glenn Davis ("Mr. Outside"), and the team improved again, to a 7-1-1 record—but lost once more to Navy. The two Army-Navy games of 1942 and 1943 were played, by order of FDR, in the home stadiums at Annapolis and West Point, where they were attended only by small, mostly local crowds, including old grads. This wartime pattern had been set by Duke and Southern Cal when they played the January 1, 1942, Rose Bowl game in Duke Stadium at Durham, N.C., for fear of a Japanese attack on California.

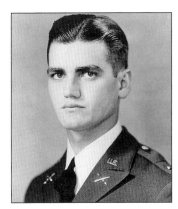

In 1944, Felix "Doc" Blanchard ("Mr. Inside") took over at fullback and became—many football aficionados believe—the best college player ever at that position. Blaik actually could put on the field two alternating teams of roughly equal skills (save for Mr. Inside and Mr. Outside and quarterback Arnold Tucker leading one of them). In an unbeaten and untied season, Navy was defeated for the first time in six years—and for the national championship, no less! The game was played before 70,000 fans at Baltimore's Municipal Stadium, with wartime restrictions, by then, relaxed and the rip-roaring atmosphere of pre-war college football restored. Moreover, fans attending the game enriched the government by buying $59 million worth of war bonds.

Former Superintendent Eichelberger—then serving on General MacArthur's staff in the

"My boys—sort of"

—by Hugh Sidey

I WAS FAMILIAR WITH THE WEST POINT legend when I landed there in the winter of 1946 as a private first class, at the bottom of the heap of that strange cadre of detached servicemen who keep the Military Academy running. But I had little notion of its deeper meaning.

I shoveled the snow and carried out the garbage of General Max Taylor, when he became superintendent. I helped position the velvet rope when the beautiful New York women arrived as weekend "drags" and was chewed out for my clumsy maneuvers by Cadet George S. Patton, IV, already certified in Patton family flamboyance.

I cleaned up after both the glorious public celebrations and private debauches of June week, the first after the end of World War II, with victorious soldiers from so many battlefields back to the Plain that formed them, watching young men who would take their places. I made eleven bucks (a huge windfall for a pfc) by being strategically placed to give first salutes to the newly-commissioned second lieutenants. Tradition demanded a dollar for each salute.

I parked cars for the hordes who came to see the final gridiron exploits of Don Blanchard and Glen Davis, quaffed a few beers down at Bennie Havens', got to know the legendary Marty Maher, the real-life hero of John Ford's *The Long Gray Line*, and mopped up the puddles of water after the demonstration of artillery trajectory with what the Cadets called "Colonel Hayden's pissometer," nothing more than a large hose and a variable nozzle but with me behind the mop at present arms.

Other events and sounds began to rise over the routines of life around the Academy and I began to understand better its methods and its purpose in our national life. When I helped bring the Corps on buses to New York to march in the Armed Services Day parade I stood on a sidewalk and watched them swing down Fifth Avenue flawless in gray in a misty rain. I thought: my boys—sort of.

Ike and Bradley came back to West Point one day, crammed in what I recall as a ridiculously small command car, the two of them apparently just looking around, actually talking more to each other than looking. I fumbled a salute and they gave me a clumsy response through the car window. I suppose it was really quite a pain with every G.I. rushing in the car's path so they could claim to have saluted the great Generals Dwight Eisenhower and Omar Bradley. What would they do now, I remember thinking? War over and so many unemployed generals. War, it turned out as always, was not over, just different, nor was their work ended. MacArthur visited like royalty and there was a review for Jonathan Wainwright, "the hero of Corregidor," a bent and wasted man with only the light of old memories seeming to hold him up.

When I was free of duties I would hurry to the review and often stand on Trophy Point and let my eyes and mind wander over the Hudson Valley and the ranks of the Cadets, the enduring barracks behind and the Chapel and Fort Putnam above—and history all around pressing its message to march on. What would these young men do going into an army which was melting away and into a world where the great war was over, its heroes anointed, its job ill-defined in a year of exuberant homecoming? Though I did not know it then, among those Cadets were Al Haig and Brent Scowcroft, two men who would become generals and who would play a huge part in my life—and the nation's. And in a few years when I read the news stories of fighting in Korea, I knew some of those same voices I had heard on the Plain were shouting commands at Pusan and Inchon. How many had been silenced in that strange place half a world away from West Point?

One morning I was asked to report at the Old Cemetery and help bury a long-retired cavalry officer who had fought in the Spanish-American War and World War I. There was an option to refuse such duty and yet I was pulled there by a curious emotion. The man's name meant nothing to me and I promptly forgot it. But I still vividly recall the riderless horse, the turned boots, the crunch of the caisson wheels over the gravel path, the peace and beauty of the cemetery, the surrounding graves from all of our wars and the muffled sobbing of the gaunt widow who walked behind.

I was struck by her labored dignity. How many years on her husband's miserable pay had she endured, how much of his frustration at slow advancement had he heaped on her, how many cramped and distant outposts had she endured? Yet she was there for that last short journey, him going home to the Corps, she still remembering and caring. There was the meaning of West Point.

South Pacific—listened to that 1944 Army-Navy game on Armed Forces Radio, no doubt with considerable satisfaction. MacArthur himself, a sports buff who had been Superintendent when Red Blaik was a cadet, wired with typical flamboyance:

"GREATEST OF ALL ARMY TEAMS STOP WE HAVE STOPPED THE WAR TO CELEBRATE YOUR MAGNIFICENT SUCCESS."

For the national championship years 1944-46, Blaik may have fielded one of the best college football teams of all time—a judgment many would dispute, of course, and no one can prove. But the Black Knights, as they came to be known, had a twenty-five-game winning streak in those years. Through 1947 (when Columbia broke the winning streak), Army was unbeaten in thirty-two games, although tied twice—once in the memorable 1946 game with Notre Dame in New York's Yankee Stadium, played to a 0-0 finish in a veritable roar of national attention, heavy betting and wide-open ticket scalping.

After that game, the Army-Notre Dame series was cancelled (except for the already-scheduled 1947 game); West Point officials feared that the Notre Dame games were beginning to overshadow the service rivalry with Navy.

It's been charged through the years, and was frequently at the time, that the Black Knights of Blaik, Blanchard & Davis were playing understrength teams depleted by the war service of the better players who, in happier times, would have been at civilian schools. This theory hardly detracts from the demonstrated excellence of Blaik's teams, though it was strengthened when that postwar Notre Dame squad of 1946 played Army to a standstill. Army's great wartime end, Barney Poole, left the Academy after World War II, giving further point to the criticism.

In any case, the wartime football teams gave

Above: MacArthur kept his promise to return to the Philippines, wading ashore at Leyte Gulf on October 20, 1944, with Japanese defenders not more than a few hundred yards away.

men of the Corps ample opportunity to learn to be good winners. The cadets' vocal support at every game—"the Army's twelfth man"—continued to be a vital part of the West Point football tradition. Besides, non-playing cadets knew, if opponents didn't, that the Academy made few concessions, other than a training table, to its football players. Once admitted, standards were not lowered for them. They marched, drilled, studied, walked guard, went to summer combat camp, and were expected to do well in what was essentially a difficult engineering course.

National champions on the field, they were ordinary cadets on the Plain.

For more than a century, since its opening in 1802, West Point had been the spiritual—if not always the numerical—heart of the Army. In World War I, of Pershing's forty-two divisions in the AEF, fourteen were commanded by his classmates of 1886. Sixteen others were led by West Pointers he had known as a cadet or later, as tactical officer.

The Western Front met the Eastern Front on April 25, 1945, at Torgau on the Elbe River. Anthony Gross, a British artist, painted this somewhat fanciful rendition of the encounter. The American officer standing in the boat is James M. Gavin '29, commander of the 82nd Airborne.

In World War II, Dwight Eisenhower and all the leading American combat generals—MacArthur, Bradley, Patton, as well as Arnold, the Air Corps commander—were West Point men; and twenty-four of the thirty-four commanders of army corps at one time or another had attended the Academy (twenty-three were graduates). At lower levels, the officer corps also reflected West Point; of the roughly 15,000 graduates since 1802, about 9,000—90 per cent of those still living—were on active duty in World War II—some of them older and retired officers called back to administrative and training commands, relieving younger men for combat duty. West Point graduate engineers also played large roles in such significant wartime building feats as the Burma Road, Alaska Highway and Iran pipeline.

Of the four wartime classes, more than eight percent were killed in the line of duty. The Class of 1941, with 424 members—known as "Black '41," a nickname coined by an unknown cadet—was commissioned in June 1941, barely six months before Pearl Harbor. With war already engulfing Europe, Secretary of War Henry Stimson spoke plainly in his commencement address:

> *"The world today is divided between two camps and the issue between these camps is irreconcilable. It cannot be appeased. It cannot be placated. Humanity cannot permanently make terms with injustice, with wrong and with cruelty."*

The '41 graduates were commissioned second lieutenants after that speech, and went directly into the Army. Within seven months, the first of them was killed in action—Lt. Alexander R. "Sandy" Nininger of Florida, who as a cadet had arranged for the Broadway production of the comedy *Arsenic and Old Lace*, with Boris Karloff, to come to West Point. Nininger died leading an infantry unit in a fierce counterattack against Japanese forces on Bataan in the Philippines. For his heroism in that action, he was awarded the Congressional Medal of Honor (the first and only member of Black '41 to win that

highest of American military awards).

Only a year before his death, Nininger had marched with the Corps of Cadets in Washington on January 20, 1941, for the third inaugural parade for Franklin Roosevelt. In a later letter, Nininger told how he and other cadets were then given liberty from 8 to 11 p.m. before being expected back on "sleepers" for the overnight train trip to West Point and a full day of classes on Jan. 21.

At the time, he was taking a horseback riding class three times a week. Today he is honored at the Fourth Class Clubroom in Central Barracks—called "Nininger Hall."

Sandy Nininger was by no means the only notable member of the Class of '41. Another, distinguished in life rather than by death, was George S. Brown—a marked man from the start of his career. He flew ably for the Eighth Air Force in World War II, a few years later was director of operations for the Fifth Air Force in Korea, then became an assistant to the chairman of the Joint Chiefs of Staff. In 1968, he donned a fourth star (the only member of the Class of '41 to rise to that rank). President Nixon selected General Brown to be Chief of Staff of the Air Force and he continued to serve in that high office for Presidents Ford and Carter. He died of cancer in 1978.

The cadet who stood first in Black '41—Alfred Judson Force Moody—also rose high, as expected, though not to the level of some lower-ranked classmates. Moody was first an instructor at West Point, then an officer at Eisenhower's World War II headquarters in Europe, in intelligence in the China-Burma-India theater, and on Okinawa. After the war, he earned a masters degree at Yale, worked in the Pentagon for the Army Chief of Staff, held posts in France and Germany, studied at the Army War College and served in Korea.

Moody later became an assistant to the Secretary of Defense, a brigadier general in 1966, took helicopter training at an advanced age, and went to Vietnam—his third war—as second in command of the First Air Cavalry Division (commanded by a Black '41 classmate, Lieutenant General John "Jack" Norton—the business manager of *Malim in Se* on that long-ago Hundredth Night in 1941). General Moody died of a heart attack at Camp Radcliff in Vietnam in 1967 and is buried in Arlington National Cemetery.

Another member of that class thrust so quickly into combat in World War II was Edward L. Rowny. He became a three-star general in 1979, after serving as President Reagan's principal advisor on arms control and the chief negotiator for the START treaty.

Some Class of 1941 members distinguished themselves in civilian life. Brigadier General William T. Seawell retired in 1963 and was chief executive officer of Pan-American Airways from 1972 to 1982. After a combat career in the European theater, George "Bliss" Moody won a Silver Medal in the modern pentathlon at the Olympics of 1948. He retired as Colonel, U.S. Army, in 1965.

Two years later, in 1967, Colonel James Fowler, USA, the only black man to graduate with the Class of 1941, also retired. When Fowler had entered West Point, Benjamin Davis had been the only black to have been graduated from the Academy in the twentieth century. In Fowler's West Point time, well before the civil rights movement, he had roomed alone for four years; records suggest that he was not well-treated by his classmates.

One of most important incidents of the war in Europe was the discovery, in 1945, of the Ludendorf railroad bridge standing mostly undamaged across the Rhine river—a broad gateway into Hitler's Germany. Leading the patrol near Remagen that discovered the open bridge was Sears Cohen, Class of 1941, later to retire as a colonel. (William C. Westmoreland '36, decades later the Army commander in Vietnam, also fought for the bridge at Remagen.)

By the end of World War II, 40 members of Black '41's 424 cadets had been killed in action. Another eleven had died in Air Corps training

accidents, a total of fifty-one dead, to be joined by four more killed in the Korean War—about 12 per cent of the class. In 1964, however, over half the class members still were on active duty; but after 1970, when the class had reached the thirty year point, only twenty remained in the Army. The last of them to retire—Brigadier General Charles Schilling, then the head of the USMA Engineering Department—shed his uniform in 1980.

The succeeding class, that of 1942, was featured in 1966 by *Fortune* magazine as "The Backbone Class of 1942" at West Point. It produced invaluable officers not just for World War II, the magazine reported, but for a modern Army and ". . . a world where parade drill has become a minor facet of military psychology, where continental defenses call for guided missiles, and where communications involve radios, computers and satellites."

That tribute—coming just before the war in Vietnam became an American disaster—was well deserved. Mustered in at West Point in 1938, fourteen months before Hitler set off World War II with his invasion of Poland, the 483 cadets of '42 were Depression babies, some of them at the Academy not for the love of "duty, honor, country" but mostly for a free education. They served into the years of America's prosperity and world eminence, when high technology took a leading place even in warfare.

The Class of 1942, however, also "paid its dues" in combat. By 1976, seventy-two of its members had died in combat in three wars, or in war-related accidents—mostly air training crashes. Collectively, the class had won four Distinguished Service Crosses (three posthumously), more than 40 Silver Stars, over a hundred Distinguished Flying Crosses, and more than 125 Purple Hearts, as well as numerous other medals.

Lucius D. Clay Jr., a much-decorated flyer in World War II (and the son of the prominent general who became High Commissioner of Germany after that war) rose to the highest rank—major general—of any class member.

After World War II, Class of 1942 members served in assignments around the world, and many attended the Army War College and the Command and General Staff School, or civilian universities. They earned eighty-seven masters' degrees and several doctorates. By 1966, according to Fortune, only thirty-four members of the Class of 1942 had resigned from the Army and the magazine could list these outstanding "backbone" men:

Clay, then the commanding general of Twelfth Air Force at Waco, Texas; Brigadier General John D. Crowley Jr.—at West Point, ranked last in the class—a high-ranking logistics officer in Vietnam; Brigadier General Thomas M. Rienzi, supervisor of developing the "side-looking airborne radar"; Brigadier General John Deane, a Harvard MA in business administration, formerly a member of the Korean armistice commission, and chief of staff for U.S. Field

This ten-foot-long replica of the ballistic case of "Fat Man," above, the atomic bomb dropped on Nagasaki, Japan, on August 9, 1945, is in the West Point Museum. General Leslie R. Groves, top, Class of November 1918, directed the Manhattan Project that produced the bombs that ended the war with Japan.

The Class of 1945 marches to the podium to receive their diplomas. These men may have missed out on World War II, but many of them would see more than their share of action in the Cold War.

Forces at Nha Trang in Vietnam; and Colonel Robert H. Offley, project director for early U. S. missile tests.

These outstanding graduates in the Class of 1942, the magazine said, were only a few of the class's "diplomats, engineers and scientists." All had come a long way from the Depression days of their plebe year.

In 1939, when the successor Class of 1943 was mustered in at West Point, its members, too, joined what was still an antiquated and under-sized peacetime Army—130,000 total strength and about 14,000 officers. For the latter, promotion came slowly, if at all, owing mostly to congressional penury. Even the between-wars career of so outstanding an officer as Dwight Eisenhower '15, was typical: a lieutenant colonel in wartime 1918, back to major in 1920, down to captain in 1922, a major again in 1924, returned to his 1918 rank only in 1936. Eisenhower himself, recalling those years in Crusade in Europe, noted rather sadly that "some of the officers in the long years of peace had worn themselves deep ruts of professional routine with which they were sheltered from vexing new ideas and troublesome problems . . . seniority was the only basis for promotion . . . "

No books or magazine articles seem to have been written about the Class of 1943 although its members too were commissioned lieutenants upon graduation in January and June 1943, and sent directly into the Army. Forty-four of them were killed in action and thirty-two in accidents—again, mostly pilot-training crashes. Eighty-eight per cent of the survivors served on active duty for twenty years or more. One distinguished member of the class, Roger Hilsman, served in the 1960s as a high official of the Johnson Administration with much responsibility for operations in Vietnam.

The Class of 1944, too late for most of World War II, included a future West Point superintendent, Lt. Gen. Ernest Graves Jr., who had finished second in the class, and a future academic dean, Brigadier General Frederick Smith. Nor was John Eisenhower the only member of the class who was the son of a leading general. So was Donald Alfred Gruenther, whose father in the 1950s was to succeed Dwight Eisenhower in command of NATO forces.

General Eisenhower gave son John a quick lesson in how West Point training differed from actual warfare. While spending a two-week graduation leave with the Allies' commanding general, Lieutenant John Eisenhower spotted a line of vehicles moving bumper-to-bumper, shattering Academy doctrine.

"You'd never get away with that if you didn't have air supremacy," he declared to his father—who promptly put him down: "If I didn't have air supremacy, I wouldn't be here."

In 1939, when the Class of 1943 took the oath, the Army and the nation were finally beginning—barely—the mobilization that sustained, after Pearl Harbor, nearly four years of war on two fronts. Thus, the class had the distinction of seeing the last of the old horse-drawn Army, while many still remained active in the age of jet aircraft and space exploration.

Recalled in their 50-year book was a song they sang—to the tune of *The Caissons Go Rolling Along*—at West Point as motorization belatedly but inevitably came to the Army:

See the red guidon stuck
on the offside of a truck
with horses and caissons all gone.
Gone are nose bags and grass
as we feed with oil and gas,
make tracks with the pieces hooked on.

7
INTO THE COLD WAR: 1946-1964

BY DENNIS E. SHOWALTER

"A feeling came over me that the expression 'The United States of America' would now and henceforth mean something different than it had ever before. From here on it would be the nation I would be serving, not myself."

—Dwight D. Eisenhower, 1952, remembering his first day at West Point

■ Major General Maxwell Taylor became Superintendent and revised and modernized the curriculum. The Board of Consultants included the Presidents of Massachusetts Institute of Technology, Williams College, and Louisiana State University.

■ New instructors selected in advance of assignment to West Point to permit them to attend civilian universities for graduate study.
■ Horsemanship dropped from the curriculum.
■ Army and Notre Dame tie, 0-0.

■ Colonel William E. Morrison retired as Professor of Modern Languages, in grade of Brigadier General, after "long and distinguished service," first professor to be so honored.

■ Course in Military History redesignated History of the Military Art.

■ Graduates 1802–1950: 18,016; 1941–1950: 5,777.
■ Statue of General George S. Patton, Jr. dedicated in front of the library, August 19, first of the statues of the heroes of World War II to be emplaced at West Point. Melted into the bronze hands of the statue are four silver stars worn by the General and a gold cavalry insignia worn by Mrs. Patton.
■ Korean War begins.

■ Pursuant to Department of the Army directive to release 25 per cent of Regular Army officers for field and staff assignments necessitated by the war in Korea, retired and reserve officers were assigned to the various academic departments.

■ Dwight David Eisenhower was elected President of the United States, member of the USMA Class of 1915, "the class the stars fell on."

PRECEDING SPREAD: American soldiers walk through the middle of a burning village during the Korean war. Over 150 West Pointers died in the seesaw struggle for the Korean peninsula. Inset: General Matthew Ridgway '17 rallied the demoralized Eighth Army in the winter of 1950-51, after the disaster on the Yalu River.

"Everybody thinks we're knights. And we are—a military brotherhood vowed to poverty, obedience, and unchastity!" That rueful capsule definition of West Point by a contemporary cadet suggests as well the U.S. Military Academy's position in 1945. "The Point" had never stood higher in America's status structure. In contrast to the Civil War, no political soldiers like John Logan emerged to trumpet the sovereign virtues of citizen colonels and amateur generals. In contrast to World War I, no National Guard lobby systematically took claims of discrimination in command assignments to the national press. Between 1942 and 1945, the U.S. Army had demonstrated beyond reasonable doubt that war was too important to be left to amateurs. Its wartime graduates had proven themselves at battalion and regimental levels, as tacticians, logisticians, and leaders. Its senior alumni had provided a stable of division and corps commanders uniquely competent among all the combatants, despite severely limited interwar opportunities to develop the skills required for higher command.

Some rituals never change. In their last moments as civilians, below, plebes check into West Point in 1926. Except for their clothing, they could have been the frightened plebes of the 1950s. Bracing (right) was an extreme posture of attention that upperclassmen demanded as an assertion of dominance over plebes.

The Academy stood alone after 1945 as a matrix for lieutenants and a nurturer of generals. Other components of the army, the National Guard and the Organized Reserve, defined their war-fighting effectiveness in terms set by West Point. The ROTC programs that increasingly proliferated in colleges and universities took their cues and their standards from models asso-

■ Field Marshal Viscount Montgomery of Alamein addressed the three upper classes on "Leadership" 9 April.
■ End of Korean War.

■ USMA Archives, a branch of the National Archives, established to assemble and preserve the permanent records of the U.S. Military Academy.

■ President Dwight D. Eisenhower visited during June Week participating in graduation exercises and the fortieth reunion of class of 1915.
■ Motion picture *The Long Gray Line*, directed by John Ford, released.

■ Conversion of Riding Hall to an academic building, renamed Thayer Hall, begun.

■ At the Graduation Parade, when the graduating cadets were supposed to form for "Front and Center" to review the Corps, one company after another began breaking ranks and running across the Plain until the whole class was celebrating wildly all over the field. Only two companies held their positions.

■ Cadet Pete Dawkins won Heisman Trophy in Army's best football season [8-1] in eight years.

■ *West Point Atlas of American Wars*, edited by Colonel Vincent J. Esposito, Professor and Head, Department of Military Art and Engineering, with maps by Edward J. Krasnaborski, published in October. Deemed "the most significant work ever undertaken in the field of American military history."

During "Beast Barracks," left, the young men of the Class of '52 begin to shape themselves into soldiers.

The cartoon below suggests the legendary terrors of the plebe year.

ciated with West Point, rather than any variant of part-time soldiering.

West Point benefited as well because the aftermath of World War II did not experience a turning away from military issues to anything like the degree of the post–Civil War and post–World War I eras. With the Cold War emerging almost immediately, even the intellectual/academic community retained militarized attitudes and militarized rhetoric. Paul Fussell makes the point that profanity became another general legacy of the Second World War experience in social and occupational classes that previously shunned rough language as a mark of low breeding. "Tough-mindedness" was high praise among professors, politicians, and policy-makers alike. As the Cold War intensified during the 1950s, an image as a no-nonsense producer of no-nonsense men was among the best things a publicly funded institution could enjoy.

West Point possessed that reputation in the highest degree. Feature films like *The Long Gray Line* and a successful TV series, *Men of West Point*, testified to the Academy's commercial appeal. Young adult and juvenile books, often written or fronted by West Point "insiders" like Colonel Russell Reeder, the wounded hero of D-Day who returned to his alma mater and became a

WEST POINT IN THE MOVIES

More than thirty movies have been made about West Point, from the pioneering *A Day at West Point Military Academy, New York*, made by Thomas Alva Edison's company in 1911, through the promotional films *Inside America's Military Academies: Conquering Summer*, in 1999. While most of these have been documentaries, the Academy has proven irresistible to commercial film makers as well.

Early on, a spate of musicals included Nelson Eddy's giddy *Rosalie* (1937), in which a West Point football hero falls in love with a girl from Vassar (Eleanor Powell), who turns out to be a princess. Cole Porter wrote the music, which includes *In The Still of the Night*, and Ray Bolger dances.

Dick Powell in *Flirtation Walk* (1934) played a cadet who falls in love with a General's daughter—Ruby Keeler, the great dancer, who unfortunately was trying to break out as a straight actress in this film and doesn't dance.

In *The West Point Story* (1950), starring James Cagney, a Broadway director tries to stage a show at the Academy but keeps running afoul of the rules. Not one of Cagney's triumphs, the movie also starred Gordon McRae as a singing cadet, with Virginia Mayo and Doris Day as assorted love interests.

Inevitably, West Point figured in several historical melodramas, and inevitably the best known revolve around George Armstrong Custer. In 1940s *The Santa Fe Trail*, the dashing yellow-hair is played by none other than Ronald Reagan, who gallops off with J.E.B. Stuart (Errol Flynn) to pacify Bloody Kansas. That the historical *Continues next page*

Film producers found the sheer visual drama of West Point irresistible. The still opposite, from Rosalie, shows off the film's gaudy Busby Berkeley style. Above, Dick Powell marries Ruby Keeler in Flirtation Walk, another film from the 1930s, when war seemed only distantly related to West Point.

The Entertainment Triumph Of The Year!

TYRONE POWER

MAUREEN O'HARA

IN JOHN FORD'S

THE LONG GRAY LINE

CINEMASCOPE
Color by TECHNICOLOR

Co-starring
ROBERT FRANCIS · DONALD CRISP · WARD BOND · BETSY PALMER · PHIL CAREY
Screen Play by EDWARD HOPE · Based upon "Bringing Up the Brass" by Marty Maher and Nardi Reeder Campion
Produced by ROBERT ARTHUR · Directed by JOHN FORD · A COLUMBIA PICTURE

The Long Gray Line, advertised in the poster at left, was directed by John Ford, and is the best-known of the West Point movies. It told the story of Marty Maher, an Irish immigrant who began waiting tables and became one of West Point's most beloved gym instructors. Below, Tyrone Power (as Maher) hoists a tray in the mess hall. More typical of the cinematic portrayals of the Academy was the forgettable The West Point Story, *which starred, left to right, Alan Hale Jr., Virginia Mayo, James Cagney, Doris Day and a singing cadet, Gordon McRae.*

WEST POINT IN THE MOVIES

Continued

Custer was only a boy when Kansas was bleeding so badly didn't phase Hollywood. *They Died With Their Boots On*, from 1941, also featured the doughty Flynn, this time as Custer, getting his final demerits at the Little Big Horn. Olivia de Havilland co-starred. *MacArthur*, premiering in 1977, was Gregory Peck's ambitious but thin biopic of the great General.

Another sub-genre of West Point films depict the Academy as The Great Americanizing Influence, as in *The Duke of West Point*, in 1938, in which a snobbish Englishman learns true American values as a cadet. The best of these is also the best West Point film, *The Long Gray Line*, released in 1955.

John Ford directed *The Long Gray Line*, which starred Tyrone Power as Marty Maher, the feisty young Irish immigrant who starts out working in the kitchens at West Point. His cocky independence gets him in trouble with the Academy's rules, but his spirit earns him the sympathetic interest of Ward Bond, playing the Athletic Director, who takes him under his wing.

There, Marty finds a wife, Mary O'Donnell (Maureen O'Hara), another Irish immigrant, and a calling, as he becomes one of the most inspiring athletic instructors in West Point history. When their son dies, Maher and his wife transfer that love to the cadets, whom they support and encourage and then, in one heartbreaking scene, send off to war. Dwight Eisenhower appears in several scenes, both as a young cadet, and later, as President, when Maher was being forced into retirement, and went to ask Ike to let him stay on. The movie is long (138 minutes) but steady and affecting, with good characters, and it honors the best of the spirit of West Point. A true story, it's based on Maher's autobiography.

Dress Gray (1986) was originally a TV miniseries: the script is by Gore Vidal. When an underclassman whom he befriended is murdered Cadet Alec Baldwin risks his career to find out who did it and uncovers far more than he asked for. *Assault at West Point* (1994) dealt dramatically with the controversial court-martial of black cadet Johnson Whittaker. While it does a good job of presenting the injustice of Whittaker's persecution, the film never comes to life as drama.

The nadir of all West Point films, though, must be 1952's *Francis Goes to West Point*, in which the intrepid and sarcastic mule provided new insight into Beast Barracks.

Worth watching only because Leonard Nimoy, who later played another character with interesting ears, appears briefly.   —C.H.

legend in its Tactical and Athletic Departments, presented West Point affirmatively—not in rosy colors, but by stressing its rite-of-passage elements. The challenges of cadet life were by no means unappealing to adolescents whose civilian male role models in the 1950s often wore either gray flannel suits or frilly aprons like the one donned by Jim Backus, the unforgettably ineffectual father in *Rebel Without a Cause*.

What exactly, however, were soldiers supposed to do in a global, nuclear age? The Cold War army required a defining image. West Point provided one: a national citizen army raised by selective service had a national officer corps whose permanent members were provided by the Military Academy. In terms of raw numbers, Academy graduates were in the minority of the Army's Cold War officer corps. Fewer than 700 were commissioned annually. Nevertheless they set the tone. During the Cold War proper, the West Point model was never significantly challenged. Each year a legally-mandated Board of Visitors, congressmen and Presidential appointees, tours each service academy and submits a report. These documents, while not exactly whitewashes, seldom incorporate serious criticisms or reservations. West Point's reports for the Cold War era, are, however, extraordinarily affirming even by the standards of the genre. In 1958 the Visitors

described cadet morale as "excellent." Every officer observed was "alert, eager, and interested." Recommendations for change focused on such minutiae as building an additional barracks and providing the chaplain with an assistant. In 1961, with Vietnam still no more than a cloud on America's horizon, the Board again found cadet morale excellent, officers "enthusiastic and interested in their work," and methods of instruction "modern and effective." The Military Academy clearly had what amounted to a free hand from the government, as well as from the people, its graduates served.

West Point during the Cold War stood alone in other ways. The creation of an independent Air Force, and the accompanying departure of its cadets to their own academy in Colorado Springs, significantly narrowed the academic and professional focus of the older institution. The split was inevitable. About 60 per cent of the first and second classmen had applied for aviation training when it was first offered in 1942. Air cadets subsequently did much of their training at Stewart Field, twenty miles from the Academy. As a result two distinct subcultures developed, even though air cadets and ground-pounders were required to perform the same drill field and parade ground exercises. With well over a third of the postwar classes seeking Air Force

RING ISSUE

SEPTEMBER 10, 1954

For members of the First Class, the presentation of class rings at the beginning of the year was a special moment. At a ring hop cadets were photographed with their dates in the circle of a giant ring, like the one on the cover of The Pointer *of September 10, 1954, above. Traditionally the cadet wears his ring with his class crest toward him, whether he's right or left handed, until he graduates, when he turns the ring so that the Academy crest faces him, symbolic of his commitment to duty, honor, country.*

commissions, and given the Air Force's single-minded postwar drive for a separate identity, sustaining a common purpose for both services in the same academy was at best unlikely. The post-Air Force Academy West Point nevertheless lost the input of cadets and officers with an essentially different professional orientation.

In the rapidly changing postwar West Point lost another set of contacts as well: with the civilian academic world, and particularly the Ivy League. Beginning around the turn of the century, the Military Academy had borrowed significant aspects of its socialization from its neighboring institutions. The process was initially heavily dependent on athletic interaction, as cadets dated women and imitated men from

the schools to which they traveled for games. The relatively low social standing of cadets compared to their civilian counterparts at Yale, Harvard, and Penn further encouraged acculturation to collegiate norms: imitation is a sincere form of flattery.

It is not stretching too far to see parallels between the Academy's burgeoning emphasis on varsity athletics and that prevailing in the college world of the real-life Hobey Baker or the fictional Dink Stover. The limited intellectualism of the interwar Military Academy had its counterpart in the civilian world's "gentleman's C." The companies into which the Corps of Cadets were organized acquired some of the characteristics of college fraternities, becoming most cadets' everyday world for the months and years between Beast Barracks and graduation. Transfers among companies were almost as unusual as a civilian fraternity brother's resigning and pledging another society. Even though until 1957 the only principle of selection was height, companies possessed and sometimes cultivated individual identities. Rick Atkinson's *The Long Gray Line*, discussing West Point in the early 1960s, describes some companies as using plebes as "manservants rather than slaves," while others were much harsher on first-year men as a matter of principle.

West Point's connections to the college world began to erode with the tectonic shift that hit the American academy after World War II. The Cold War and the influx of GI-Bill undergraduates combined to create an atmosphere far more intellectually oriented, far more narrowly academic, than anything that had existed previously. West Point, with neither reason nor desire to follow the same path, increasingly stood alone.

West Point became isolated in another way.

"THE DAY WEST POINT WENT CO-ED!!"

"About two hours later a very strange sound echoed through the division. It was a combination of high heeled tapping on a stairway plus the rattle of keys against a guard's saber. I wouldn't have believed that one unless I had seen it with my own eyes. As soon as the guard saw my head sticking out the door, she started towards my room. She was a vision of loveliness in her little gray suit with the black pinstripes. She sidled up to me, and in a low, husky voice said, "What're you doin' up after taps, big boy?" I asked her if we couldn't be friends and talk the whole thing over sensibly. I invited her to come in and have a Pepsi with me. Being duty bound, she refused, and started out the door of the division. I made a frantic grab to bring her back, and—thud! I found myself lying on th floor beside my bed."

Excerpt from a spoof in
the April 1, 1955 *The Pointer*
—Cadet Bob Christiansen

An article from The Pointer *April 1, 1955, The Day West Point Went Co-ed, found the idea of women attending the Academy to be an impossible dream. The impossible became fact in 1976.*

Long before 1945 the Military Academy had been the soul of the Army, focus of a nostalgia sharpened by the bleak and dreary nature of so many peacetime garrisons. During the Cold War it became as well a public shrine, a place of pilgrimage and tourism recognized by the Academy's official designation in 1961 as a historic site. Increasing amounts of energy were required from successive superintendents to balance the claims of a shrine, which is by definition a memorial, and the needs of a living institution with ongoing and changing responsibilities.

The Academy's status as a site of memory was reinforced by what a current faculty member calls the tendency of Academy graduates to believe viscerally that West Point was at its absolute peak during their first-class year, and that everything since has taken the institution downhill. The aphorism can be tested—and affirmed—by reading the letters in any given issue of *Assembly*, the Academy's alumni magazine. It is particularly true for senior officers. A 1958 study reported that since the Class of 1910 twice as many graduates from the top fifth of their class as from the bottom fifth had become generals. Success as a cadet, in other words, was significantly predictive of success in the army— a fact likely to discourage serious consideration among senior officers of significantly altering for any reason the cadet experience as they remem-

bered it. Alumni nostalgia is not an exclusive military phenomenon, but even the most successful and powerful graduates of Harvard, Wisconsin, or Colorado College are unlikely to be in a position to institutionalize their memories by using command influence and command authority to avert change!

As West Point stood increasingly above and apart from the wider American society, it continued to develop internally as what social scientists called a "total institution": one in which every aspect of life—work, play, and rest—are performed in the same place, with the same people, under the same authority, and as part of the same plan. Bill McWilliams entered the Academy in 1950, and learned there was a system for eating. Plebes were required to

> Cut off a piece of food no larger than a sugar cube and convey it to the mouth with a fork lifted from the plate in a curved motion, enabling us to keep our eyes on the fork. Before chewing, as slowly and deliberately as cattle, we returned our forks to the plate by the same route and placed our hands in our laps.

Nor was personal hygiene a personal matter. In their first weeks in "Beast Barracks" new cadets were marched in formation to the showers and notified:

You each have two minutes in the shower. As your turn comes, step out of your slippers and set them in order next to the wall. Hang your bathrobes and towels on the hooks you see outside the shower door. Time begins when you are under the shower . . . . You have one minute— thirty seconds—ten seconds—five seconds— time's up! Next man! Go! Go! Go!

Beginning with Sylvanus Thayer, the U.S. Military Academy had evolved a distinctive administrative and cultural structure that had proven highly functional relative to the perceived needs of the Academy itself, the U.S. Army, and American society. It was based on

three principles. One was organic unity, based on the concept of transferable experience. Every aspect of Academy life, from the most arcane mathematics classes to the most demanding athletics programs, contributed directly to common end of developing military leaders. A second principle was philosophical idealism, with ideas like duty, honor, and country presented as having an essential existence. "Honor," for example, was not a subjective concept but a reality, to be sustained, in Dwight Eisenhower's words, with the same comprehensive zeal as the physical chastity of one's mother or sister. A third was the definition of knowledge as the deduction of immutable truths through mental and emotional discipline. A professor of mathematics writing in 1958 described his subject as "an intellectual discipline, not a tool for compilation . . . a pattern of thinking, not . . . a manipulation of symbols." The long-standing requirement that every cadet recite in every subject every day was intended to institutionalize that kind of discipline by establishing academic habits that became mental patterns—for better or for worse.

This system, the West Point way, faced four significant challenges between 1945 and 1964. The first involved mission definition. Was the Academy's principal task to prepare cadets primarily for the relatively specific duties of junior officers, or to give them tools for the broader responsibilities that might confront them later in their careers? Prior to World War II the question had been essentially moot. West Point existed to produce second lieutenants. Further intellectual development would be undertaken in a growing structure of advanced professional schools like the Army War College, or Fort Leavenworth's Command and General Staff School.

Rapid wartime promotion patterns, however, had thrown a good many graduates into the deep end of situations where the conventional Academy education proved a limited resource. Since the war, moreover, the Army confronted unprecedented technological change. Apart from the question of whether nuclear weapons left soldiers anything beyond constabulary and mop-up roles, developments in conventional weapons systems provided new and comprehensive challenges to their users. Increasingly complex organizational structures created a corresponding need for administrative and management skills. The Army's conversion to a permanent force of short-service citizen conscripts, most of them young unmarried men, created new leadership demands; commanders could no

longer count on "old-timers" knowing what to do without being told. Finally, the unprecedented economic demands of waging a Cold War against a background of nuclear Armageddon meant the Army had to justify its claims for funding more comprehensively and convincingly than had been the case even in the darkest days of the Depression.

In such contexts adaptability and breadth of vision were arguably as important, even for junior officers, as the "heroic" characteristics historically inculcated by a West Point system that even prescribed how to chew food. Academy superintendents are not appointed by accident. It was once one of the Army's highest-profile assignments, a stepping-stone to the highest ranks and appointments when performed well. The general officer who held it was there to make his mark, as Douglas MacArthur had done in the 1920s. From 1945 to 1949, the superintendent's post was held by Maxwell Taylor. As commander of the elite 101st Airborne Division in the European theater of operations, he had established himself as the very model of a modern major general—handsome, fit, photogenic, and intelligent. When he declared that West Point was not "a mill for producing second lieutenants," he was making a statement—specifically, to the academic departments.

Historically these had been oriented towards the purpose of preparing officers. They were headed by "Permanent Professors" who had sacrificed promotion beyond field rank in order to remain at the Academy beyond the usual ages for retirement. Their

The Korean War began with a rout of South Korean forces by the North. UN forces, mostly American, rushed to help South Korea. The drawing below by Herbert Hahn depicts MacArthur's daring

landing at Inchon, which outflanked the Communists and started the UN forces driving north again. General MacArthur (inset) observes the landing. UN forces pushed all the way to the Yalu River, where

the Chinese came into the war, sending the Eighth Army into headlong retreat. General Ridgway '17 (right), carrying his characteristic infantryman's rifle, led a remarkable comeback.

years of experience made them key members of the Academy's official and unofficial power structures. Their junior faculties composed of serving officers assigned for short tours of duty, and West Point's departments remained focused on cadet, e.g. undergraduate, instruction at a time when American higher education was becoming increasingly oriented towards research and graduate training, with professors at all kinds of

institutions expected to earn doctorates and pursue individual research. As late as 1964-65, of the 388 officers on West Point's teaching faculty (physical education staff excluded), 316 were MAs while only thirty-five held Ph.Ds.

It is, however, impossible to communicate what one does not know. Steadily increasing numbers of faculty or faculty-designates, especially in the humanities and social science fields, were sent for specialized graduate training, usually at top-ranked civilian institutions. Classroom structures became more flexible, with

KOREA
1950-1953

6 MARCH 1918

10 OCT.

THE
POINTER

Your Communist Enemy In Korea
SEE PAGE 2

MAY 4, 1951

This stained glass window (left) in Washington Hall honors the Korean War. Above, The Pointer of May 4, 1951, tried to define the enemy in the conflict. The politics of the Cold War overshadowed the fighting throughout.

daily recitations being supplemented—supplanted in some departments—by quizzes, examinations, and instructor-led discussion. Department structures, once as seemingly inflexible as the tides, were changed. As early as

1946, for example, a Department of Electrical Engineering was created from what had been the Department of Chemistry and Electricity.

The mental flexibility demanded even of a modern junior officer was not best fostered by

Three commanders: Omar Bradley '15, later Chairman of the Joint Chiefs of Staff, confers with Matthew Ridgway '17, left, and James Van Fleet '15, the man who replaced him as commander of the Eighth Army. The battered helmet below, from the West Point Museum, came through the bloody UN assault on Pork Chop Hill in 1952.

classroom environments emphasizing detail and memory. The Superintendent's Curriculum Committee reported in 1958 that " . . . greater flexibility in the educational process is mandatory. Problems of strategy cannot be foreseen; they come from unforeseen quarters; and they demand solutions for which there is no precedent. The intellectual formation of the cadet requires his growth in wisdom; information is only one phase of the total intellectual formation."

The authors of a standard work on military education published in 1957 mused that cadets needed "a little more opportunity . . . to sail on uncharted seas, to wander out of the safe waters of established fact." The Curriculum Study Committee recommended less frequent grading and less emphasis on reaching "school solutions" based on doctrinal or theoretical principles. It urged developing advanced sections of existing courses. It went so far as to support allowing cadets in their last two years to take a single elective—as an overload, on a voluntary basis, in the one free hour of the afternoon schedule. This proposal scarcely opened the door to curricular anarchy. Not until 1960 were cadets allowed to take two electives, in their first-class year when presumably they would be sufficiently mature to handle such heady freedom responsibly. Nor was critical thinking established as central to the West Point classroom. In the words of another contemporary report, "skepticism frequently breeds indecision, and to turn out a man beset by doubts is hardly the proper objective of Service Academy training."

The quest for certainty at West Point was encouraged by the Korean War. In theory at least, it was a regular force led by Academy graduates that went into Korea—and reeled back in near-rout before a North Korean army that attracted no American attention before it began hammering American soldiers. Direct responsibility for the debacle scarcely could be assigned to West Point. Nevertheless the first three months of the Korean War established a pattern that seared itself into the institution's memory and its unconsciousness. For the first time in American military history, trained soldiers did not follow their officers. Time after time, men posted by daylight drifted back to headquarters and field kitchens by ones and twos during the night. Time and again, platoon movements begun at full strength dwindled to a half-dozen hard chargers in the lieutenant's immediate neighborhood. Matters were not helped later in the war, as army units subjected to the massive Chinese attack across the Yalu River disintegrated, while the 1st Marine Division, "attacking in a different direction" from Chosin Reservoir, brought out all its wounded and most of its dead.

For some recent graduates it seemed at first unreal. Harry Maihafer, Class of 1949 and an armor officer, was under orders to the Far East in June 1950. "Do you suppose this Korean thing means I'll be going into combat?" he asked a lieutenant colonel whom he had just defeated in a tennis match. "Not a chance, Harry" was the reply. "It'd be stupid to send West Point second lieutenants into combat—the attrition is too great. . . . You fellows are too much of an asset to squander as platoon leaders." By mid-August, Maihafer was on the line in Korea—commanding an infantry platoon.

He had plenty of company. About half the Academy graduates of 1949 and 1950 went to Korea in a similar capacity. Over 150 graduates were killed in action in Korea. Most were lieutenants. The Class of 1950, pitchforked directly into combat, paid with forty-one killed and eighty-one more wounded, from its 670 graduates. That was a long way from the colonel's prediction to Maihafer that "you'll no doubt end up in some cushy headquarters job." It was an Academy graduate, General Matthew Ridgway, who revitalized a shaken Eighth Army after the debacle at the Yalu River, turning it into a fighting machine for a limited war. It was Academy graduates who took over battalions, regiments, and divisions, often from other graduates who failed the test of command, and kept them on the line as the politicians talked of a peace that refused to come. And it was the lieutenants and captains who set the tone of command in the rifle companies, mentoring World War II-era reservists and filling gaps in the military educations of ROTC graduates.

Those graduates who survived have recorded no significant criticism of their alma mater for preparing them poorly. Memories of Korea nevertheless bit deeply into the Academy's consciousness. They worked in particular to reinforce advocates of focusing the system even more closely on producing junior officers who could both lead and command the soldiers the country gave them—even if their skills in higher mathematics and their understanding of Clausewitz suffered in the process.

No amount of classroom experience, no amount of field training, can really prepare anyone for combat. West Point's Tactical Department recognized this, but also responded to the Korean experience by steadily increasing the pressure to militarize Academy training programs. That approach was facilitated by an emerging rivalry between the academic and tactical wings of the Academy. The Tactical Department's historic functions had been disciplinary.

Under Maxwell Taylor, however, tactical officers were also expected to provide role models and positive reinforcement to their cadets. As a result the Tactical Department included more and more hard-charging field soldiers, men for whom academic standing was less important than warrior spirit. The department to a degree

A machine-gun crew of the U.S. 3rd Division fires on Communist hillside positions in the summer of 1951. Above: Long Tom howitzers fire off the heavy charges known as Van Fleet Loads.

■ Graduates 1802–1960: 23,281; 1951–1960: 5,265.
■ Major General William C. Westmoreland succeeds Lieutenant General Garrison H. Davidson as Superintendent.

■ Sylvanus Thayer Award presented to General of the Army Dwight D. Eisenhower, USMA 1915.
■ Vice President Lyndon B. Johnson delivered commencement address June Week.

■ General of the Army Douglas MacArthur received the Thayer Award at West Point and gave his famed "Duty, Honor, Country" speech.

■ Navy, an eleven-point favorite, won the Army-Navy football game in Philadelphia 21-15 on Pearl Harbor day, when final seconds clicked off the official time. Army was only two yards away from the tying touchdown as bedlam in the stadium kept Army quarterback Carl Stichweh from getting off the final play.

■ Public Law 88-276 decreed an Academy expansion program almost doubling the strength of the corps by 1973.
■ New Library completed in March with capacity of 500,000 volumes.
■ Plebes granted Christmas leave for the first time.
■ Americanization of Vietnam War.

prided itself on representing the "goats," those cadets in the low academic sections who despite that—or because of it—often blossomed into first rate fighting men.

Historically, the Academy had done little during the academic year to teach small-unit tactics, as opposed to drill. Physical fitness was considered a natural consequence of the constant physical activity. Summer training programs for upperclassmen had been regarded as less than taxing by cadets who survived the previous nine months. As one plebe expressed conventional wisdom, " . . . we will drive tanks, jets, and every other army vehicle there is, besides that there is a lot of recreation . . . . You always get the afternoon of (sic) and there is always something to do." During the 1950s, however, third-year cadets underwent increasingly demanding, physically-oriented combat-arms training similar to that of the elite army rangers. Second classmen had been able to look forward to a summer spent leisurely touring various military posts with an eye towards branch selection. "We will . . . have hops at Ft. Lee, Ft. Eustis, Ft. Benning, and Maxwell Field, and an outdoor roast at Eglin Field. At Eglin we will get a chance to go deep sea fishing and water skiing." That fun too was curtailed in favor of assignments to field units in quasi-command roles, or to summer plebe training, previously a first-class responsibility.

While highly visible appointments like regimental commanders remained permanent, increasing numbers of lower command and staff assignments for example, were rotated among cadet officers at the semester, instead of being made for the entire year. The intention was to train cadets in assuming a broader spectrum of responsibilities on short notice; the subtext was to diminish the arrogance of callowness that led some graduates to act as though cadet rank persisted after graduation.

Branch schools, and the army in general, grew increasingly satisfied with the results of both Academic and Tactical Department innovations. Far more public, arguably of greater institutional significance as well, was the cheating scandal that hit the nation's headlines in 1951. Its taproot lay in the growing importance of varsity football to academy life since the 1920s. Army's increasingly successful team was a source of favorable national publicity, with influential congressmen lobbying for it to come to their home states and play their favorite teams. West Point's football culture offered some concessions to a "normal" collegiate atmosphere. Football weekends were date weekends. For the unattached cadet, they broke a routine often as boring as it was demanding. No less significant was the widespread conviction in the West Point community, and the Army in general, that football was the sport that above all others exemplified "transferable experience" by its combination of intellectual sophistication, quick thinking, physical force, and will power. "I want an officer for a secret and dangerous mission. I want a West Point football player," was a quotation frequently attributed to World War Chief of Staff George C. Marshall.

Like other American colleges, West Point in the 1940s recruited "student athletes." Unlike its big-university counterparts, the Academy did not relax the requirements of its compulsory curriculum. Instead it provided opportunities of several kinds for extra instruction. What happened, while not inevitable, was predictable. Beginning in the 1940s a few selected players received unauthorized assistance once or twice in the academic year—help sessions, for example, based on the specific material in a quiz or examination given to earlier sections. By 1950, in the words of one author, it had evolved into

On June 3, 1952, Mark Clark '17 and James Van Fleet '15 lead other generals along a Korean trench. (Both Clark and Van Fleet had been wounded in WWI trench fighting.) Far right: Dick Shea '52, a track star at West Point, chose to serve his country rather than try for the personal glory of an Olympic medal. He died in hand-to-hand combat on Pork Chop Hill. Below: General Maxwell D. Taylor, '22, posed for a formal portrait as Superintendent of West Point.

"a full-time conspiracy, aimed at keeping every football player [academically] proficient at all times." As much to the point, it had begun spreading to the athletes' friends and roommates, and to other cadets as well.

The Tactical Department was already hostile to what it considered special privileges extended to varsity athletes that drove a wedge into the homogeneous cadet community. It played a key role in exposing what by then was legitimately described as a ring, with elaborate methods of passing information among participants. The Academic Department, also hostile to what it considered varsity athletics' encroachment on the curriculum, made common cause with the tacs.

Eventually ninety cadets were dismissed. The details of the Academy's handling of the situation are correspondingly less important than the challenge it posed to the Academy's moral center: its honor system.

The essence of the West Point honor system in its pristine form is widely familiar: A cadet does not lie, cheat, steal, or tolerate those who do. Its most demanding tenet is that every cadet is honor bound to report any breach of honor coming to his attention—including his own unintentional violations! That ethic challenges a long-standing American tradition of contempt for the informer, no matter how noble his principles. It also challenged a specific element of the West Point ethos: comradeship. From their first days as plebes, cadets were conditioned to stand together, to cooperate and help each other. Was it, for example, dishonorable to assist a struggling teammate or classmate academically, but honorable to let him sink for want of a helping hand? For graduates, "the brotherhood of the Corps" was not an empty phrase. In principle, the honor system was a cadet institution, administered and implemented by cadets. In practice, honor was

West Pointers on the Covers of Time

West Point has produced more than its share of notable leaders, as this sampling of Time covers testifies. Some, like Douglas MacArthur and Dwight D. Eisenhower, were cover subjects many times over. MacArthur appeared first in 1935 as the Army's controversial Chief of Staff. Eisenhower would be Time's Man of the Year, first in 1945 and later as President. The others on this spread were singled out for their achievements as warriors—except for Maxwell Taylor, the World War II hero, who made it as John F. Kennedy's most trusted military advisor.

January 1, 1945
General Dwight D. Eisenhower,
Commander of the Western allies.

March 25, 1935
Douglas MacArthur's first appearance—
as Chief of Staff during the Depression,
fighting for a larger army budget.

December 4, 1944
Lt. General Omar N. Bradley,
the soldier's general at the
German frontier.

April 9, 1945
Lt. General George S. Patton,
driving into the heart of the Reich.

July 28, 1961
Maxwell Taylor—
the former
Superintendent
becomes JFK's
military mentor.

March 5, 1951
Lt. General Matthew Ridgway, rallying a
battered Eighth Army in Korea.

February 19, 1965
General William C. Westmoreland, presiding
over American escalation in Vietnam.

regularly used to uncover rule-breaking. In 1945 Dwight Eisenhower wrote to new superintendent Maxwell Taylor;

> *. . . my most unfortunate experience while I was myself a cadet . . . The culprits were found by lining up the Corps and the querying of each individual as to whether or not he was guilty of this particular misdemeanor.*

What rankled Eisenhower thirty years later was using the obligation to tell the truth, without considering whether evidence existed for a particular cadet's involvement in an offense. He was not alone. As the investigation of the cheating scandal spread, the issue rapidly became not one of actual dishonesty but "guilty knowledge." Cadets, including the son of the football coach himself, were being expelled for failing to report what they knew. But what constituted "knowing?" More than moral abstractions were involved in the answer. Fifteen years later, a cadet who reported honor violations described being attacked by other cadets involved in the cheating and beaten into unconsciousness. Apparently, the assorted investigators cut their work short for fear of what they might discover if they continued to push the issue. How far could the process of cadets reporting other cadets continue before generating an effect opposite to that intended, creating a permanently poisoned atmosphere of mutual suspicion?

There was a sense in the Corps, and the Academy community as a whole, that justice had been reasonably served and the obviously guilty punished without tearing West Point apart. If some cadets, and perhaps some officers, wrestled with their behaviors in the dark of the night, the price was acceptable.

If it was in fact made, the bargain did not imply slackness. In 1956 the Superintendent comfortably observed that the cadets ". . . are well-disciplined, and they know well that if they step off base they pay for their sin." Regulations were enforced by cadets on cadets with existentialist enthusiasm. One upperclassman, recovering from having his wisdom teeth extracted, was excused from a class to see the dentist. The appointment did not require the full class period and the cadet, still shaky from the surgery, returned to his room. He was promptly asked by another cadet, responsible for checking attendance in the class, whether he had been excused for the entire period, or just for the duration of his dental appointment. That the dental patient found himself disciplined for "unauthorized absence" is less remarkable than the positive spin he put on the story when recounting it.

Honor representatives as well tended to "specialize in honor." Some approached the system with black-and-white absolutism and applied it with the rigor of zealots. Others stressed the distinctions between bad judgment or simple mistakes, and dishonorable behavior. A discrepancy of a few minutes in reporting might become the potential matter of an honor board hearing, with dismissal or resignation as an outcome. Or it might be dealt with *ad hoc*, by an honor representative considering probable intentions. Taunts that the rigorists were "honor Nazis" unable to distinguish between the honor system's letters and its spirit were met with countercharges of being too permissive about the principles that were the core of West Point. The dissonance would have significant consequences for the Corps and the Academy in the 1970s.

Changes in cadet culture segued into the Academy's final challenge: expansion. The size of the Corps of Cadets had stabilized at 1,400 in the 1930s. During World War II, it was enlarged to around 2,500. Growth brought diversification of activities: there were too many cadets to use the same facilities at the same time. Growth made it more difficult—indeed for practical purposes impossible—for a cadet to have more than a nodding acquaintance with more than a fraction of his fellows. Small-group allegiances, to a cadet company or an athletic team, developed as a reaction. These specific loyalties were frequently cited as a factor in the cheating scandal and similar, lesser affairs; and as correspondingly detrimental to the Academy's collective identity.

Never before in its history had the Military Academy mounted overt recruiting campaigns to attract desirable candidates. But now, increasing numbers of appointments were remaining vacant. In his report for 1957, however, Superintendent Lieutenant General Garrison Davidson asserted that "the competition for potential leaders from among the students of the secondary schools is becoming continually more keen. . . . Unless the Military Academy adopts an aggressive program to interest this type of youth in the Military Academy, and in pursuing a military career, the Army will not get its fair share of potential leaders from among the youth of the country."

Even before Davidson's report, West Point had been expanding its admissions programs, undertaking active recruitment in competition with other service academies and elite civilian schools. That did not mean, at least initially, revising the ethnic and social bases of the Academy to incorporate more minorities and more youths from underrepresented economic classes. General Davidson, like almost all of his military and civilian contemporaries, accepted the notion of a steady-state pool of potential "leaders" coming from traditional sources. West Point throughout this period was for all practical purposes a white institution. In 1948 the Corps of Cadets included

General Douglas MacArthur, fired as commander of the UN army in Korea, received a ticker-tape parade (above) through New York City in 1951.

nine blacks, five of them plebes. The Class of 1966 would graduate three. Those blacks who enrolled and survived did so by adapting, just as did their white classmates. Now, at least, they were not subject to "silencing," as Benjamin Davis had been in the 1930s: rooming and eating alone, spoken to only in the line of duty.

There were other subtle changes. The Corps of Cadets also included increasing numbers of men who perceived themselves as having chosen the Academy, as opposed to the other way around. West Point was hardly overrun with self-serving egocentrics. But by the end of the 1950s, more and more high school students were pursuing a process later called "résumé padding": not only

THE BRITISH WEST POINT

—by Alistair Horne

My first sight of West Point was as a teenaged "Bundle from Britain" during World War II, when I used to spend some of the summer holiday months at Garrison. Garrison stands right opposite the great gray college across the Hudson river. In the summer of 1942 I first set foot in West Point for the graduation ceremony that year. I remember thinking how incredibly smart the graduation Seniors were in their gray, nineteenth century uniforms, hurling their caps in the air in a rare moment of breaking with discipline.

By 1943, they would be leading troops ashore at Sicily and Salerno, and in the South Pacific.

At the end of the World War I found myself as an officer cadet, selected for the British Coldstream Guards, at Sandhurst, which in wartime had become our army's Armoured OCTU (Officer Cadet Training Unit). We were being schooled in tanks for the Guards Armoured Division, which had then just had its baptism of fire in the bloody battle for Normandy.

Despite wartime austerities, we were instantly—and forcibly—aware of the great institution's traditions and background. The first RMA (Royal Military Academy) was established in 1741 at Woolwich, on the then outskirts of London, to train "gentlemen cadets" for commissions in the Royal Artillery and Royal Engineers; it was known as the "Shop." By the end of the century, however, it was clear that Britain and her

army were going to need a generally higher level of officer training if it was to compete against Napoleon's highly efficient, modern forces.

One day late in 1798, an ambitious young cavalry colonel, John Gaspard Le Marchant, was traveling by coach across southern England and set to thinking about the state of the British Army. That same year, though Nelson's victory of the Nile had won Britain's navy mastery of the Mediterranean, her army had—once more—been humiliated in Egypt. Four years previously her expeditionary force had been ignominiously expelled from Flanders. Le Marchant saw it as a rabble of criminals and drunks led by easygoing, amiable aristocrats. Promotion was bought and had little to do with ability. To get to be a lieutenant-colonel cost £3,500—£5,400 for the elitist Guards. Arriving at his inn, Le Marchant started putting down on paper some ideas for educating the officer corps as a whole. The following year his ideas were picked up by the Duke of York and a staff school for young officers established at High Wycombe. The first Commandant was Le Marchant. In 1801 it became the senior department of the Royal Military College (RMC), and the next year a junior department, to train cadets for commissions in cavalry and infantry, was opened. In 1812, as the British Army faced a new challenge against the young United States, and with the ultimate test of Waterloo on

the horizon just three years ahead, the junior department moved to Sandhurst, into what is now called the "Old Building" (and where I was housed in 1944-5). In 1858, it was joined by the Staff College, with a separate establishment, across the way at the "New Building."

To become an officer in the cavalry, infantry, or Indian Army all had to pass through the RMC; to reach the higher ranks, all had to graduate from Staff College. An undistinguished career at the former, however, did not necessarily always spell failure in future life; Bernard Law Montgomery, for instance, was little short of disaster at Sandhurst, narrowly escaping expulsion. He rose to become Britain's greatest commander since Wellington.

After World War II, in 1947 the RMA (at Woolwich) and RMC combined to reopen under the present name of Royal Military Academy Sandhurst. Since then some 25,000 officer cadets have passed through Sandhurst. Compared with the six months highly compressed training of our wartime Sandhurst, the RMA now operates more like a university with three terms of fourteen weeks each—plus two separate weeks of "adventure training." Its intake is now highly democratic, and unelitist; though, inevitably, there remains a residual penchant for the progeny of former officers. Still, as in wartime, the primary instructors remain the senior NCOs, often with fearsome voices

and matching personalities.

Wartime Sandhurst had a very different atmosphere to wartime West Point. Instead of the smart gray-blue uniforms, everyone was in khaki. The tank park was covered with camouflage, against possible Focke-Wulf attacks. There were certain joint bonds between the two colleges. First of all, the British Brigade of Guards and West Point shared the same steely discipline, immaculate turn-out (even in wartime British Battle-dress) and impeccable morale. Superbly brain-washed, we are trained to kill Germans and Japanese. That was what we were there for; and we relished the opportunity. The training was tough, constantly testing us to breaking-point.

Despite wartime, some traditions lingered at Sandhurst. For instance, the Adjutant stiffly astride his white horse would ride up the steps of the Academy at the end of a graduation parade, down through the corridors, and out through the back door—attentively followed by a cadet with a brush and pan. (I later discovered that the adjutant to start this particular tradition—which still continues to the present day—was "Boy" Browning, later General Sir Frederick, commander of the airborne troops in the disastrous Arnhem operation of September 1944, and husband of Daphne du Maurier, the famous novelist.) In the College Chapel were the tattered remains of regimental colours from the Peninsular War, as we prayed for vic-

tory there, every Sunday.

Because I have written several books on military history, I have been invited back on various happy occasions to West Point. I recall giving one lecture, to the plebes class in the late '70s, in the aftermath of Vietnam. It was the first lecture I have ever given when the first two rows of the audience were fast asleep, even before I started speaking. When I inquired later of one plebe why this triumph of Lethe, he sprang sharply to attention and said,

"Sir! It's the jogging."

"Then why do you do so much jogging?"

"Sir! It's the only way we can get away from being shouted at!"

Returning to West Point in the '90s, in the wake of the Gulf War, shortly after the fiftieth anniversary of both D-Day and VE Day, I found it a very different place. For one thing women now shared the cadets' accommodation. Some males grumbled about this unwelcome propinquity; however, on the other hand it may well have had an effect on sharpening up the cadets, and keeping them awake during lectures—and possibly off jogging.

Nevertheless, whenever I see the lean, upright and erect silhouette of an unmistakable West Pointer, or meet battlefield commanders like General "Stormin' Norman" Schwarzkopf, I feel the reassurance that the ancient academy along the Hudson has served, and continues to serve its country and the Alliance well—just as our Sandhurst as.

going out for as many activities as possible, but excelling in all of them with the expectation that it would enhance their prospects for getting into a "good" college. "But when you got to the Point," a graduate from the 1960s stated, "you found out fast that you couldn't excel in everything the way you had. But we were used to standing out. So we specialized: some in a particular varsity or intramural sport, some in a particular academic discipline, some in being 'military.'"

The levels of individual self-awareness and individual self confidence among incoming cadets were also sufficiently high that the traditional "plebe system" was less effective in socializing new cadets. Instead of being understood as a rite of passage into a desirable system, the regimentation, the discipline, the rote compliance invited interpretation as a year-long exercise in petty tyranny administered by petty tyrants. Instead of integrating cadets into a community, the system arguably encouraged "playing it cool—acting as though the s—t is important, but not believing it" in the words of one 1962 graduate.

"Playing it cool" could extend to other areas of Academy life—including its understood primary purpose of developing professional officers for the U.S. Army. Even the conservative 1958 curriculum study conceded that the certitude of a military career in the traditional sense of twenty years or more was "probably infrequent" among new cadets. The study recommended as well "That the requirement for Fourth Classmen to memorize vast quantities of immaterial data be severely curtailed." "Plebe knowledge," however, endured. So did mealtime rituals that virtually guaranteed fourth classmen left every meal hungry. Meanwhile, Davidson's successor Lieutenant General William Westmoreland was widely considered to have been assigned to enlarge the corps even further. Between 1964

In 1955, during his first term, President Dwight David Eisenhower (left) attended his fortieth reunion at West Point. Ike was one of the most beloved presidents of the 20th century.

and 1972, the Vietnam years, the number of cadets nearly doubled, to 4,400.

When the Academy's changing human dynamics between World War II and the Vietnam Era are placed in the context of the multiple stresses presented earlier in this essay, the question is less why cadet withdrawal rates increased, or why some cadets "gamed" the system, than how West Point continued to meet the human needs of an overwhelming majority of its cadets, respond to the uncertain trumpets of the Cold War, and maintain its privileged position in American society—all without changing its essential character. It is easy to see what West Point was not. It was neither a nursery of military intellectuals nor a training ground for platoon commanders. It was neither a custodian of tradition nor a focal point for change. The red thread running through the West Point experience from Maxwell Taylor's appointment in 1945 to William Westmoreland's departure for Vietnam in 1963, is adaptability. The U.S. Military Academy adjusted to changing needs while recognizing historic strengths—even those that, like the plebe system, could not be fully explained rationally. In that sense the Point served itself, the Army, and the nation well: far better than would be conceded as America lurched through the Vietnam War.

8

FIELDS OF FRIENDLY STRIFE

BY GEOFFREY NORMAN

"If we have athletes, we shall
never be without soldiers."

—Herman J. Koehler,
Master of the Sword

There is a window on the second floor of West Point's Herbert Hall that is dedicated to the memory of the members of the Class of 1967 who died in the service of their country. Thirty names. What is not mentioned on the plaque—there is no reason it should be—is that half of these men played intercollegiate sports at West Point. And that two of them were All-Americans in their sports.

The thirty deaths is a somber datum, but no surprise. West Point exists for a reason and no graduate, no cadet, not even the lowliest plebe, is confused about what that purpose is. Neither is it a surprise that half of those thirty men should have been athletes. While West Point—unlike many civilian colleges and universities—does not make special cases out of athletes (as late as the 1970s, Academy football players were going to classes Saturday morning, before games), it has long understood, and celebrated, the importance of athletics in the life of the Academy and the growth of its cadets. Many of West Point's most distinguished graduates competed on what General Douglas MacArthur memorably called "the fields of friendly strife," then went on to those other fields of the General's memorable formulation where they also performed well, sometimes at ultimate cost.

It was MacArthur, in fact, who during his tour as Superintendent, brought West Point into the modern age in athletics. He was a vigorous, energetic, and innovative Supe in athletics as in so many other things. When he arrived in 1919, Army was playing only five intercollegiate sports: baseball, football, polo, basketball, and hockey. Lacrosse had been played intermittently before being dropped.

During MacArthur's three years as Superintendent, the Academy began intercollegiate competition in tennis, boxing, wrestling, cross-country, outdoor track, rifle, soccer, swimming, and golf. lacrosse was also restarted. MacArthur was also responsible for the annual hockey competition between West Point and the Royal Military College of Canada. This began in 1923, after MacArthur left but in response to a letter he had written to Major General (Sir) Archibald McDonald in 1921, and is the longest-running continuous international sporting event in the world.

It is a home and home affair, complete with military pageantry and competitions in events like rifle and pistol shooting and karate, among others. For many years, in the spirit of military honor, penalties were not called. The first called penalty was, unfortunately, on a West Point goalie. The Canadians, as might be expected, won or tied the first sixteen games, but as Americans learned hockey and West Point acquired the services of a legendary coach, Jack Riley, the Academy caught up and now leads the series. In recent years, West Point has dominated. Hockey players who have competed in this singular event wear a small gold maple leaf on their letter, as athletes who have competed against Navy wear a gold letter "A." And those who have competed against Air Force are entitled to the same letter in silver.

While there had been athletics at West Point before MacArthur's time, he undeniably raised their importance and made them central to the Academy's mission. Before MacArthur's tour as Supe, the athletic focus of West Point had been inward. Cadets were given instruction in gymnastics, fencing, and riding which were almost self-evidently military arts. One of the two

Academy graduates to become Commander-in-Chief, Ulysses S. Grant, found a kind of solace in horsemanship while he was at West Point. He was not especially fond of the austere West Point life but he took to riding and became a first-class horseman. In the legend, he set a jumping record that stood for many years but the historians at West Point have never been able to document the story. There is much about Grant that remains ambiguous. But it is undeniable that he was a great general and horseman. And in both of those spheres, there is no escaping the profound influence of West Point.

MacArthur himself had played baseball while he was a cadet—though he was not much of a hitter and spent most of his time safely in right field, out of harm's way. He had also been man-ager of the football team. (Another, future Chief of Staff—and a survivor of the Bataan Death March—would also serve in this capacity: Harold K. Johnson,'33) During his time at West Point, MacArthur, like all cadets, was taught gymnastics, swimming, fencing, and equestrian arts; the instruction was first rate. From 1907 until 1916, Army did not lose a single fencing competition. Credit for this remarkable record, and for the overall excellence of the physical training at the Academy, belonged to Herman J. Koehler, whose title was "Master of the Sword." Today, he would be Chairman of the Department of Physical Education.

Koehler's emphasis was on athletic training and competition within the Academy. Until 1890, intercollegiate competition was virtually

Throughout the 19th century, fencing was the main sport taught at the Academy. The cadets in this early photo are practicing sabre thrusts.

The Academy's first organized sports team was its 1890 basketball team, left. The Fencing team, below, won national honors under the Master of the Sword, Lieutenant Colonel Herman John Koehler, seated on the right. Koehler's discipline and intensity inspired Douglas MacArthur's lifelong enthusiasm for sports; as Superintendent MacArthur greatly expanded the athletics program. Here MacArthur (middle row, seated at right) poses in his cadet uniform with the upper-class baseball team. He played an undistinguished right field.

unknown and the conservative leadership of the time was not inclined to change this. There was pressure from below, however. Junior officers and cadets were eager to compete against other schools. In 1890, West Point (where Abner Doubleday, the Civil War soldier who has often been credited with "inventing" baseball, had been a cadet) played a baseball game against Riverview College in New York. This was a first. But the event that changed attitudes about intercollegiate competition most profoundly occurred that same year when Annapolis challenged West Point to a game of football. This was pressure of a different, irresistible order. With pride at stake, the challenge was accepted.

Navy already had a team. Army hastily assembled one for the game and lost, 24-0. That game is, of course, legendary and its legacy is a rivalry that is widely considered the greatest—certainly the purest and most enduring—of all of sports. There is, quite simply, nothing like an Army-Navy. But there is a poignant lesson in that game.

The cadet who accepted the Navy challenge was Dennis Michie (for whom the stadium at West Point is named) and the star for the midshipmen was Worth Bagley. Both men were killed in action in the Spanish-American War.

MacArthur's own wartime experiences, along with his own prior love for sports, were motives for his overhaul of the Academy's outlook on athletics. He had seen, in France, both too many out-of-shape soldiers and too much undeniable evidence of the value of fitness and the competitive spirit. In his *Reminiscences*, MacArthur wrote that what he had been taught as a cadet, by Master of the Sword Koehler, had been validated vividly on the battlefield. Koehler had said, "If we have athletes, we shall never be without soldiers." Now MacArthur set out to insure that West Point had athletes in

Clockwise from top left: West Point cadets and opponents leave the starting line in a 1906 meet. The presence of the Hudson encouraged rowing; this group of oarsmen was photographed in 1887. In 1904 the cadets did calisthenics on the parade ground. Below, Hap Arnold '07, future Chief of Staff of the Army Air Corps, leads the pack in a 1906 race.

many sports, both intercollegiate and intramural, with all cadets competing under the mantra, "Every man an athlete."

The success of that campaign is undeniable.

The flagship of Army athletics is, of course, football. MacArthur followed the fortunes of Army football passionately, long after he had left the post of Superintendent and had taken on other, even larger, responsibilities. When he was named head coach of Army football in 1933, Gar Davidson was informed that every Monday during football season, he was to write

The First Army-Navy Football Game

As a cadet Dennis Mahan Michie (above) engineered the first Army-Navy game, bottom, in 1890.

IN 1890, FOOTBALL was widely popular among American colleges, including the Naval Academy at Annapolis. Yet only two West Point cadets had ever played: Cadet Leonard M. Prince, and Dennis Mahan Michie '92, the high-spirited son of Peter Smith Michie (Class of 1863), Professor of Natural Philosophy and head of the Academic Board.

Dennis Michie loved football, and he had an undeniable influence over his formidable father. So it was young Michie who launched Army's football career, when he persuaded his father to allow West Point to accept a challenge from the Naval Academy to a game of football.

The first game went predictably. Navy had been playing organized football for years; West Point's team, with young Michie as the coach and trainer, had been allowed to practice only on a few rainy Saturdays when the weekly parade was called off. Michie's coaching seems to have been fairly informal. When Navy's team came out on the field and began warm-up drills and exercises, the cadets looked on in shock.

At the line of scrimmage, Navy's quarterback began to bark out commands in nautical terms. "Tack ship" indicated a run to the right, "Wear ship" a run to the left. The Army quarterback, Kirby Walker, caught on fast, and began shouting out his signals in Army turns— "In battery, heave!"

Since at this time the basic tactic in football was the flying wedge, allowing for none of the finesse of the modern game, the game was all brute force—war by another means. Army's inexperience accentuated the havoc. Kirby Walker was knocked out four times, and was finally taken off unconscious to the hospital, but the game went on. A *New York Times* reporter noted, "There is not much football in this struggle but the fighting is immense." Navy exploited its sophistication, at one point running a fake punt, which caught Army so off guard the play went for a touchdown. The referees shrugged off Army's indignant protests that a man who professed he was about to punt was honor bound to kick away. Navy won the game 24-0.

The defeat spurred a robust effort at fielding a better team. Every regiment in the Army contributed money for uniforms and a part-time coach, as well as for sending the team down to Annapolis for a rematch. In 1891 West Point played six home games, winning four, and one away game—at Annapolis, where the cadets recorded their final victory over Navy 32-16.

Even before he graduated, Dennis Mahan Michie had founded one of the great American sports rivalries; as a player he scored in Army's first victory. Before him lay a future shining with promise. But he was cut down almost before he could start. He died in the Spanish-American War, at the Battle of San Juan Hill. In the tradition of naming sports facilities for Academy graduates who died in action, Michie Stadium is named for him.   —*C.H.*

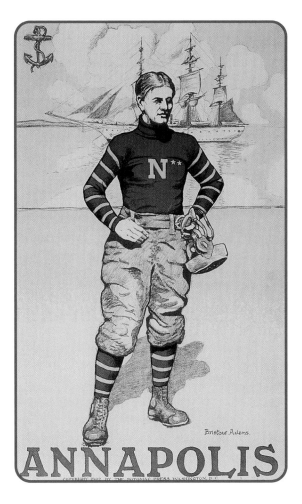

ANNAPOLIS

WEST POINT

MacArthur, by then Chief of Staff, and provide him with an analysis of the previous Saturday's game. MacArthur knew that war was coming and he was doing all he could to make the Army ready. But there was still time for football. After Army beat Navy in 1944, MacArthur cabled Coach Earl Blaik: THE GREATEST OF ALL ARMY TEAMS STOP WE HAVE STOPPED THE WAR TO CELEBRATE YOUR MAGNIFICENT SUCCESS. The General was being playful, but only slightly. He cared almost that much about Army football.

And the teams have, in truth, been vital to West Point and to the history of college football in America. There were seasons of glory—undefeated seasons and national championships. There were single games when Army and its opponent—usually Navy or Notre Dame—seemed to concentrate the attention of the entire nation for a few hours on a Saturday afternoon in the fall. Some 120,000 fans watched Army and Navy play to a 21-21 tie in Chicago's Soldier Field in 1926, making it the largest crowd ever to watch a college football game.

Three Army players (Glen Davis, Doc Blanchard, and Pete Dawkins) have won the Heisman Trophy. And, of course, one Army football player rose to the rank of General of the Army, commanded the coalition of forces that liberated Europe, and served two terms as President of the United States.

Dwight Eisenhower's football career as a running back was cut short by a knee injury in 1912. He lettered and it was a good year for Army. The team went 6-3, but lost to Navy, always a heavy consideration. If Eisenhower had been able to finish out his eligibility on the 1913 and 1914 teams at the Point, he would have tasted football immortality. The 1913 team went 8-1. The 1914 team went 9-0, was the first undefeated and untied Army team, and would have been national champions if there had been such a thing in those days.

Eisenhower was certainly not the only notable West Point figure of those times who played football. Nor the only one to pay a price for it. George Patton also had to give up football after he broke both his arms. Omar Bradley played

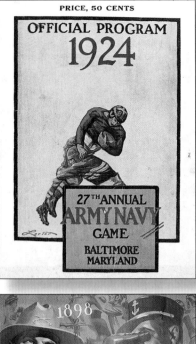

OFFICIAL PROGRAM
1924

27TH ANNUAL
ARMY NAVY
GAME
BALTIMORE
MARYLAND

The Army-Navy Football Game quickly became a major national event, its excitement captured in the programs shown on these pages. Played on a neutral field at the beginning of the holiday season, the encounters drew tens of thousands of spectators, often including the President of the United States. Theodore Roosevelt began the presidential practice of sitting on one team's side during the first half, and changing to the other side at halftime. In 1941, at the peak of the game's popularity, the Pennsylvania Railroad ran forty-two special trains direct to Philadelphia's Municipal Stadium. Although eclipsed today by the plethora of postseason bowls, the Game is still first in the hearts of its fans, especially the players. As Army linebacker Adisa King said in 1999, "Last year we were 3-8, but it was a successful season because we beat Navy. I was on an Army team that beat Navy. I can take that to my grave."

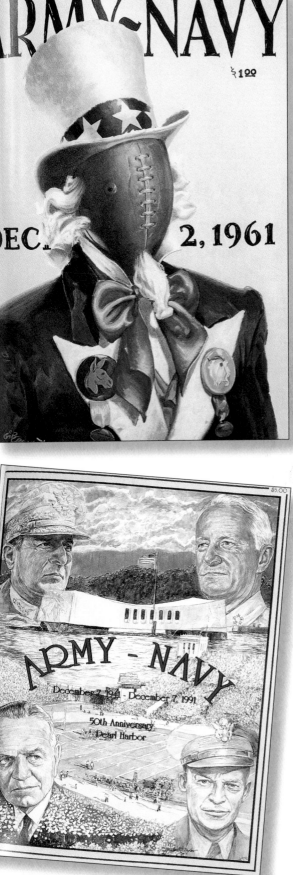

Earl "Red" Blaik '20, seen here as a cadet lineman in the 1919 season, would coach the most successful football teams in Army history, introducing such innovations as the Lonesome End. The postcard below shows Michie Stadium from the air. The stadium is named for Dennis Michie, who pioneered football at West Point, and was one of the few battle deaths in the Spanish-American War in Cuba.

WEST POINT

MICHIE STADIUM

he was shooting an unfamiliar weapon. Bradley also played baseball.

There were other former football players who went on to achieve high rank and distinction and to distinguish themselves on MacArthur's other fields. General James Van Fleet commanded divisions in World War Two and the Eighth Army in Korea and said that his Army A was as valuable to him as a DSC—and he was awarded three of them. Robin Olds became a fighter ace in Korea and almost accomplished the same feat again in Vietnam and served as Commandant of the Air Force Academy. General Charles Gabriel became Chief of Staff of the Air Force. General George Joulwan retired as Supreme Allied Commander Europe in 1997. These men all played football at the Academy.

Then there were the former football players who made their contributions on those other fields as field grade and company grade officers. Charles Meyer, known affectionately as "Monk," was the quarterback of the Army team in the late 1930s. As a battalion commander with the 127th Infantry in the Pacific, he won a Distinguished Service Cross, two Silver Stars, and two Purple Hearts. He also served in Vietnam before retiring as a Brigadier General. Among the men captured in the surrender of Corregidor in the Philippine Islands was Colonel Paul Bunker who had been an All-American football player at two positions, halfback and tackle, while he was at the Academy. It was Bunker's melancholy duty to lower and burn the American flag when the capitulation became inevitable. He saved a portion of the flag and concealed it from the enemy. Before he died in captivity, he passed that remnant of the flag on

and lettered (he was a member of the 1914 team) and said later that he believed "No extra-curricular activity could better prepare a soldier for the battlefield."

Eisenhower, Patton, Bradley. These are among the most recognizable, honored, and resonant names in the history of the United States Army. They were all athletes at the Academy. All played football but were not exclusively football players. Patton competed in the 1912 Olympics in Stockholm as a fencer and in the modern pentathlon and came in fifth because, he said later,

How Army Got Its Mascot

IN 1899, AT THE ARMY-NAVY GAME, the Navy football team appeared with a mascot, a handsome if smelly goat. Army fans looked hastily for a mascot of their own. The Army mule was already legendary for its toughness and endurance, so the mule was obvious. A quartermaster in Philadelphia stopped a passing ice truck, and the big white mule pulling it became the first Army football mascot.

Dolled up in leggings, a collar and a gray blanket, with black gold and gray streamers fluttering from his ears, this mule met the Navy goat and--according to West point legend—"hoisted that astonished goat toward the Navy stands to the delight of the laughing crowd." Army won the game, too, 17-5.

Few other mules have actually gone into combat but some of the great white mule's successors have also passed into legend. The first official mascot, Mr. Jackson, a pack mule from the regular Army, arrived at West Point in 1936, and remained until his death in 1961, at the astonishing age of thirty-five. Retired from active service, he remained stabled with other mules, and would bray plaintively when he saw them led out to events.

Pancho, a little Ecuadorian burro, was a gift of the Ecuadorian ambassador. She appeared at the '42 Army-Navy game got up in a goat's skin and horns, her rider dressed in a middie's uniform, and galloped up and down the sidelines to the amazement and applause of the fans. Trotter, who had begun as a pack animal for the regular army, was a rarity, a four-gaited mule.

The mules live at the Veterinary Station Hospital, under the supervision of the Post Veterinarian. Each spring the Corps selects a mule rider from the fourth class, based on horsemanship and character, and as each progresses upward through the classes he or she rises in the ranks of the mule riders to become, in the first class year, cadet-in-charge.

—*C.H.*

The cartoon above shows the Army Mule presiding over the steamrolling of Navy's Goat and its handler. In the photo, a modern mascot poses with its mule rider, two players and a coach.

to another prisoner and told him to deliver it to the Secretary of War. That scrap from the flag at Corregidor is preserved at the West Point Museum.

The football team of the war years featured the most celebrated players in the history of Army football—Doc Blanchard and Glen Davis, Mr. Inside and Mr. Outside. It is safe to say that in those years—during and just after World War II—Army was the dominant football team in the country or, at the very least, that it shared that distinction with Notre Dame.

The Army-Notre Dame rivalry was notable for many things, including the first use of the forward pass as the centerpiece of a team's offense. Notre Dame used the pass to beat Army 35-13 in 1913. It was the only game Army lost that year and those were the only points scored on Notre Dame that season. Army, as it happens, was Notre Dame's opponent in 1928 when

"ON BRAVE OLD ARMY TEAM"

In this 1940 Howitzer painting an Army player gains yards. That year the fortunes of the Army football program were at a low ebb, as the team won only one game, tied one, and lost seven.

Knute Rockne gave his famous "Win One for the Gipper" pep talk that immortalized him and, later, Ronald Reagan. The two teams played to the most famous scoreless tie in the history of football in 1946. This game was probably the most eagerly anticipated and thoroughly reported sporting event of the year—the Super Bowl of its day.

Still, those teams, like all Army teams, were made up of future officers. They were good football players, even great football players, and those were good teams and even great teams. But football players at West Point faced obligations—duties in the strictest sense of the word—beyond the football field. Tom Lombardo, captain of the 1944 National Championship Team, was killed in action in the summer of 1950 in Korea. So was John Trent, captain of the 1949 team that went undefeated and was ranked fourth in the nation by the Associated Press.

While this grim news was making its way

back to West Point, the football team was going through its own ordeal. This was the famous honor code crisis of 1951, which resulted in the dismissal of thirty-seven members of the football team. The controversy surrounding this episode still simmered fifty years later, with *Sports Illustrated* magazine devoting many pages to a rehash and reappraisal.

The crisis was especially hard on a nation accustomed to success on the battlefield that now found its forces struggling on the Korean Peninsula. It was a crisis that had been preceded by what was, in all the years of Army football, surely its time of greatest glory. From 1944 through 1950, the Army football team had gone 57-3-4. The 1950 team was undefeated and on its way to a likely national championship before losing to Navy in the kind of upset only that special rivalry seems capable of regularly producing.

Things would be different, many thought, in 1951. This would be the year for Army to take care of some unfinished business.

However, some cadets were troubled by the existence of a clandestine system of leaking exam questions. The system seemed to favor athletes, especially football players, and was made possible by the fact that the Academy had been expanded due to the manpower requirements of war. Two separate regiments would be given the same exam on different days. The temptation to pass along information was virtually irresistible. But the requirements of the Honor System—another MacArthur legacy—were inflexible. "A Cadet does not lie, cheat, or steal. Or tolerate those who do."

There was poignancy to the whole affair. The Academy had been troubled by the status of football in the greater scheme of things both at the Point and within the Army. In 1946, Major General Maxwell Taylor decided, in his capacity

During the 1930s, '40s and '50s the Army-Navy Game had the spectacle and glamor of a Super Bowl today. This article by the popular writer Paul Gallico ran twice, in 1934 in the New York Daily News and in 1951 when it was reprinted in Esquire.

MUNICIPAL STADIUM DURING A PAST GAME

MORE THAN A BALL GAME...

By PAUL GALLICO

ALTHOUGH THIS APPEARED IN THE NEW YORK DAILY NEWS BACK IN 1934, IT IS JUST AS TRUE IN 1951. HERE ESQUIRE'S PAUL GALLICO GIVES HIS IDEA OF WHAT AN ARMY-NAVY GAME REALLY IS...

ARMY-NAVY game . . . Eleven kids against eleven others. Bands, crowds, spectacles, chevrons, and gold lace, brass hats, officials, politicians and dignitaries and still, just a football game. But, of all the thousands of football games played all over the country from October to December, this is the one game that really matters, the only one at some later day, many, many years hence, might still exert its influence in some way that might affect the millions of people who inhabit this country. To me this adds spine-chilling thrills to that annual encounter. I look forward to it as I do to few others. The Army-Navy game is the yearly parade of the future commanders of the armed defenders of the United states. This is serious business. Watch these boys play. Watch them think. Watch their moves. Our lives may some day be in their hands.

*As the lives of all of us are reckoned, football games are written on water—a few hours entertainment, a story in a newspaper, a few minutes idle gossip and Monday morn-*ing quarterbacking. *A lot of the youngsters who play football are profoundly impressed by the game, often to their own detriment, but that hardly affects us. But these players on the field at Philadelphia today will some day be in charge of our line of defense, at sea, on land, in the air. These are their habit forming years. The lessons learned, the habits formed, the friendships made, every element that goes in their making as soldiers and gentlemen may some day be our concern.*

To begin with, these twenty-two boys who face one another on Franklin Field today are successful boys. They have achieved a goal. With intelligence, self-denial, courage and fine bodies, they have won the right to represent the Services of the United States. They are fine physical specimens or they could not play the game. They are not brainless physical hulks or they wouldn't be in either academy. They have maintained fine scholastic standing in two of the most difficult curricula in the country. There

(Continued on page 24)

Arnold Tucker '47 (far left) arrived at West Point after a stint in the Navy. A three-time All-American, he went on to quarterback the best Army team ever. Glenn Davis '47 and Felix "Doc" Blanchard '47, here on this Life cover photo by Alfred Eisenstadt, were "Mr. Outside" and "Mr. Inside," in their era the foremost pair of running backs in football. Red Blaik called Blanchard "the best built athlete I ever saw." Below, Blanchard, number 35, breaks into the open.

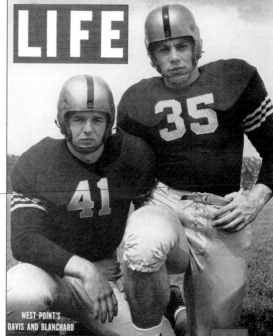

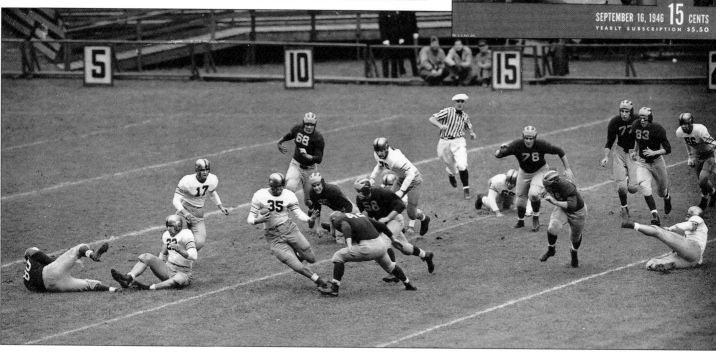

as Supe, to cancel the Notre Dame series because the game had become too much of a spectacle. Football, some thought, had become a separate fiefdom, an elite under the control of the Academy's first civilian coach, Earl "Red" Blaik.

A 1922 graduate, Blaik had been a star at end and a favorite of MacArthur who asked him to come to the Philippines and serve as his aide-de-camp. But career possibilities were scarce in the Army of those times and Blaik had resigned from the regular army for civilian life. In 1940, he left Dartmouth, where he had been a success as head football coach, to take the same position at West Point.

Blaik, because he was still a reserve officer, used the title "Colonel" as much as "Coach." And there was a duality—perhaps fatal—in this. He was a power at the Academy, still a friend of MacArthur, and in the eyes of some, an empire builder and ruler unto himself. The honor system worked its way mercilessly through Blaik's team. He lost a Heisman candidate, the team captain, and, most harshly, a quarterback who was his own son. Robert Blaik was not a cheater—he didn't need help on his exams—but he had failed to report honor code violations. He was one of ninety cadets allowed to resign from the Academy.

Blaik himself considered resigning. His old mentor, MacArthur, who was back in the United States after being relieved of command in Korea, met with Blaik at the Waldorf Towers in New York City. They were closeted for two hours. MacArthur told Blaik, "Earl, you must stay on. Don't leave under fire."

Blaik stayed.

Many offices thought the Academy's action in the cheating scandal draconian. Others thought it necessary to preserve the honor and integrity of the corps. These included General Matthew Ridgway, who wrote to Secretary of State George Marshall from Korea that he hoped "With all my soul" that the violators would be "relentlessly" removed from the rolls of the Academy.

Controversial as the entire affair was, and remains, one thing is beyond dispute. In a nation that seems to debate ceaselessly the role of athletics—especially football—in the culture of higher learning, West Point acted decisively and with the health of the institution, not football, uppermost in its mind. West Point did not have to be dragged into an investigation by the NCAA. It did not dissemble and it did not embroider the truth. It was faithful to its own code. The Academy did what no other football power in America had ever done by taking such forceful action against its own team and its own athletic fortunes for the sake of principle. The argument has always been "was the Academy too stern and too severe in an effort to make sure that it did not give special consideration to athletes?" It was the furthest thing from a cover-up, the polar opposite of a whitewash.

And however one answers that question, it remains undeniable that the Academy did return from the desert of self-exile to win again. After a 2-7 season in 1951 (remarkable enough under the circumstances), Army went 4-4-1 in 1952. In 1953, a 14-7 win against a powerful Duke team on a late goal line stand was the sign that Army had returned. Army beat Navy, went 7-1-1 and was presented the Lambert Trophy for football supremacy in the East. In the history of college football, it is hard to find a comeback as honorable.

Players on those teams also had their rendezvous with other duties on other fields. A very good player on that Lambert Trophy team was later called upon, by coach Blaik, to change

Blaik, seen above with his son Robert, who was expelled in the cheating scandal of 1951, produced not only great football players but great coaches. Vince Lombardi and Sid Gillman, among others, served as his assistants. Pete Dawkins (right) won the Heisman Trophy playing for Army. Here he breaks a tackle during the Colgate game. Pete Dawkins, inset, appeared on this cover of Life Magazine for April 8, 1966, now a hero in Vietnam.

Russia vs. Red China | Britain's Train Robbery

LIFE

A ROMANCE GOES SOUR | **STILL A SUPER RIDDLE**

Army's All-America Rhodes Scholar, Now in Vietnam

CAPTAIN PETE DAWKINS KEEPS ON WINNING

Captain Pete Dawkins is honored with the Vietnamese battalion he advises

APRIL 8 · 1966 · 35¢

Bobby Knight coached the West Point basketball team before moving on to a spectacular career at Indiana. Here he is seen at a National Invitational Tournament in 1969, with fellow coaches Bob Cousey of Boston College, left, and Ray Mears of Tennessee.

positions. Because of an injury to the regular starter in 1955, Don Holleder would move from end, where he had been an All-American, to quarterback, a position he had never played before. Holleder agreed, for the good of the team, to go with what was being roundly denounced as "Blaik's Folly." After a faltering start, and a lot of second guessing, Holleder made it work and in his last game, led the team to a 14-6 win over Navy. After graduation, Holleder returned to West Point for a tour as an assistant football coach. Then in 1967, while serving with the 1st Infantry Division in Vietnam, he was killed in action after ordering the pilot of a helicopter he was flying in to land so he could evacuate some wounded soldiers. The Holleder Center for Sports and Recreation is named in his honor. All of the athletic buildings and facilities at West Point, for that matter, are named after graduates who were killed in action, a point that is not lost on visiting high school athletes who are thinking about going to West Point.

After Vietnam, Army teams no longer played for National Championships. Football had become a lucrative career for the best players and they went to schools where football was the most rigorous part of their lives and where they could move directly from the campus to the NFL. West Point could offer them neither an easy life apart from football nor the opportunity to play professionally as soon as they graduated. Army played football and played hard enough to go to four bowl games in the '80s and '90s; the first bowl games the Cadets had ever played. In 1966 after an 8-2 season—Tom Cahill was voted Coach of the Year—Army had been invited to play in the Sugar Bowl. Gen. Harold K. Johnson, who had been a football manager at the Point and was now Chief of Staff of an Army at war, decided that the team should decline. Cadets piled tables to the poop deck in the mess hall and then put sugar bowls on top of the tables in protest. Johnson did not relent; but there were no punishments, either. It was the old question of whether or not football was being given too much emphasis at the Academy.

When Army did at last accept bowl invita-

tions, it won two and lost two. In one close loss, Army ran for 350 yards against an Alabama team whose defense was ranked fifth in the nation. Army became one of twenty-one schools in the nation to have won 600 football games. Three Army teams in the '90s led the nation in rushing. The 1996 team finished the season ranked twenty-fifth in the nation with Coach Bob Sutton named Coach of the Year. Army teams still played hard, played for pride and for what General MacArthur understood was the fundamental purpose of football—indeed, all athletics—at West Point: Every man an athlete.

And while football remains the flagship sport, many other Army athletes have made their marks on both playing fields and battlefields.

In 1903, Cadet Joseph Stilwell organized the first basketball game played at West Point against outside competition, a victory over a YMCA team from Yonkers. Stilwell also lettered in football and was captain of the cross country team. After he'd been commissioned, he returned to the Academy for a tour with duties that included

coaching the basketball team. These were the days when each score was followed by a jump ball and under Stilwell, Army recorded two shutouts and a record of 49-17 from 1907-11.

Stilwell, of course, became a general known best by his nickname "Vinegar Joe" He led an Allied force in Burma in 1942 and after superior Japanese numbers had forced him to retreat to India, he was asked, in a press conference, about this glorious retreat.

"There is no such thing," he answered, "as a 'glorious retreat.' I claim we got a hell of a beating. We got run out of Burma, and it is humiliating as hell. I think we ought to find out what caused it, go back, and retake it."

The same principle, as articulated by MacArthur in a cable to Blaik before a Navy game, would be: "There is no substitute for victory."

That Stilwell later accomplished his objective in what was called the China-Burma-India theater is especially remarkable in light of the political as well as military obstacles he faced. As a basketball coach, however, Stilwell is less well known than Bob Knight, who coached at West Point from 1964 to '71. Knight's teams were, unsurprisingly, disciplined and tough and not put off by the kind of hard, repetitive practices that he insisted on and that made them into well-drilled units. Knight's players routinely practiced diving for loose balls, a form of individual infantry tactical training done not on bare earth but a hardwood floor. In three of Knight's six seasons, his teams were ranked first defensively in the nation. His teams went to the NIT tournament five times and never lost to Navy. His record, when he left the Point, was 102-50.

The captain of Knight's 68-69 team was Mike Krzyzewski, who later returned to West Point and coached the basketball team for five years. He built a 73-59 record before moving on

to Duke and routine Final Four appearances. (One of his players in 1978, Garry Winton, was good enough to be drafted into the NBA; he chose a career in the Army instead.)

Knight and Coach K are two conspicuous cases of legendary coaches who have made career stops at West Point and have both left something behind and taken something with them when they left. Vince Lombardi was an assistant coach under Earl Blaik. Bill Parcells was an assistant football coach from 1967 to 1969. Jack Riley was one of the finest college hockey coaches in the history of the sport and coached the American team to a gold medal in the 1960 Olympics, long before the famous American underdog victory at Lake Placid in 1980.

But the coach who, more than any other, stood for the values of West Point was a graduate of the Academy, though it took him six years to accomplish the feat since he was always less interested in academics than athletics. But it was, to say the least, prudent of his superiors to give Red Reeder a series of second chances. He was captain of the 1926 baseball team that beat Navy and was rewarded for this accomplishment at commencement with a bigger hand than that given the class goat.

Reeder made much larger contributions in uniform, though he could have left the Army and played professional baseball for the New York Giants. He was famous in the peacetime Army for what he did as athlete. When war came, he continued to distinguish himself in three theaters, right up until the time he won the DSC and lost his leg in France.

In 1947, he was back at the Point where he conducted a leadership course that was avidly attended by cadets though he claimed, characteristically, that he got more from the cadets than he gave. "West Point cadets are the finest people produced in our country," Reeder said. "They inspired me."

Reeder also coached baseball and wrote books—some thirty-five of them—mostly about the adventures of a cadet named Clint Lane. One of Reeder's books became the basis for the film *The Long Gray Line*, directed by the legendary Hollywood figure John Ford, who had been in command of the Navy vessel that had evacuated the wounded Reeder from Europe.

At West Point, Red Reeder was the embodiment of that fusion between athletics and military leadership that was the MacArthur vision. He was a profound influence and inspiration to an entire generation of cadets who remembered him for his unfailing optimism and can-do attitude. When he was crippled with Guillan Barre Syndrome in 1975, Reeder cheerfully went into therapy and convalescence saying, "Most mortals have to learn to walk once. I've had three chances."

Until his death at the age of 95, in 1998, Reeder would visit with a group of Cadets before the Army-Navy game and reminisce. He remained what he had been—a coach and a leader. Though it had been a long time since he had taken the field, the legend remained fresh.

Coaches like Reeder were at West Point to make the athletes—and the athletes, according to Koehler's dictum, were there to make soldiers. The soldiers came from many sports. Richard Shea '52 was captain of the indoor and outdoor track teams and set several Academy records. A little over a year after he graduated and was commissioned, with the Korean armistice less than two weeks away, Shea led a counterattack against Chinese forces at Pork Chop Hill—he was wounded but refused evacuation and was last seen, according to the citation for his posthumous Medal of Honor, "in close hand-to-hand combat with the enemy."

Paul Bucha '65 was a two-time All-American swimmer at West Point and served as a company commander in the 101st Airborne in Vietnam where, in 1968, his unit was attacked and pinned down. Bucha single-handedly destroyed an enemy bunker and, though wounded, remained in command of a shrinking perimeter throughout the night. Using a flashlight to direct the air evacuation of wounded men, he exposed himself to enemy fire and when daylight came led the recovery of the dead and wounded from his unit. Bucha said of his Medal of Honor, that the award belonged to the men of his company.

Robert Foley, who was captain of the 1963 Army basketball team, also won a Congressional Medal of Honor in Vietnam. Foley retired as a Lieutenant General. There are others, many others, who played on the fields of friendly strife and later performed honorably as soldiers on those other fields.

Nearly a century has passed since General MacArthur embraced the Koehler dictum: "As long as we have athletes, we shall never be without soldiers." West Point has fielded great teams, and individual Army athletes have turned in great performances, and many West Point athletes have gone on to glory on those "other fields." Maxwell Taylor, who went on to command the 101st Airborne at Normandy and then to serve as Chief of Staff, was captain of the tennis team while he was at the Academy. Gar Davidson, who coached the football team and wrote those Monday letters to General MacArthur when he was Chief of Staff, returned to the Academy as Superintendent. The footprints left by athletics are all over the Academy archives.

Jack Mackmull '50 was a star pitcher at West Point and after a distinguished career, retired as a Lt. General. James Hartinger '49 was an All-American lacrosse player and retired with four stars after commanding NORAD and the USAF Space Command. Others from West Point went further in flight, if not in rank. Buzz Aldrin, an Academy track man, became the second man to walk on the moon. Ed White, first man to walk in space, played soccer at West Point. He died in the tragic Apollo fire. And Frank Borman, like MacArthur and Harold K. Johnson, a football manager while at West Point, commanded the first ship to fly around the moon. Borman, ironically, later chaired a commission that studied and revised the Honor System at West Point.

But while the past is rich, the present is still exciting. Women came to the Academy in 1976 and began playing winning basketball almost immediately. The Lady Knights went 21-5 in the '78-'79 season and finished third in the Prince-

ton Invitational Tournament. In 1984, Pam Pearson became the first West Point woman to become an All-American in basketball. Shelby Calvert had already been there in swimming in 1980. In 1986-87, swimmer Marie Wycoff became Army's first woman national champion. Tracy Hanlon and Alma Cobb were honored as All-Americans in track in 1981.

While it is still early and opportunities have been mercifully limited, women athletes from West Point have also distinguished themselves on those "other fields." Kristin Baker was the first woman at West Point to serve as first captain. She lettered in soccer as a plebe and later commanded a company in Bosnia. Jillian Boice (Schwitzer) was a star diver at the Academy, Division II All-American, and later won a Bronze Star with V in Desert Storm.

Women at West Point are plainly athletes and soldiers and while the old cry of "Every man an athlete" may have been altered to "Every cadet an athlete," neither the mission of the Academy nor the purpose of athletics at West Point have changed since MacArthur's time.

You are reminded of this whenever you arrive on the Post from Highland Falls and see the cadets out running to stay in shape or in formation for intramurals. In the afternoon, the fields are full of cadets at earnest play. If it is Navy weekend and you had forgotten, you will be reminded of it by the signs that say, laconically, "Beat Navy." What else needs to be said? That game, indeed the whole universe of competitive athletics, remains a vital part of life at West Point and the Academy's mission, as a memorandum from the Supe in late 2000 makes clear:

"The mission of the United States Military Academy is to prepare cadets for commissioned service in America's Army, an institution that is morally obligated to fight and win the nation's wars. There are no trophies given on the battlefield for 'most improved army,' and unlike all other endeavors, where it can be easy to rationalize lack of success, there is no justifiable alternative to 'winning' in the profession of arms. As should be evident . . . we see competitive athletics as an important component in the process of developing a winning attitude in our cadets. I believe it is important that all members of the West Point community understand why we are firmly committed to this principle and, more specifically, just what is my commanders' intent for our competitive athletic program. Bottom line: I intend for the Academy to field competitive teams that win championships the 'right way' with future officer-leaders."

Which is exactly the spirit: of the words General MacArthur composed and ordered carved into stone above the entrance to the Academy gymnasium.

Upon the fields of friendly strife
Are sown the seeds
That, upon other fields, on other days
Will bear the fruits of victory.

West Point cheerleaders, by now both male and female, and a cadet suited up as the Black Knight, pose with the Army Mule for this photo for Life Magazine, *May 1980.*

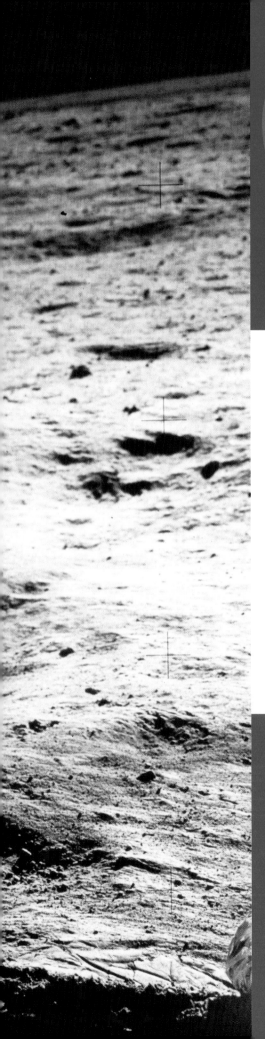

9

FOUR DECADES OF TUMULT

BY BRIAN HAIG

"Today marks my final roll call
with you, but I want you
to know that when I cross the
river my last conscious
thoughts will be of
The Corps, and The Corps,
and The Corps."

— General Douglas MacArthur,
speaking at West Point, May 12, 1962

■ Colonel Ed White II '52 became the first American to walk in space. He would die in an accidental fire at Cape Kennedy January 27, 1967.

■ Wesley Clark graduates first in his class. A Vietnam combat veteran, he would become Supreme Allied Commander Europe in 1997.

■ Ex-President and General of the Army Dwight D. Eisenhower visited the Military Academy to dedicate a mural depicting D-Day at the Normandy beachhead at the West Point Museum.

■ West Point Equal Admissions Opportunity Program established; minority cadets increased from seventeen in 1968 to seventy-seven in 1969.
■ Mrs. Elizabeth Lewis, librarian and art history instructor, appointed as first female faculty member.

■ Major Mike Collins '52 and Colonel Edwin E. [Buzz] Aldrin '51 accompany Neil Armstrong in moon shot in July.

■ Graduates 1802–1970: 29,498; 1961–1970: 6,217.
■ Major General Samuel W. Koster '42 relieved as Superintendent in fallout of My Lai Atrocity investigation. Later retired as Brigadier General. Replaced by Major General William Knowlton.

■ Moments before the 1971 Army-Navy football game, a black stretch limousine entered Philadelphia's JFK Stadium amid rumors President Nixon would attend. To a thunderous ovation from the middies, Bill XVII, Navy's goat mascot, stepped out smartly.

I t was May 12, 1962, a glorious day, and a slightly stooped, still regal Douglas MacArthur peered from the lectern at a sea of gray suits. "As I was leaving the hotel this morning, a doorman asked me, 'Where are you bound for, General?' and when I replied 'West Point,' he said, 'Beautiful place, have you ever been before?'"

The General grinned. Of course he'd been before: as a cadet when he broke academic records, and right after the First World War when as superintendent he'd pushed through reforms that helped shape the modern Academy. And a hundred other times over the years. He knew his beloved West Point was not only achingly beautiful, but serene, a gift of nine years of peace. It was a place that worked its way into his heart, a touchstone that had seen him through countless battles and trials, a foundry that forged great men for great purposes. A dozen of its graduates were living legends; one of whom—MacArthur's former aide—had just stepped down from two terms as president. A cadet uniform could still get you half-fare at the Essex House and Mama Leone's, invitations to escort the fetching contestants at the Miss America Pageant.

The Academy's reputation had never been higher, its image more illustriously polished. Two generations of Americans had witnessed West Pointers in action where it most dearly counted; in the trenches of the First World War, destroying the world's two most powerful dictatorships in the Second World War, and in the sweeping dash through Inchon and north to the Yalu. The man at the lectern had earned his spurs in all three, and a little over two thousand admiring young men listened to the old warrior sternly warn, "You now face a new world—a world of change."

None guessed on that radiant spring day how agonizingly prophetic those words would prove, how suddenly they'd be awash in war, contro-

versy, suffering, and ultimately change so blunt it would engulf them like a tidal wave. The shadows were there. By the late fifties, the Army had dwindled to 860,000 and Air Defense Artillery was its largest branch—two of many reflections of a national strategy dominated by nuclear weapons. A recent bestseller, The Uncertain Trumpet, had disemboweled that strategy and the ways it was misused to justify inexcusable neglect of the Army. Its author, Maxwell Taylor, another former superintendent, warned the nation it was planning for the wrong kind of war, fielding the wrong kinds of weapons, ignoring the wrong kinds of enemies.

Less than twenty black faces gazed up at MacArthur from the audience. Only seven hundred miles away, Freedom Riders were being murdered and Martin Luther King, Jr., was bouncing in and out of jails.

Had anyone suggested a woman would in a few short decades become First Captain of the Corps of Cadets he would've been pelted with laughter. Graduates of West Point went into the combat branches. It was a place that changed boys into men and sent them out to do men's business.

When MacArthur mentioned change, the halls of West Point echoed with other debates. Should cadets be permitted to wear mufti on weekends? Should the fifteen mile drinking limit be docked closer to Academy grounds to curb the annual toll of drunken cadets dying on the torturous curves from Snuffy's Bar and Tavern? And only months earlier, the Superinten-

PRECEDING SPREAD: Edwin "Buzz" Aldrin '59 was the second person to walk on the moon, one of the most dramatic moments of the highly dramatic 1960s. Right: To the modern cadet, the heroes of World War II seemed truly larger than life, figures like George S. Patton set in unapproachable bronze.

| 1972 | 1973 | 1974 | 1975 | 1976 | 1977 | 1978 |

■ In December 1972, compulsory chapel attendance for cadets ended after the U.S. Supreme Court ruled that mandatory religious services were unconstitutional.

■ January. Paris Peace Agreement marks withdrawal of U.S. troops from Vietnam.
■ Cadet James J. Pelosi, the 31,500th graduate of USMA, was commissioned. The Cadet Honor Committee had previously found him guilty of cheating. The decision was reversed. Ostracized by fellow cadets, Pelosi would later spend twelve years in the Army.

■ Eisenhower Hall, a large cadet activity center containing a 4,500-seat auditorium, restaurants, and other facilities, formally opened 30 May.
■ Cadet Robert E. Johnson '75 became first black to be elected Captain of Army Football Team.

■ Pocket-sized electronic calculators replaced slide rules in math, science, and engineering courses.
■ Academy makes extensive preparations for the July 1976 admission of women into the Corps.

■ United States Bicentennial celebration observed by a historical symposium on the American Revolution and by partial restoration of Fort Putnam.
■ Cheating scandal.
■ First female cadets arrive.

■ After almost being cancelled by television for perceived lack of viewer interest, the Army-Navy football game on November 26 outdrew all games broadcast during the season. Army won 17-14.
■ A board headed by astronaut Frank Borman '50 to examine West Point policies and environment in the wake of the 1976 cheating scandal recommended more civilian and non-USMA graduates on the faculty.

■ Luis Eduardo Caldera graduated from West Point and spent five years as a Military Police officer before resigning his commission. In June 1998, Secretary of Defense William S. Cohen swore him in as the seventeenth Secretary of the Army.

---

dent, General William Westmoreland, received the nod from President Kennedy to begin planning a decade-long expansion that would double the number of cadets, enlarging the corps from two to four regiments, expanding the faculty and causing the largest construction boom in the school's history. Changes, large and small, were contemplated, though nobody foresaw the tsunami that was already cresting the horizon.

As MacArthur spoke, over 11,000 military advisers were already in Vietnam; among them the first downpayment of many thousands of West Pointers that would be sent into a cauldron that was to last twelve grueling years, that would gradually escalate from limited military assistance to an all-out inferno, a bitter conflict that gave appalling context to the term "Selective Service," and that separated cadets and graduates from the public as no war before.

By 1966, whole divisions were being flung into Vietnam's jungles. As the casualties steadily mounted, the need for infantry lieutenants became so stark that West Pointers were pipelined straight from graduation to Ranger School, to a plane bound for Southeast Asia.

Second Lt. George Crocker, a recent graduate of the Class of '66, had only just landed at Bien Hoa before he was rushed onto a truck and then a helicopter. "The sun was setting when the Huey dropped him off in a jungle clearing. As he ran out from beneath the whirring rotors, he could hear small arms fire, distant at first and then suddenly much closer. He felt confused, lost. Where the hell was he? Somewhere near the Saigon River in Warzone C, but other than that he wasn't sure. He had been in-country for about six hours and already he was on the fringe of a firefight. As a cadet he'd been told repeatedly to go to the sound of the guns, but he never expected to be asked to do so this quickly."

His class graduated 579 new lieutenants. Thirty were killed. More than a hundred were wounded. It was the highest toll paid by any class in the war. Proportionately, the numbers exceeded even the Class of 1950 that graduated and was rushed headlong into the meatgrinder of the Korean War. It was more than the total number of West Point graduates killed in the First World War.

It was an age-old challenge for the Academy, motivating young men deluged by death notices of recent graduates, friends, and faculty members who had taught and coached them. This time, though, it was more daunting. This time, doubts about the war and its strategy were swarming across the nation, and inevitably into the minds of the corps and faculty. Soon, there was even the flabbergasting spectacle of brand new graduates suing for Conscientious Objector status.

MacArthur came to West Point in May 1962 to warn the nation's future military leaders that they faced a different kind of war. The years to come would prove him even more of a prophet than he knew. Here the 82-year-old general, in a banker-like suit and homburg, greets the brigade officers of the Corps of Cadets.

The Cemetery

DEAD MEN MAY NOT TELL STORIES, but their graves certainly do. For those inclined to listen, the West Point Cemetery has long been the most inspiring, heartrending, and entertaining spot on campus.

The site is majestic, a promontory overlooking the Hudson River and Constitution Island. It is also that rare piece of flat highland, which is why its original service was as a vegetable garden for the Continental Army's garrison. As a cemetery, it predates the Academy by twenty years. The first man buried there, in 1782, was Ensign Dominick Trant of the 9th Massachusetts Regiment, a native of County Cork "which place he quitted from a thirst for military glory & an ardent desire to embrace the American cause."

Major General George W. Goethals, chief engineer of the Panama Canal, from which excavation his headstone was mined. Or the hunk of Jerusalem stone standing over Colonel David "Mickey" Marcus, Class of 1924, who became an Israeli general and was mistakenly killed by one of his own sentries during the 1948 War for Independence. Or the cannon-topped Cadet Memorial, erected in 1817 in honor of the first cadet killed in training, to which the names of other fallen cadets have been added ever since, some as young as fifteen.

The cemetary is one of the most hallowed in the U.S., the final resting place for two centuries of heroes. Above, the chapel, a Greek Revival edifice, was built in 1836 and moved to its present site in 1911. Far left: The cross on the rock marks the grave of Clarke Churchman '98, killed in Cuba within a month of his graduation. The obelisk, left, is the Custer Monument. Above right are the gravestones of Lucius Clay and Edward White, with, appropriately, a boulder for George Goethals, builder of the Panama Canal.

As Trant embraced the cause, so has the cause embraced him. He has since been joined by some 7,000 others, primarily West Point alumni and their families. A walk through the cemetery is an exercise in random thrill. The famous and the unknown, the old soldiers and their young children lie side by side. (Among the first women to be buried here were the Warner sisters of Constitution Island, who taught Bible to the cadets.) Because it is not a national cemetery, the uniformity of headstones is not required. Uniformity is, in fact, roundly ignored. Thus the immense, football-shaped marker belonging to Red Blaik. Or the low-slung, craggy stone of

The cemetery's entrance is guarded by the Old Cadet Chapel. Built in 1834-1836, it stood originally near today's library. When the Chapel, along with several other buildings, was slated for demolition during the Academy's Centennial expansion, many alumni decried the plan. "All the others might go, the barracks, the adjutant's office, and the academic buildings," wrote Morris Schaff '62, "but when the architect laid his hand on the Chapel, there was feeling at once." The Chapel was instead relocated, stone by stone, to the present site. Its most puzzling plaque, in a section commemorating the feats of Continental Army gen-

erals, lists only a 1740 birthdate and the rank of major general. The name, long left blank, once read "Benedict Arnold."

From the Chapel, the cemetery loops out and back in a circle, a design created by Brigadier General Egbert L. Viele, Class of 1847. An influential landscape engineer who helped design Central Park and Prospect Park in New York City, Viele did not charge the Academy for his work on the cemetery. He did, however, award himself the most ostentatious tomb on the grounds, a gargantuan pyramid replete with sarcophagi, an inscription in Etruscan, and a pair of sphinxes. The sphinxes are not the originals, which were said to have been found too buxom by Viele's wife, who ordered them dumped in the Hudson. (One salvaged sphinx now graces a residential garden on campus.) Viele's neighbor, Major General Daniel Butterfield (who wrote "Taps" but did not graduate from West Point), rests beneath an equally ostentatious tomb. Shortly after those two men were buried, it was decided that, uniformity or not, humongousness would no longer be allowed.

Alas, a great many great men lie beneath subtle stones: Sylvanus Thayer, the D-Day general Norman D. Cota, the astronaut Edward H. White II, the spirited West Point gym teacher and den father Marty Maher. Here lie sixteen Medal of Honor winners and eighteen U.S.M.A. Superintendents; here lie sports heroes and Buffalo Soldiers; here lie, in Area XXXIV, too many men from the Class of 1966, Frank Rybicki and Donald Judd and Dennis Loftheim and Buck Thompson among them. It is a known fact that death is a by-product of the soldiering life; still, coming upon the tight rows of the Vietnam dead, that fact is rendered impotent.

Tourists occasionally make their way to the gravesites of Marty Maher or Edward White or Mickey Marcus. Or George Armstrong Custer, who may or may not lie beneath his marker. He was originally buried with his men at the Little Big Horn; when an expedition was sent a year later to recover Custer's remains, his bones had been scattered, and the recoverers took their best guess.

Most tourists, though, don't come near the cemetery. Nor do most cadets, now that the P.X. has moved—the route to the old P.X. ran right past the cemetery. It is considered by many to be West Point's most overlooked treasure. Two of its foremost scholars came to their obsessions quite by accident. Marie T. Capps, a former U.S.M.A. librarian, used to lead her Girl Scouts through the cemetery to discuss its grand old trees; at length she decided she might as well teach her girls about its grand old soldiers too. Conrad Crane, who is writing a book about the cemetery, first stumbled upon it as a boy: his parents were Army football fans, and, on winter gamedays, sought out the cemetery's heated bathroom. In the late 1960s, Crane began to notice new gravestones, bearing the names of the football players he'd only recently rooted for. Crane went on to graduate from West Point and teach history there. He took to asking his students why they'd come. "A few of them said they wanted to be doctors, or make a million dollars on

1. Old Cadet Chapel
2. Dade Monument
3. Margaret "Molly" Corbin
4. Colonel David "Mickey" Marcus
5. The Anderson Fountain
6. General Lucius Clay
7. Colonel Edward H. White, II
8. Major General George W. Goethals
9. Major General Frederick Dent Grant
10. Wood's Monument
11. Ensign Dominick Trant
12. Susan & Anna B. Warner
13. The Cadet Monument
14. Lieutenant General Winfield Scott
15. Colonel Sylvanus Thayer
16. Major General George A. Custer
17. Brigadier General Robert Anderson
18. Major General Daniel Butterfield
19. Brigadier General Egbert L. Viele

Wall Street," Crane said. "They didn't understand what it meant to be a West Pointer. That's when I started taking all my students on a tour of a cemetery—to say to them, if you want to make a million dollars, this is what one West Pointer says the cost might be."

—*Stephen J. Dubner*

General William C.
Westmoreland '36, seen
below at Da Nang with
three Hawk anti-aircraft
missiles, commanded
American forces in the
most unpopular war in
our history, one the
Army was never allowed
to win. As this New
York Times headline
(right) attests, every
request for more troops
in Vietnam ratcheted up
the public outcry.

k Times

Te... ...
44. Full U.S. re...

SECTION ONE

40 CENTS

60c beyond 80-mile zone from New York City, except Long
Island. 75c beyond 200-mile radius. Higher in air delivery cities.

RCH 10, 1968

WESTMORELAND REQUESTS 206,000 MORE MEN, STIRRING DEBATE IN ADMINISTRATION

Enemy Hammers 7 Sites On the Outskirts of Saigon

FORCE NOW 510,000

Some in Defense and State Departments
...Oppose Increase

By TOM BUCKLEY
Special to The New York Times

SAIGON,
Sunday,
cong...
ear...

Vietnam, namese police said that 4 per-
Viet- sons had been killed an
tacks wounded, all civilian
...tacks.

But equally daunting were the numbers and their implications. In eleven years of combat, only eight colonels and three generals were killed. The number of lieutenants killed was seventeen hundred. It was a different kind of war. And the cadets at West Point were keenly aware of it.

But what was happening on other campuses by the end of the sixties only added to the pain. Across the country ROTC programs had their doors nailed shut as students carried North Vietnamese flags and launched mammoth protest marches on Washington. Glamorous actresses and musicians flew to Hanoi to show their support for the enemy's cause, while prominent politicians blasted both the war and those who fought it. The men of West Point felt socially and politically ostracized, even forsaken.

Some tried to balance those frustrations with mordant wit, as on the day protesters from Vassar came to West Point and began handing out flowers. Several cadets graciously accepted . . . then promptly ate them. But wit couldn't begin to eclipse the planeloads of flag-shrouded caskets, the solemn funeral processions wending their way through West Point's verdant cemetery, the sight of battle-hardened veterans—many still recuperating from terrible wounds—pouring into faculty ranks.

It was a bleak, jarring trial for the institution. Draft evaders were regarded in many quarters as heroes; professional soldiers as murderous automatons, the Army a soulless killing machine. In 1968 the My Lai scandal broke and the Academy's superintendent, General Samuel Koster, was implicated and asked to resign. At Homecoming Weekend, 1972, Don McLean, singer of

A MILITARY MAIN STREET

—by David Halberstam

I am always moved when I go there. Part of it is the sheer beauty of the site, located on a cliff above the Hudson, the view absolutely magnificent, or more accurately perhaps, majestic. But more importantly, it is the sense of the past which is so palpable there, the idea that this is where so many great American military figures arrived from their small towns, eighteen years old, completely raw and unfinished, filled with the notion of serving their country, and in fact went on to do precisely that. When I am at West Point my imagination runs free and I can see the young Ulysses Grant arriving here in another century and, then earlier in this century, that remarkable crew of young men who would bring such honor to America during World War II, Eisenhower and Bradley, and in time, my special favorite and hero, Matthew Ridgway. They were small town boys most of them, more often than not from very humble backgrounds, and they brought only their hopes and their ambitions; their notion of duty was formed here. The MacArthurs and the Pattons with their talents and their greater vainglory tend to be the exception: the quintessential West Point graduate is more likely to be like an Eisenhower or a Bradley.

I am impressed by this place because it is so uniquely American, small town, god-fearing America at that; it may have on occasion in the past have helped to create an elite within the military itself, and certainly in an earlier era if not in this one, there was a distinct career advantage in having the West Point ring, but it was not as occasionally happens in other countries, part of a self perpetuating elite, an elite which on occasion tends to look down on the ordinary citizenry around it. Sometimes there is a sense of obligation which can be found generation after generation in a particular family like the Truscotts, where going to West Point seems to be in the DNA, but in America our military academy is not part of a self perpetuating (and self isolating) class.

For one thing the place itself is simply far too demanding, and the rewards, particularly in an America which now offers talented people a chance at a very fast track, are on the surface at least too small. By its very nature it is self-selective of a certain kind of young American: the admissions system tends to find good committed kids from all over the country; the combination of the demanding curriculum and the harsh daily regimen suffices to warn off most of the more privileged children of the upper middle class. The people who come here tend to bring a certain hunger with them; it is one of the principal attractions that the education is both very good and free. As such it is more meritocratic than France's St. Cyr which has tended to reflect a certain kind of French elite and, in the past, a somewhat ideological one at that, and Britain's Sandhurst, which has traditionally reflected more of England's upper class.

I think we are very lucky in this country. Unlike the military in other countries, the American military has rarely been politicized; it tends to be more conservative than the general societal norm, but that is a most natural and normal phenomenon. Over the years those generals with serious political ambitions, like Douglas MacArthur, have tended to give off the wrong scent to their fellow Americans and their political ambitions inevitably crash; it is those more modest officers who tend to reflect the culture of this special place, like Eisenhower, men who do not even want to run for office that badly, whom their countrymen tend to trust. And in no small degree I credit West Point with its unique selection process and its codes for that. Over the years I have come to know a number of distinguished generals who went here— Matthew Ridgway, Hal Moore, who so brilliantly commanded the American soldiers at the Ia Drang in Vietnam in November, 1965, and Bob York—as good and honorable a man as I have ever met—and I was always moved by the combination of strength and honor and humanity in all of them.

For West Point has always seemed to me to be unusually close to main Street in middle America; it is a place without glitz which without consciously trying to do, reflects both the norm, the center, and the diversity of America. Again and again it turns out good people of significant personal modesty and a powerful sense of obligation. One of my favorite West Point stories is of the gifted, talented, but relatively poor Dwight Eisenhower leaving his Mennonite home in Abilene, Kansas. His mother, Ida Stover Eisenhower who hated the very idea of war, was virtually unable to watch his departure, and returned from the train station to burst into tears.

When I was a reporter in Vietnam in the early sixties, the young American advisers there were almost exactly my age, and a significant number of them were from the Point. We talked easily and naturally, because we were all the same age and we were, I a a reporter, they as officers, all volunteers for this assignment. A number of them were very good to me, young and green and scared as I was at twenty-eight; on my first operation in the field I was escorted by Captain Ken Good, West Point Class of 1952, and then the next time by Captain Jim Torrence, Class of 1955. And I was impressed as much as anything else, by their sense of decency and obligation; they reminded me very much of the young Americans I had already met in Africa who were serving in the Peace Corps, in their sense of duty, their modesty, and, for this is an old fashioned word, their innate goodness.

Ken Good was killed early in the war, during his first tour in January 1963, and Jim Torrence, who I thought was surely going to be a general, went back for a second tour and advised a Vietnamese regiment in 1970. His story seems to me to embody everything that is special about this place; he was the West Point son of a West Point graduate, born on location during a time when his father, the senior Jim Torrence, taught math there. He had never considered going anywhere else, and he had never considered any other career. Because the family moved around so much when he was young, he always thought of West Point as his one real home. He had gone to Vietnam as I had in 1962, full of enthusiasm for the cause, but by the time he was ordered back for his second tour as the senior adviser to a Vietnamese regiment, in our old stomping ground of the Delta, he was deeply skeptical and full of misgivings; he was disillusioned with the war, but had accepted his assignment, and was killed there in May 1971 in the crash of a command helicopter. I think of him often and Ken Good and another young officer I knew, Don York Class of 1954, who was killed there in those early days, and now when on occasion I go back to the Point to teach a class, it is their names I seek out on the long list of men who died serving their country.

Michael A. Hood '67 helps a wounded South Vietnamese soldier. As Washington approached the edge of the quagmire in the early 1960s, President John F. Kennedy (above, back to the camera) confers with his Secretary of Defense Robert MacNamara (left), and his chief military adviser Maxwell Taylor (center).

the popular ballad *American Pie*, was invited to West Point for a concert. He opened with the announcement he was going to "donate the proceeds from this concert to Veterans Against the War." The hall fell silent. A number of faculty members and their wives stood up and left. The war and all its galling complexities kept oozing over the ramparts.

Could the Academy still attract the best and brightest to fight a malignantly divisive, prolonged war? Would Vietnam unhinge Westmoreland's doubling of the Corps? Would it inflict long-lasting divisions between officers and their political masters, between professional soldiers and their society? These were very compelling

concerns to the faculty of the late sixties and early seventies.

In the summer of 1971—the heyday of the war's unpopularity—the class of 1975 reported to West Point 1,339 strong. The swearing-in ceremony was packed front-to-back with bright and able young men willing to fight an unpopular war in an unpopular place. The Academy had passed the first two of its tests.

But on that third concern, the record was and remains blurry, not only among West Pointers, among the officer corps generally. If the old saw about literature being a reflection of the soul holds water, the stoic harmony between the military and its political masters was one more casualty of the war. The books written during and afterward by faculty members—from Josiah Bunting's *The Lionheads*, to Andy Krepenevich's *The Army in Vietnam*, to H.R. McMaster's *Dereliction of Duty*—all were harshly

General Creighton Abrams '36 (above left) took over from his classmate Westmoreland with orders to "Vietnamize" the war. Here he confers with General George I. Forsythe. Above right: General Earle Gilmore Wheeler '32, Chairman of the Joint Chiefs of Staff as the war escalated, stands to brief civilian leaders at the White House, including Lyndon B. Johnson, seated at the head of the table.

resentful of the way the war was fought, pointing reproachful fingers at everyone from the political and senior military machinators in Washington to the command bunkers in Saigon.

But perhaps none described the anguish more poignantly than LTG (ret) Hal Moore, Class of '45, in his bestselling book *We Were Soldiers Once and Young*:

> "We were the children of the 1950s and John Kennedy's young stalwarts of the early 1960s. He told the world that Americans would 'pay any price, bear any burden, meet any hardship' in the defense of freedom. We were the down payment on that costly contract, but the man who signed it was not there when we fulfilled his promise. John F. Kennedy waited for us on a hill in Arlington National Cemetery, and in time we came by the thousands to fill those slopes with our white marble markers and to ask on the murmur of the wind if that was truly the future he had envisioned for us."

It seemed MacArthur in his Farewell Address had foreseen this too: ". . . and through all this welter of change and development, your mission remains fixed, determined, inviolate—it is to win our wars." Well, the Vietnam conflict had not been won. Neither had it been an outright defeat, but near enough to concoct the same embittered feelings and regrets and after-doubts.

West Pointers had done their best; they'd showed valor, commitment, and leadership; 273 gave their lives. Five earned the Medal of Honor, and countless others the Distinguished Service Cross, Silver and Bronze Stars, Purple Hearts. But by the time the war finally ground to its agonized halt in 1975, the Army was demoralized and shaken to its roots by rampant drug use, racial tensions, and epidemic disciplinary problems. The term 'fragging' had been coined to depict the too-common murder of officers by their troops. The service that had been most cruelly debauched by the war's burdens and costs, that had slogged through the jungles and rice paddies, that had stomached the highest casualties, now had to bear its ugliest recriminations.

To some, the blame landed squarely on West Point's doorstep. It was the breeding ground for the Generals who led the forces, who promised a "light at the end of the tunnel" that flickered but never shone. To the critics, it did not matter that the Army had been given an impossible mission in an impossible place. It did not matter that Westmoreland and Abrams and the troops who followed them had done their duty in a strategic straightjacket not of their own making or choosing.

Anthony Herbert in his foreword to the blisteringly critical 1972 book, *West Point: America's Power Fraternity*, wrote: "For the first time in the history of this great nation we have lost a major war—the full aftermath of which is yet to hit us. Somehow, on the field of battle our Army—manned by the very best of raw material, the cream of America's youth, and they were the cream: bigger, better, healthier, better educated, brighter than any who came before them, and at least as brave; backed by the most willing, sup-

portive and patriotic citizenry of the world, the people of the United States; armed with the most horrendous weaponry ever entrusted to the hands of man anywhere—managed to lose. To lose decisively to what can be considered at best a fifth-rate military, and even less than a fifth-rate economic power."

While the fingers of blame were still gesturing, the Army leapt to fix the problems roiling in the war's dispiriting wake; turning its focus back to the Soviet threat; demobilizing to 781,000; shifting to an all-volunteer force; developing programs to overcome racial hostilities and drugs, restoring discipline and morale in the ranks.

Then, in the spring of 1976, a cadet appended a note on his take-home Electrical Engineering exam that he'd received unauthorized assistance. That note let loose an avalanche: alerted, the Department initiated a wider survey and quickly found another 117 cadets suspected of cheating, and after a more extensive second look, another 150 suspects.

It was, as one chagrined faculty member put it, "a damned if you do, damned if you don't" moment. It would be hard to envision a worse time to expose the largest cheating ring in the Academy's history. And it unleashed fresh barrages of criticism and external intervention. The

school got no kudos for unmasking and disclosing the scandal. The honor system was the school's sine qua non; the central noun of its cherished motto; the heart of what West Point and its graduates stand for. And if it was rotten, well, then, what wasn't, asked its critics? The Academy was accused of being overly insulated, blind to its own sins, entrenched in archaic

The Holy Cause

—by William F. Buckley, Jr.

WHEN HENRY KISSINGER RECEIVED the Sylvanus Thayer Award in September, 2000, he spoke forthrightly about the Vietnam mission of—yesteryear, is probably the best way to put it. The two most prominent West Point graduates in attendance that night had both worked for him, and he paid them ample tribute. General Al Haig and General Brent Scowcroft acknowledged the salute of the statesman who was the right hand of the commander-in-chief, Richard M. Nixon, from 1969 until 1977. In his speech, Dr. Kissinger defended the purpose of our military expedition in Vietnam. He had of course given his position on Vietnam extensively in his autobiographical books. Now he spoke of his mortification over how it all ended. It was good to hear that voice, saying those things, to that audience.

In 1971, I spoke at the Military Academy at a commencement exercise. At that time, the clouds of self-disparagement were heavy. John Kerry, who is now a United States Senator, had made extraordinary charges about the behavior of the American military in Vietnam. I remember thinking then how dumbfoundingly passive the United States Military Academy has to appear to be when the public mood turns sour, and the whole idea of a military career is made to seem savage and even anachronistic.

John Kerry, who returned from Vietnam with personal honors for heroic action, cursed not only the venture (this is not difficult to do—an honorable case can be made for saying we should never have got into Indochina), but the professionals and their surrogates who carried out the assignment. West Pointers were heavily engaged in Vietnam and understandably accepted responsibility for the behavior of their subordinates on the field. Mr. Kerry ascribed to our soldiers in Vietnam barbarous practices, proscribed explicitly by the West Point code, and alien to the West Point spirit. Mr. Kerry had delivered his indictment in full military dress, before the Senate Committee on Foreign Relations.

What he said was that in Southeast Asia, he saw "not isolated incidents but crimes committed on a day-to-day basis with the full awareness of officers at all levels of command." He gave tales of torture, of rape, of Americans who "randomly shot at civilians, razed villages in a fashion reminiscent of Genghis Khan, [who] shot cattle and dogs for fun, poisoned food stocks, and generally ravaged the countryside of South Vietnam in addition to the normal ravages of war."

What would be the consequences of such action? Dead people, cattle, and dogs to be sure. But, he warned us in 1971, we have "created a monster, a monster in the form of millions of men who have been taught to deal and to trade in violence, and who have returned with a sense of anger."

In the thirty years since that indictment was handed down, we have not seen that anger raging, nor any fruits of it in our military establishment.

But the slur against West Point, the matrix of military conduct, remains on the record. It is reassuring that the charge against the military is generally dismissed as the act of a veteran whose judgement was affected by the awful tribulations of war. But worth recalling, on this anniversary of the Military Academy, to remind us of the holy cause of the military profession.

Cadets at the United States Military Academy necessarily ask themselves from time to time the analogous question of the priest's most agonizing moments: Is there a God? Young men and women studying among other things how to fight ask: Is America worth it?

The assault on the military is an assault on the proposition that what we have, in America, is truly worth defending. The military is to be loved or despised according as it defends, contingently, that which is beloved, or perpetuates that which is despised. The root question is, to say it again, Is America worth it?

Without organized force, and a credible threat to use it as required, there is little prospect of sustained freedom. Without freedom, there is not true humanity fulfilled. If America were the monster of John Kerry, cadets would do well to forswear their calling. My own conviction remains that we owe much to their dedication. And that, from time to time, we do well to register our debt to those who devote themselves so completely to the republic's needs. In Saigon, they had experience with military failure. The United States Military Academy has much to learn from reflection on the lessons to which Dr. Kissinger alluded.

1979	1980	1981	1982	1983	1984	1985

■ Cadet Vincent K. Brooks is first black to be named Brigade Commander in the history of the U.S. Military Academy.
■ Andrea Lee Hollen became the first woman cadet to win a Rhodes Scholarship for two years of study at Oxford University.

■ Graduates 1802–1980: 38,081; 1971–1980: 8,583.
■ First women graduated; sixty-two women were among the graduates, having survived hostility and enmity, proving themselves capable of meeting the demands of the institution.

■ On May 27, 1981, President Ronald Reagan gave the commencement address at West Point. In closing he said,
"Do your duty. Keep untarnished your honor, and you of the corps will preserve this country for yourselves, for all of us, for your children, and for your children's children. God bless you and keep you."

■ Ground was broken for the Jewish Chapel at West Point. Designed by former cadet Max Abramovitz, the structure was being built into a bluff between the existing Cadet Chapel and the Catholic Chapel. In 1982, Jews number only forty-nine out of 4,400 cadets.

■ General James H. "Jimmy" Doolittle, who guided 16 twin-engined B-25's in a daylight raid on Tokyo on April 18, 1942, received the 1983 Sylvanus Thayer Award on September 29, 1983. Presented annually by the Association of Graduates, it recognizes citizens who exemplify the Academy's motto, "Duty, Honor, Country."

■ Army defeated Michigan State 10-6 in the inaugural Cherry Bowl, in Pontiac, Michigan, the first post-season bowl game in which the U.S. Military Academy had been allowed to compete.

■ The student chapters of the American Society of Civil Engineers at West Point and City College of New York sponsored a Concrete Canoe Race at Round Pond. The students of seven colleges competed, building canoes built only of concrete and reinforcing materials as a test of their engineering skills.

habits, not tradition-bound . . . tradition-enslaved. Study groups descended in flocks and every aspect of cadet life was dissected, criticized, scrutinized, and re-scrutinized.

Age-old questions were revisited with fresh urgency and skepticism. Had the precarious balance of an officer's education become lopsided; too academic or too military? Was the honor system, like communism, congenitally flawed, or did the seeds lie elsewhere? Perhaps with the school's leaders; with superintendents that were too weak or too strong, or Academic Boards that were either powerfully hidebound, or too impotent to resist capricious change? Or was the problem with contemporary cadets; did baby boomers lack the ethical DNA of past generations, coming to West Point too pampered, too morally elastic, too materially corrupted to fit into West Point's character? Or was it what was done with them afterward; either given too many liberties, or too few; their lives too over-structured or not structured enough?

On these and many other vexing questions the studies inevitably came to contradictory conclusions. And the authoring groups clashed, against each other, and within themselves. Then the toxic self-doubts lurched from bad to worse. Some of the country's preeminent engineering graduate schools notified West Point its graduates were too academically soggy for the rigors of graduate courses—that a West Point education was no longer what it once was.

The nation's very first engineering college, the school that produced America's most fabled builders, the men who mapped the West, who tamed the nation's waterways and carved out its railroads and created awesome dams and the Panama Canal, who oversaw the development of the atomic bomb and inspired the greatest civil engineering feat in history—the construction of the national highway system—was being told its graduates were too academically feckless for advanced studies.

A double-barreled shotgun had been fired at the school. Not only the Academy's ability to forge soldiers of character, also its specialty of turning out credible engineers were under assault.

A new azimuth of soul-searching was sparked and the previously verboten words, optional majors, were suggested as a remedy. But to many members of the Academic Board optional courses weren't the remedy; they were the cause the problems in the first place. In their view, the decline of the Academy's engineering reputation traced right back to the introduction of electives back in 1960, to what began as a pinched concession—a tiny program of four electives—that mushroomed over time into over a hundred courses and instigated an internal battle for cadet intellectual wattage. Something had to give—but nothing had. By the mid-seventies, cadets were the distressed rope in a pedagogical tug-of war; required to pass forty-eight courses to graduate when external boards advised only forty, surely creating an impulse to cheat. As cadets of that era liked to say, they were getting a hundred thousand-dollar education stuffed into their ears a nickel at a time.

In the in-house civil war that was ignited, departments were pitted against departments. The engineering and mathematics apostles fell back on their traditional argument; that the pointy logic of arithmetic and engineering were peerless cerebral foundations for future officers. They taught ordered, dispassionate, tangible ways of analyzing problems, at achieving precise, workable solutions. Theirs were sciences of diamond-hard clarity; other academic fields were mushy, wantonly opinionated, imprecise. The other departments just as fiercely defended their

■ General Fidel V. Ramos became Chief of Staff of the Philippine Army, two years before he would become Secretary of National Defense. He graduated from West Point in 1950.

■ Brigadier General Fred A. Gorden became the first black Commandant of Cadets. The only black cadet to enter West Point in 1958, Gorden had grown up in the Jim Crow atmosphere of Alabama before moving to Michigan, where he secured a nomination to the Military Academy.

■ General Lyman Louis Lemnitzer [1899–1988] died at age eighty-nine. A brilliant organizer and diplomat who qualified as a parachutist at the age of fifty-one and rose to become chairman of the Joint Chiefs of Staff, Lemnitzer graduated from West Point in 1920.

■ Kristin M. Baker became the first female First Captain in the history of West Point. Although women had attended West Point since 1976, they comprised only ten percent of the student body.

■ Graduates 1802–1990: 47,892; 1981–1990: 9,811.
■ Gen. Colin L. Powell, a child of the South Bronx who rose to become the Chairman of the Joint Chiefs of Staff, gave the graduation address. "I'm the first active duty R.O.T.C. graduate to address a West Point graduation," he said.

■ President George Bush gave the Commencement address at West Point with a theme of racial and gender equality as practiced by the military. "Government's responsibility," he said today, "is to enhance, not redistribute, opportunity, to insure that all people get a fair chance to achieve their dreams."
■ Gulf War

■ James Alward Van Fleet, a U.S. Army General who led his troops ashore on D-Day and later commanded the American forces in Korea, died on his ranch on September 23, 1992 aged 100, the last survivor of the Class of 1915.

THE BLACK EXPERIENCE —by Wallace Terry

Almost sixty years separate the West Point class of H. Minton Francis and that of Brian Thomas. They are divided by a social gulf as wide as all those years. In the 1940s, Francis was ostracized as a black cadet. In the new century, Thomas, also black, has been embraced as a cadet leader. Francis had no white friends. Thomas's best friend is a white cadet, from the same Southern soil as he. But both Francis and Thomas have a common connection besides their color—a deeply felt love for their alma mater. Throughout the painful, uncertain and growing times that characterize the 130-year history of the black experience at West Point, black cadets, like Francis and Thomas, for the most part, maintained their faith in the ideals of the Academy.

From its creation in 1802 until 1870, West Point had no black cadets. But during Reconstruction the War Department, anxious for a small cadre of black officers, pressured the Academy to admit blacks, if not to graduate them. From 1870 to the turn of the century twenty-three blacks were appointed of whom twelve attended and just three graduated. From 1887 to 1929, not a single black appeared at West Point.

In 1932, Benjamin O. Davis Jr., the son of the first black Army general, entered West Point. He had to endure the same silent treatment that was given to black cadets sixty years before. "I made my mind up that I would continue to hold my head high," Davis wrote. Davis finished thirty-fifth in a class of 276, and received his diploma from General John J. Pershing. He was the first black to graduate in the 20th century. There would be no lasting friendships from those days. But Davis would win fame in Europe as commander of the first black Army Air Corps unit, known as the Tuskegee Airmen, and later would retire from the Air Force as a lieutenant general.

H. Minton Francis was in the middle of his first year at the University of Pennsylvania when his father told him, "You're going to West Point." Why, he asked. His father replied, "Hitler is in Poland." Upon arriving at the Academy, a white officer asked young Francis, "Why do you niggers want to come here?" Francis was the only black in the class of 1944. Clarence Davenport, Class of '43, recalls, "In all of the time there, not one white cadet had a cordial conversation with me. And when *Life* Magazine came on campus, I was ordered to move out of the way of the cameras." Davenport later retired as a colonel, and Francis served as Deputy Assistant Secretary of Defense for Equal Opportunity under Presidents Ford and Carter.

The numbers of black graduates remained fairly static through the 1940s, in part due to the inability of some black cadets to measure up in a still racially difficult environment. But the climate improved in the 1950s in part due to the 1948 orders of President Truman integrating the Armed Forces. And the last vestiges of segregation on campus were gone by the end of the Korean War. The 1951 Class yielded—for the first time more than two—five black graduates, including Roscoe Robinson Jr., who would become the first black four star general in the Army. Conditions for black cadets continued to improve in the sixties as the nation responded to the Civil Rights Movement.

Above top: The first second generation black graduate of West Point, James D. Fowler Jr. '67 gets some advice from his father, Colonel James D. Fowler '41. Above: Recognition Day marks a milestone for plebes—the day when the upperclassmen finally "recognize" them as full-fledged cadets, and they put the horrors of plebe year behind them. Here, Vincent K. Brooks '80, right, who would become the first African-American First Captain, recognizes an ex-plebe.

■ General Matthew Bunker Ridgway '17, died in Pittsburgh aged 98. His remarkable career culminated in his appointment as Supreme Allied Commander in Europe, succeeding Gen. Eisenhower.

■ A kick once again decided the Army-Navy game. A 52-yard field goal by a near-sighted cadet, Kurt Heiss, in the fourth quarter provided the winning points today in a 22-20 victory. Heiss, a left-footed senior, could not see the football go through the goal posts.

■ The year in Army-Navy football was immortalized by John Feinstein in *A Civil War: Army vs. Navy: A Year Inside College Football's Purest Rivalry*.

■ Army beat Navy 28-24 in the biggest come-from-behind win in the history of the rivalry. At one point Army was behind 21-3.

■ President Bill Clinton delivered the commencement address in which he told 896 graduating cadets that expanding the North Atlantic Treaty Organization to former communist nations would enhance U.S. security.

■ General Hamilton Hawkins Howze, '30, who was credited with developing helicopter warfare tactics used in the Vietnam War and beyond, died at age eighty-nine. As head of the Army Tactical Mobility Requirement Board, which became known as the Howze Board, he came to champion airmobile warfare.

■ President Clinton posthumously pardoned the first black graduate of the U.S. Military Academy at West Point, Henry O. Flipper, '76, whose military career was tarnished by a racially-motivated discharge. "This good man has now completely recovered his good name," Clinton said.

Joseph Anderson, a celebrated member of the Class of '65, recalls none of the harsh experiences of earlier generations of black cadets. "I always had white roommates," he says today, "and I was the lead singer in the glee club. The Academy had crossed the bridge of integration, if not the bridge of full opportunity." Anderson was appointed to several leadership roles, but never felt that a black cadet could achieve the highest brigade rank. He would later be heralded for his Vietnam War leadership in the Oscar-winning documentary, *The Anderson Platoon*, and would serve as a White House Fellow.

The Vietnam War was a stimulant to Academy integration, too. The Department of Defense did not fail to notice that the ratio of black Army officers to black enlisted men and NCOs fighting in Vietnam was very low. In July of 1969, forty-five black cadets could be counted in the entering Class of '73. "I don't feel that we were singled out for anything, good or bad," Col. Andre Sayles, a member of that class, recalls. For the first time in my life I felt the same as everybody else."

Meanwhile, the Academy staff was integrated. In 1966, Maj. James Hill, in chemistry, and Capt. Reginald Brown, in social science, became the first black faculty members. And the following year, Maj. Roger Blunt, Class of '56, was appointed the first black tactical officer. As their number grew over the next decade, black staff members informally organized themselves into a support group called Black Officers at West Point. Their primary mission was to mentor minority cadets.

But nothing was more transforming as a measure of social change at West Point in the seventies than the selection of Vincent K. Brooks of the Class of '80 as the first black to serve as first captain and brigade commander of the entire corps of cadets. Brooks and his family were establishing their own tradition at the Academy. He had followed his older brother, Leo, who became a regimental commander. It was the first time two sons of a black officer on active duty had come to the Academy. And the father, like B.O. Davis, Sr., would himself become an Army general.

The number of black cadets graduating rose to seventy-nine in 1985. In 1987, Brig. Gen. Fred Gordon, a member of the Class of '62, became the first black commandant, putting him in charge of the military training of the corps. Black graduates were also appearing as trustees of the Association of Graduates.

As the 20th century came to an end Sayles was leading the electrical engineering and computer science department as the first black department head in West Point history.

Despite all the symbols that now connect West Point to its black heritage and despite the striking success of its black cadets and instructors, a racial gap remains. And it is in the failure to attract and graduate more black cadets, despite working very hard to do so. The number of those graduating since the days of Henry Flipper passed the 1,000 mark in 1991. And most entering classes since the 1990s have included at least eighty blacks. But they have amounted to only six or seven percent of the entering classes, well under the Academy goal of 10 to 13 per cent, a figure more representative of the black population.

Lt. Col. Timothy Rainey of the History Department and Robert Johnson, now deputy director of admissions, are trying to change the image of West Point in the black community by bringing black educators to the campus and sending black graduates to high schools across the country. "The kid we want can get into any school in the country—he's the Harvard kid," Rainey says. "And here he has a five year obligation. But unlike Harvard, we pay your way." As Johnson notes, "The education and the desire to be an Army officer appeals to black kids, same as most kids. We let them know we will look out for them when they get here."

To see the children of black graduates and staff members in an incoming class or joining the faculty is not unusual anymore. Tereh Sayles, the daughter of Col. Sayles, graduated in the Class of 2001. And in 2002, Capt. Frederick Black Jr., Class of 1994, will return to teach, as did his father.

West Point today is fully integrated. Yet a black culture exists within the larger culture. "Blacks tend to hang with each other," Brian Thomas from the Class of '02 says, "and whites with each other, like any other institution. But the good thing about West Point is that it is structured to force you to interact. My office mate is white. My roommate today is Hispanic. My roommate during basic training was a white guy, Brian Smith. He is my best friend now. And his parents are like my surrogate parents.

"The atmosphere here is certainly a far cry from the days of Flipper or Colonel Francis," Thomas observes. "There is no open discrimination. But sometimes it becomes apparent that we are not where we need to be in terms of numbers. I feel it when I am the only black in my classrooms."

Thomas enjoys visiting reunions of classes from the 1940s and 1950s so that their black members can see his progress. "Blacks have been given the opportunity today," he says, "and we are taking advantage of it. One of the things the Academy teaches is to look long term. Leaders look long term. You can't get bogged down by right now situations on race or anything else. I know that once we graduate we will be on a level playing field. Not black, not white. Just lieutenants. And that is what gives me the greatest satisfaction."

These sentiments echo across generations.

One hundred nineteen women entered West Point as plebes in 1976;
sixty-two graduated in 1980. Barry McKinley portrayed this pioneering
group of women in this photo (below) in Life Magazine, May 1980.

versatilities, the crucial importance of history, of geopolitics, of social sciences, of English and philosophy, and a dozen other subjects needed in the kitbags of modern officers.

This was no petty, arbitrary debate: it was a passionate battle for West Point's intellectual heart and soul. For 180 years, West Pointers performed two inviolate purposes; they defended the nation and they built and maintained its infrastructure. How much of the brilliance of past warriors stemmed from their training as engineers? How much of the Academy's value to the nation would be lost?

West Point, after all, was never intended to be like Ivy League universities that packed their student bodies like shotgun pellets to achieve excellence in all fields—to spew out graduating classes that could achieve fame as writers, musicians, scientists, business people, lawyers. West Point selected "whole men" rather than "whole student bodies." And then targeted them like sniper's bullets to achieve excellence in only two fields—leading soldiers and engineering.

By 1982, an anguished, discordant consensus was finally reached; for the first time in history West Pointers would be offered sixteen optional majors. The decision was not universally popular. It led to a stream of faculty retirements.

Coinciding with this frenzy another question was being asked: Why were there no women at West Point? In 1975, the then-superintendent, General Sidney Berry, told Congress the reasons for the exclusion were as well-justified as they were timeless; that the Academy was not set up for women; that male bonding in a masculine climate was essential to produce great battlefield leaders; that graduates went into combat

branches from which women were excluded. Regardless of his views—shared by many at that time—Congress and the President ordered the Academy to pry open its doors in 1976.

Generations of West Pointers had been taught to regard disagreeable orders with a snappy salute and the Academy found itself hoisted on its own petard. The decision was handed down less than a year before a new class was to report. A rushed effort ensued; a last-minute campaign to attract enough qualified females to fill out a class, arrangements for living quarters, latrines, uniforms—all the mundane details of cleaning up a male locker room and making it habitable for women.

But no matter how energetically West Point prepared, problems were inevitable. And they came. It was the most radical change West Point had ever been required to swallow and some did not do so gracefully. The most recalcitrant were upperclassmen who saw West Point's compliance as a Titanic surrender to a preposterous blunder. One upperclassman wrote that, "I feel it is my duty to the alumni and the entire Army to run out as many females as possible." One hundred nineteen females passed through the sallyport on July 1, 1976; only sixty-two were destined to graduate. That first class of females found themselves taunted, ridiculed, even threatened by upperclassmen. The press watched with hostile eyes for every embarrassment, every misstep, any sign the Academy was either diffident or sheepish in its adoption of women into the Long Gray Line.

Actually, the faculty and leaders of the Academy were anything but skittish. If anything, the opposite. They lunged for complete integration;

THE FIRST FEMALE FIRST CAPTAIN

Kristin Baker was to the army born; her father, Robert M. Baker, was USMA Class of 1966, and served as commander of the Proving Grounds at Yuma, Arizona, while his daughter went to West Point. Baker was a presidential appointment, majoring in Human Factors Psychology. At the Academy, she played soccer and went cross-country skiing and sang in the choir. She was picked out early for her leadership qualities and military bearing. The woman who said her style was "to encourage people to do things for themselves" was Command Sergeant Major as a plebe, and Regimental Commander during the "Beast Barracks," Cadet Basic Training, in 1989. Her ability impressed her superiors—her straightforward bearing, discipline, especially her ability to see to the essence of a problem—and in her senior year, she was appointed First Captain.

If following in the footsteps of other Cadet Captains like Pershing, MacArthur and Westmoreland rattled her she never showed it. She performed superbly. She received some crank mail, and anti-feminist Phyllis Schlafly publically questioned what such world tough guys as Saddam Hussein would think, but Kristin Baker just went right on and made history, the first woman to command the cadet corps at the United States Military Academy.   —C.H.

At her graduation First Captain Kristin Baker posed with Colin Powell, then Chairman of the Joint Chiefs of Staff.

mixing men and women together in the barracks, issuing identical uniforms, eradicating as many lines of separation as practicable. It was a risky strategy but maintaining a unified Corps of Cadets was the only course they felt would work in the long run.

Still, the Academy found itself inventing rules on the fly, struggling to manage situations it had possibly foreseen but not fully comprehended, inescapable situations when men and women live in close quarters, from romantic relations between male and female cadets, to handling sexual infractions, to pregnancies.

In her book *In the Men's House: An Inside Account of Life in the Army by One of West Point's Female Graduates*, Carol Barkalow, a member of that first class, recalled that, "The Plebe Hop was the first time our whole class came together for a party . . . This caused some unanticipated distress among certain members of the administration, who were reportedly perturbed by the sight of mirror-image couples dancing in short hair and dress gray trousers. A rule was subsequently passed declaring that women could attend all future hops in trousers, but they had to wear skirts if they wanted to dance."

One of the more notorious incidents concerned a male and female cadet caught in bed together behind closed doors in the barracks. When the punishments for "acts of affection prejudicial to the discipline and good order" were posted on a public board the names of the two cadets were deleted. This was a good sign; the Academy obviously understood the need for discretion in such delicate matters. Yet to everybody's consternation and puzzlement the male cadet received a more severe punishment than the female.

Female officers were rushed into faculty assignments to serve as role models, female teams were added, physical standards were adjusted, even the mess hall diet was modified. Many alumni howled that the school was being emasculated, but the school's leaders argued that the dramatic changes were needed to make the integration succeed.

West Point limped into the eighties, licking its wounds and reeling from nearly two decades of bone-jarring criticism and somersaulting changes. The Army was aware the Academy was wounded and off-balance. It needed help. The decision had been made that future superintendents would serve four years and West Point would be their final assignment, a necessary step to add stability and free up superintendents to do their jobs without having to look over their shoulders, without worrying how it would impact their careers. Civilian professors were added to the faculty, as the Naval Academy had been doing for decades, to add academic stability. General Andrew J. Goodpaster came willingly out of retirement with a one-star reduction to help usher in the reforms and cauterize the resulting trauma.

Alison Jones in Nairobi

ON AUGUST 7, 1998, Cadet First Class Alison Jones '99 was in Nairobi, close enough to the American Embassy that she felt the shockwave when it blew up.

"In seconds, the streets turned to chaos," Jones recalled. The twenty-one-year-old cadet from Baltimore had come to Nairobi as a summer intern, writing a paper on HIV for the U.S. State Department; she had only been in Kenya for a month. "I heard women and children screaming and I just ran, on instinct, toward the embassy. Black smoke was pouring out of the back of the building, which sustained the most damage. By this time, people were in complete shock." Reaching the scene, Jones quickly organized a four-person rescue team and led it into the ruined building.

Starting at the top floor they searched the wreckage for trapped and wounded victims. "It was difficult to see as there was dust, smoke and electrical wires everywhere. We didn't find anyone alive on the fourth or third floors, but we could hear someone screaming on the second floor."

On the second floor Jones and her team found a man whose leg had been crushed under fallen debris. They freed him; Jones improvised a splint from a piece of ceiling beam and talked the man through the painful process of applying it. While two of her team carried him out, she and the other person kept up the search, "but after that, everyone I found was dead."

One of those she found dead was a personal friend. "He was chest-deep in rubble," she recalled. "I had been screaming his name, desperately looking for him. Once I saw him, I said, 'He's dead.' But as soon as I said it, I wanted to take it back, as if taking it back would somehow make it less real.

"For that split second, my emotions took over," she said. "But [I knew] I had to shift back into 'mission mode.'" I needed to focus and react, and I remember thinking, 'What can we do now?'"

Leaving the building, she recognized the developing security problem. "Though much of the smoke had cleared by that time, there was still chaos. People were climbing in and out of the back of the building and street kids were just wandering in and out. Some of the engineers in the area said the building was quite unstable." Jones took charge, roped off the front of the building and set up a central medical and supply-collection point. "People were arriving with ropes, blankets, shovels —anything to help. The most important thing was to create order from chaos."

For her cool-headed heroism, in 1999 Alison Jones became only the second West Point cadet in ten years to receive the Soldier's Medal, awarded for acts of extraordinary bravery in peacetime. Social Sciences Instructor Maj. Kimberly Field, one of her mentors, said, "Her West Point training in combination with her natural abilities served those around her extraordinarily well," praising Jones' "maturity, adventurous spirit, discipline, deep-thinking ability, enthusiasm, humility, compassion and athleticism." Jones tried to keep the whole thing in perspective. "I have mixed emotions about the award. I'm happy I'm getting it, but I just did what was right to do. People from the street gave all they could give to help, and I don't think I gave any more than anybody else." Graduating in 1999, she has gone into the Military Police. —*C.H.*

When General Palmer became superintendent in 1986, he laid the keel to overturn the Fourth Class System. Known pejoratively as the Plebe system, the tradition had been a cornerstone of the Academy experience for nearly a hundred years. And had been controversial from the start. Some swore it was an inalienable test of fire to sift the weak from the strong, the animating ingredient in the alchemy that transformed shy, fidgety youngsters into bold, confident leaders. Others saw it as arbitrary and cruel, a system that often veered into abuse, that taught negative leadership and eliminated as many good cadets as bad. Generations of plebes had marveled at the

The old riding hall was remodeled into Thayer Hall, now a major classroom building. Above: The structure's roof was removed but the original footprint retained. The two photographs come from a 1959 Howitzer.

biting irony of being forced to memorize and recite Schofield's Definition of Leadership—that opens with that celebrated verse, "The discipline which makes the soldiers in a free country reliable in battle is not to be gained by harsh and tyrannical treatment." One graduate of that era remembered being to forced to recite Schofield's Definition with ten upperclassmen screaming abuse in his face, leaving him to wonder "hadn't they read it?" But regardless of its merits or demerits, thousands of living graduates had survived the Plebe System and believed in it, some with theological zeal. The screaming and yelling, the pressure to memorize volumes of data and quotations and military facts, and spout them instantly and flawlessly under scorching pressure, the whole year-long ritual of plebe duties, and bracing, and eating squared meals, were ingrained into the West Point myth.

What replaced it was a system with the bulky title of CLDS—Cadet Leadership Development System—that emphasized more inspiring forms of leadership, expanded responsibilities for the upperclasses, the development of motivational skills that convey directly into the style of leadership expected of troop officers in the Army. Hazing, yelling, and insulting abuse were out. Cool, dispassionate, professional conduct was in.

Even as all these changes were ushered in, West Point fell victim to a new trend. Throughout its fabled history, whenever asked to prove its

value, West Point could always point proudly to the Army's general officer corps and the dominance of graduates in its ranks. In 1960, nearly 70 per cent of the general officers corps wore the distinctive ring on their third finger. It was a rare feat—a mark of great distinction—for an OCS or ROTC man to battle his way to the top. By 1985, according to a series of skeptical articles in the *Armed Forces Journal*, only 27 per cent of Army generals were graduates.

The reasons were many. The dominance of West Pointers with stars bred a sense of favoritism that—no matter how doggedly denied—resulted in animosity, distrust, and complaints of discrimination among other officers. West Pointers were referred to as "ring-knockers" and it was not intended as a compliment. Also, because of the irascible and prolonged nature of the Cold War, America's peacetime army was kept large and the proportion of officers who marched out of the fortress on the Hudson shrank steadily, notwithstanding the doubling of the Corps.

Still, questions about West Point's muscularity were inescapable. And of equal concern to the Academy rose the fear that non-grads who acquired three and four stars felt no loyalty to the school: they wouldn't energetically defend it, preserve its funding, come to its aid in times of crisis, fend off its critics in Congress.

So how to justify the Academy in this new

The West Point Band (here at top right, with the Cadet Corps parading in front of the statue of George Washington) was first formed in 1817. Its uniforms have remained unchanged for 100 years: dark blue tunics with red piping and white chevrons and service stripes, white cords and waist belts, and blue side pouches. Starting with Ulysses S. Grant in 1873, the first West Point graduate to become President, the band has played at many Inaugurals.

era? If it was no longer the incubator of future generals, what was it? If less expensive commissioning venues—OCS and ROTC—were manufacturing officers of equal caliber, what then justified the comparatively greater cost of a West Point lieutenant?

These were difficult, nagging questions without clear answers. And even as West Point wrestled with the reasons, it was suddenly blindsided by a geostrategic earthquake. The Berlin Wall almost overnight crumbled into a scrapheap of concrete, and the Soviet Union—for half a century a reliably cantankerous threat—simply shattered into pieces. With barely a whisper of warning the Cold War was over. With Washington policymakers scrambling to make sense of the chaotic new world, one political philosopher even predicted it was "The End of History." But

nowhere was this bewilderment more sharply felt than West Point.

Since the opening days of World War II, the Academy always had a tactile threat, a defining mission it could point to for the harsh four year passage and ensuing career of service and sacrifice expected of West Pointers. The survival of the nation, the fate of the entire world were at stake. These were inspiring themes, and palpably real. What would replace them? And what did it mean for a corps that had grown to over 4,400 cadets, pumping nearly a thousand new lieutenants into the Army every year?

But before an answer could be found, the finger tap of fate intervened again. In 1991 Saddam Hussein's forces invaded Kuwait and a four-star graduate, Norman Schwarzkopf, was dispatched with a powerful force to vanquish Iraq's bloated military. After nine months of careful preparation, he unleashed one of the most stunning victories in the history of warfare; a brilliant battleplan that mixed cunning and lightning maneuver into a pulverizing cyclone, a stratagem he later credited in his memoir to his "first lessons in Military Art at West Point." The ground campaign was over in less than 100 hours. The world was awestruck.

It was the most televised war in history, portrayed like a long-running football match, with frequent sideline interviews, with a blitzkrieg of briefings by the generals and their lieutenants, with picturesque coverage of the parries and thrusts of battle. And the picture that zoomed into America's living rooms was an Army completely reformed and recovered from the agonies of Vietnam.

The Gulf War was a trial by fire for the Army, and it was equally a vindication for West Point and the graduates it continued to pump into the Army, of all the sweeping changes that invariably

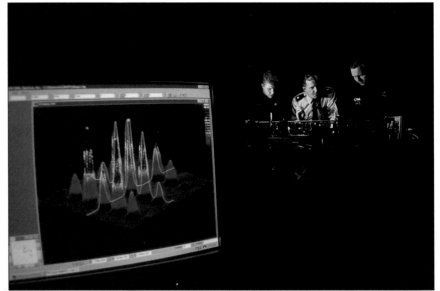

Cybertechnology has become an invaluable military tool, and no cadet goes without a computer. Left: Plebes carry boxes of computers into their barracks. The war planners above use computer simulations and projections to refine strategy and tactics.

worked their way into the leadership ranks of the service. Gone were the drug problems so prevalent in the Army of the late sixties and seventies. Gone were the racial tensions—stunningly, the Army and West Point were heralded with a cultural feat the larger society needed to study and emulate. And it was of course a test of the sexually integrated military, since over ten percent of the forces sent to decimate Saddam were women.

In one brigade from the 101st Airborne Division, the commander who trained and deployed the brigade, and his executive officer were West Pointers. Of his three infantry battalion commanders, two were West Point classmates, and the third had been a cadet who failed math, went to another military college and was commissioned right on schedule with his old classmates. The Brigade Operations officer and all three battalion executive officers were West Point classmates. The Brigade supply officer was a West Pointer, as were a large number of company commanders and platoon leaders.

On the rainy night of February 25, 1991, the lead elements of that brigade landed by helicopter next to highway 8, the enemy's main line of retreat into Iraq. They found themselves

poised precariously between two Iraqi tank brigades and a special forces division. Major Peter Kinney '75, the Brigade Operations Officer, remembered, "We were furiously erecting a berm around the Tactical Operations Center and preparing for the huge battle we knew would come in the morning, when inside my head flashed the faces of those West Point instructors and tactical officers, all Vietnam veterans, who educated me for this task . . . for this day. My beast barracks company commander, LTC Hank Kinnison, commanded the battalion directly behind my position. It was one continuous chain . . . generation to generation. It was weird. It was like that little ditty from the stanza of that song, *The Corps*, about how we all grip hands. I figured they would be proud of what I was doing, what they had done to prepare me, to get me here . . . I found myself hoping I didn't let them down."

In various incarnations, the same thinking filtered through the minds of many West Pointers in that war. General Barry McCaffrey, who earned two Distinguished Service Crosses in Vietnam and commanded the 24th Mechanized Infantry Division in the Gulf, later described it as the event "that restored the aura of glory" that Vietnam had wrenched from West Point and the Army.

That moment of glory, however, was short-lived. Within a year after the Gulf War the Academy and its offspring found themselves falling through new trapdoors. The Army was sharply downsized, losing forty percent of its maneuver battalions. The Defense Budget was slashed and

In the Gulf War, General Norman Schwarzkopf '56 delivered a Stonewall-Jackson-like left hook that destroyed the tanks of Saddam Hussein and banished the lingering ghosts of Vietnam in a matter of days. In this photo, Schwarzkopf, center, arrives at a desert command to visit with troops from other countries during Operation Desert Shield.

2000   2001   2002

■ Graduates 1802–2000: 57,552; 1991–2001: 9,645.
■ The West Point Athletic Department changed the name of the Army sports teams from the Cadets to the Black Knights, and changed the logo from a kicking mule with an A branded on its flank to a sword-wielding black knight astride a horse. They retained the Army mule as a mascot.

■ Kick-off of year-long celebration of West Point's bicentennial.

■ March 16. Founder's Day marks the two hundredth anniversary of President Thomas Jefferson's signing of the bill creating the United States Military Academy.

modernization was virtually terminated. A stream of military operations followed—Mogadishu, Haiti, Rwanda, Bosnia, and Kosovo—missions that enjoyed thin public and political support; where the soldier's bedrock quest for victory was out of character; where the combat leader's instinct for bold action was anathema.

Thousands of West Pointers left the Army's ranks during the downsizing and the years that followed. Many were encouraged to. On the June day when the class of 1992 celebrated its fifth reunion over 50 per cent were already civilians. Just as the Vietnam era faculty faced the stormy task of motivating cadets for an unpopular war, the faculty of the nineties had to instill ardor in its charges to enter a sharply downsizing army, to serve as military governors of Balkan villages, to separate warring factions, to mediate local squabbles that had at most a very convoluted relationship to American security.

Once again, West Pointers found themselves engaged in dangerous tasks while the American people debated the strategic usefulness of their missions, much less the suitability of committing the world's best war machine to operations that seemed only peripherally military in character. Still, West Pointers did as MacArthur sagely advised in his famous address. They left the political debates to others. They did their duty. They snapped off an obligatory salute and went where they were told and tried to make Amer-

ica proud of them. As they continue to do today in dozens of places around the globe, over-watching fragile ceasefires, enforcing deterrence in Korea and Southwest Asia, tying together America's farflung alliances, keeping the American Army trained and ready for war.

It is a forbidding task to sum up the ebb and flow of this tempestuous forty-year period that began with MacArthur's Farewell Speech and brings us to the present, that one West Point historian aptly titled, "The Years of Turmoil." How to characterize the Academy's accomplishments and failures, its changes and constants, what challenges and niggling doubts it bequeaths to the next group of young men and women who stumble tentatively up to that implacable Cadet in the Red Sash to begin their four year trial?

They enter an Academy that proved its quintessential purpose. Even in the grip of a prolonged, bloody, unpopular war, West Point remained a magnet for talented and courageous young patriots willing to step forward and lead troops into battle. As it continued to be throughout the most prolific economic boom in America's history—the nineties—when so many gifted young people dreamt of Porsches instead of combat boots, of homes in the Hamptons instead of puptents in the Balkans, of joining the Forbes 500 instead of leading Army platoons.

Even outside of the military sphere, its graduates and even some that spent only a year or two within its granite walls touched American life in a hundred ways and a hundred fields. There was Dr. Timothy Leary, the living talisman of the drug generation, who like Poe and Whistler, had stumbled through the wrong sally-port for his particular talents and ambitions. There were Frank Borman and Buzz Aldrin and Ed White, among the most famous of the early

astronauts, the latter of whom gave his life on the launch pad when his capsule was engulfed in flames. There were great barons of industry, from Lauris Norstad who after a full and distinguished military career became Chairman of Owens Corning, to Jim Kimsey who helped found America Online. In fact, so many West Pointers led great corporations that in the eighties the Harvard Business School convened a study to see what attributes West Point drilled into its graduates that Harvard needed to emulate. And there were Alexander Haig and Fred Buzhardt who helped hold the country together during Watergate, the latter who destroyed his health in the process, the former of whom went on to become the first academy graduate to serve as Secretary of State. And there were Brent Scowcroft, National Security Advisor to both Presidents Ford and Bush, and Barry McCaffrey, the drug czar under President Clinton.

And the Academy itself—jokingly portrayed by its inhabitants as an institution with "200 years of tradition untouched by progress"—not only changed, it adapted in ways the rest of society admires. It did not survive the turmoil; it surmounted it. Consider the Class of 2005 that joined the long gray line in the summer of 2001. Of the 1,193 new cadets that reported to Michie Stadium were 193 women, 101 black Americans, ninety-two Asian-Americans, seventy-one Hispanic-Americans, and ten American Indians. It wasn't a perfect reflection of American society. It was a reasonable shadow, though.

Nearly 50 per cent of the women in that first integrated class departed before graduation. The attrition of women in the last few years has fallen to around 27 per cent, roughly the same as male attrition, an indication of the progress that has been made.

And beyond any other measure, West Point sustained its role as the soul of the Army officer's corps. Through all the turmoil and agony, it stubbornly devoted itself to the preparation of officers for the blistering rigors and demands of battle, the distinct ethical challenges of a military career, to producing leaders. It is where future Army officers come to be inculcated with the military ethos, equipped with the mindset of Duty, Honor, Country, and the harsh recognition that sometimes the pursuit of those three cherished words requires the ultimate sacrifice. In the words of General Norman Schwarzkopf, it remained, "the keeper of the holy flame of military professionalism."

And if there is an enduring challenge that emerges from these four decades, it is that West Pointers cannot encase themselves inside a nostalgic cocoon. The moment they put on Dress Gray they inherit a Sisyphean task. They will never be allowed to rest on the wide wings of past glories and dead heroes. It will never be enough to point at the national infrastructure engineered by graduates; at the great battles and wars won; at the post-World War reshaping of modern Europe and East Asia led by Academy graduates; at the winning of the Cold War and the terrible price paid in blood every time that struggle lurched into conflict; at the more recent, lopsided victories in Grenada, Panama, and the Gulf; at 200 years of splendid service to the nation in peace and war.

On their shoulders lies the haunting responsibility to make the past prologue to the future. As MacArthur so wisely warned, ". . . always in our ears ring the ominous words of Plato, that wisest of all philosophers, 'Only the dead have seen the end of war.'"

Proud parents pin their new lieutenant's bars on two beaming graduates (left). Under difficult conditions West Point has achieved a level of racial and gender equality and harmony the rest of the nation could do well to emulate. For years the "goat"—the lowest-ranking cadet in the graduating class—received a dollar from each of his classmates. The practice was discontinued in 1977; here the last class Goat is presented with his bag of money.

Hats in the Air: The setting is the graduation ceremonies at Michie Stadium in June 1990. Men and women, minutes before members of the First Class of cadets, celebrate their new status as freshly-minted Second Lieutenants in the Army.

A Night at West Point
by Arthur Miller

A morning in 1971. The day's news at breakfast. Vietnam, like a canker sore in the mouth that will not heal. The war is killing hope in this country, where will it end, with what internal catastrophe? My phone rings, a mild surprise since it is hardly nine o'clock.

A Colonel something from West Point? A joke? He wants me to come and speak to the cadets and faculty. Oh right, I now recall a letter in yesterday's mail.

"Yes, I did get your letter yesterday, but I'm afraid you've got the wrong Miller."

"Are you the writer?"

"Yes, but I've been against our participation in this war since we got in. I spoke at the first teach-in at the University of Michigan and many times since . . . ."

"Yes, would you consider coming to the Academy?"

Can this be serious? The lion's mouth is opening to receive my head? "Okay, but let me read the letter again and I'll let you know immediately."

I read and reread the Colonel's invitation searching for an excuse to decline. A day passes, and another day. West Point is the heart of our darkness, the deaf, dumb and blind academy turning out young killers of the dream. But what excuse do I have for declining, aside from not wanting to be beaten to death, figuratively of course, by outraged heavily armed patriots? I probably owe it to my convictions to go precisely there to express them, but what earthly good could that do when they must be long past listening to anybody but their high commanders. As it happens, I decide to make the talk for a particular reason. A week or two before this phone call my wife, the photographer Inge Morath, our eight year-old daughter Rebecca and I had returned from a trip to Cambodia. Inge had wanted to photograph the temples of Anghor Wat before they utterly disappeared in the expanding war.

The lecture hall was packed with Plebes, and the back wall seemed lined with eager-looking officers, most of them quite young, their chests covered with decorations. One man, or rather one moustache, stood out. It belonged to an older Colonel whose head was bald, his uniform weighed down with medals, and a pugnacious bright red guards' moustache bristling fiercely, right and left under his nose. I immediately decided that this was the one who had come to trample me to death.

My mind-set vis-à-vis West Point was not altogether unilinear. Born in the second year of the First World War, I had grown up in the Twenties when the most blatant patriotism was in the air. In fact, by my twelfth year I was trying to convince my Uncle Moe, who had driven an ammunition wagon at the front in France, to help get me into West Point once I had finished high school. It was a time of life when I was saluting in all directions. Moe was incredulous; he had contracted tuberculosis in the service and would spend the rest of his life trying to beat it, dying in his late thirties of the disease. War, he tried to explain to my deaf ears, was hell and had to be avoided at any cost. I respected him too much to disagree openly, but deep down I would have loved to have been a soldier, an image of myself which would soon fade.

Facing the young cadets and officers, with what I believed would be very discouraging news from their viewpoint, I had a couple of regretful minutes on the platform, but there was no escape. The war, of course, was raging and men were dying, our own as well as Cambodians now.

In short, as in Vietnam itself, I believed we had no better prospects of a real victory in Cambodia that would justify the destruction we were wreaking there. The road inside Cambodia which the Vietnamese were using would doubtless be interrupted for a bit, but it would surely be reusable in short order as we had learned was the case in Vietnam itself even after dropping more bombs there than had been dropped on Europe during all of World War II. In a word, this war was impossible not because of a military failure but a political one. Inevitably to the Vietnamese and no doubt the Cambodian mind now, we had assumed the evil identity of French colonialism with all its unforgotten indignities for the masses of both countries. Finally, our cold war mentality had seduced us into believing that Hanoi and its leadership were merely lackeys of Moscow, but that the time had surely arrived when we had to confess that our opponent was indeed a genuine anti-colonial nationalist and not somebody's foreign hired gun. The tragedy was that the Vietnamese would no doubt end in a rigid Communist system that probably had no future, and that we would for a long time stand as the enemy of their aspirations for a better life. The whole war, in short, was a dreadful, bloody miscalculation on our part, and should be stopped as quickly as possible.

Silence. Questions were asked for. A cadet with a powerful build—I remember the thickness of his wrestler's neck—raised his hand. "Why is this man allowed to speak to us?" he asked, an outraged look in his blue eyes. The chairman-Colonel explained that it was important for them to hear all sides. Looking around at the young audience and their scrubbed faces, and at their officer teachers, all of them Vietnam vets who had rotated back here to teach before returning to battle, I couldn't help sympathize deeply with the dilemma which I thought I saw reflected in the cadets' eyes—their pride in their upcoming profession and their reaction to what I had tried to tell them about the war they would soon enter.

Now the colonel I had designated as my certain enemy raised his hand at the back of the hall. Oh God, I'm dead, I thought. "I was the American military attaché in Phnom Penh for nine years," he announced. There was a good long pause. "Everything this man has been telling you . . . is the truth." With which he turned aggressively and walked out of the room. Astonished, I felt choked with gratitude.

A young colonel came up to me and offered me dinner at his home. He seemed pleased with my little speech so I had no hesitation in accepting.

Dinner, as it turned out, was for not only me but half a dozen other young officers and their wives. It was very quickly obvious that these young commanders, none of them much over thirty, I thought, were physically and intellectually an uncommon lot of battle-scarred academics, in effect, teachers of philosophy, English, math, sciences. In no time they were telling me about having to change into civilian clothes on trips to New York to avoid being either cursed by passers by or actually spat on if they were in uniform. Again and again came the same litany—that the army had not wanted this war but that it had been handed them by politicians who—without saying this in so many words—were opportunistic, irresponsible men.

I left our dinner at nearly one in the morning. By that time I was feeling enormous respect for these West Point officers who were entrapped in a tragic dilemma they had not made. If they had ever believed in the war they certainly no longer did now, yet they were obliged to return to Vietnam to lead men into battle for a cause they knew was at a minimum futile and possibly even morally wrong. Driving home through the night on an empty highway, I saw them as a sort of tragic priesthood pledged to a holy cause—their country's defense even at the cost of their lives, a cause that had been bitterly traduced. For duty demanded not only their own sacrifice but that of men whom they, in effect, would be required to convince of the rightness of the killing. For me it was painful to recall the implicit hope which I thought I saw in them that I might be able to help end the carnage by writing about it in the spirit of my talk earlier that day. The fact, however, was that I believed—after all the protests and the anti-war articles and books and plays and movies—that the war had no visible end in sight.

I left West Point aware of these soldiers' anguish in a way I had not begun to imagine before. Above all, the mystery of duty hung before me; it was driven, after all, by the tangled power of a kind of love without which it would be nothing. The immensity of our Vietnam tragedy was never so moving as it was that night.

WEST POINT TODAY

A cadet in rain gear (left) directs traffic during the 2001 graduation ceremony. Trophy Point commands a magnificent view of the Hudson. The monument's guns suggest the beginnings of West Point as Revolutionary War fortress.

PHOTOS BY INGE MORATH

BORN IN GRAZ, AUSTRIA, INGE MORATH began her long and distinguished career as a photographer in 1951. She assisted master photographers Ernst Haas and Henri Cartier-Bresson; world renowned, she has won numerous awards for her work. Widely traveled, she is especially known for capturing on film the essential character of a landscape (right) and the inward drama of a human face (above). Her photographs of West Point reveal both the enormous dignity and traditions of the institution and the excitement and accomplishment of the young men and women studying here.

Douglas MacArthur (left) served as superintendent of West Point early on in his extraordinary career. Walter Hancock sculpted this statue, which stands in front of the Eisenhower Barracks. Above: Cadets wait in formation before marching to the dining hall.

*During the Sandhurst
Competition, a rigorous
test of military skills and
physical training, these
cadets (above), fully
equipped, scale a twelve
foot wall. The observer on
the right judges their form
and speed.*

One of the tests during the Sandhurst Competition is to cross a river on a single rope bridge (top). This woman cadet has almost made it across. Cadets below rush their inflatable raft into the water.

At the end of five weeks of Beast Barracks, the fully-equipped plebes (left top) march twenty-five miles to West Point. Arriving on the ski slope, they stop for an hour's rest before entering their newly assigned barracks. Above: the new cadets march past the Superintendent's house, the second oldest building on the campus. Even after twenty-five miles they keep excellent order. The young men left are airing their feet and resting after the march.

Overleaf: since MacArthur's superintendency, organized sports have been crucial to developing the cadets' physical conditioning. Soccer with its nonstop action clearly has these young men focused and intense. Insets: top: Two cadets engage in close quarters combat practice. Middle: a woman cadet works out on the gym horse. Bottom: Some cadets come to West Point not knowing how to swim. This cadet is practicing survival swimming weighed down with his full kit.

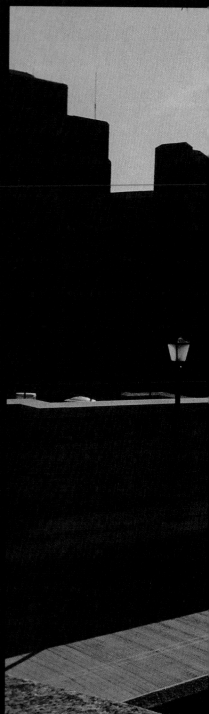

For cadets the rigorous physical training and demanding academic work pays off in visible pride and confidence. Left, top: A woman cadet walks to class. Bottom, at graduation, a female company commander beams with a sense of accomplishment. This page: top: The woman instructor taking the salute is Lt. Renecke, executive officer, the air assault school, Camp Smith, a nearby facility used by West Point. Since women first arrived at West Point they have consistently performed important jobs in areas that used to be considered appropriate only for men. Below: A sailboat on the Hudson passes beneath the ramparts of the Military Academy.

Photo Credits

ACKNOWLEDGMENTS AND CREDITS

The Editors are particularly grateful to:
Alan Aimone, Special Collections, USMA Library for his extensive knowledge of USMA history
Andrea Hamburger, Public Affairs Office, USMA for her coordination of the Bicentennial projects
Ted Spiegel for his special expertise in representing West Point history through photography

The Editors would also like to thank the following for their assistance:
Mike Albright, Athletic Department, USMA
Suzanne Christophe, Special Collections, USMA Library
Joe Dineen, Admissions Department, USMA
Mike Fusco, Creative Imaging Department, USMA
Kirk Gohlke, Admissions Department, USMA
Sylvia Graham, Editor, Publications, Association of Graduates
Colonel Seth Hudgins, President of the Association of Graduates
Laura Kreiss, Washington DC
Renee Klish, U. S. Army Art Collection, Washington DC
Alicia Malden, Special Collections and Archives, USMA
David Meschutt
Jay Olejniczak, Vice President of Publications, Association of Graduates
David Reel, Curator of Paintings, USMA Museum

PHOTO CREDITS

Museum and Archival Photography by Ted Spiegel

American Philosophical Society: 40 bottom
AP/Wide World Photos: 138-139, 188 right, 197, 198, 199 top, 229, 245, 246 bottom, 248 right, 260, 268 top, 273
Army Art Collection, U. S. Army Center of Military History: 96-97, 186-187
Art Archive, London/Musee de Guerre: 146-147
Association of Graduates, United States Military Academy: 122 top left, 123 top right
Beinecke Library, Yale University: pages 41 top, 41 bottom
Marshall Best '74: 251

Braintree MA Historical Society, Sylvanus Thayer House: 45
John F. Brewer Jr.: 211 top
Charleston Renaissance Gallery. Robert M. Hicklin Jr., Inc., Charleston SC: 91
Chicago Historical Society: 28-29, 84-85
Corbis: 54 middle, 62 top left, 82 bottom right, 140 (Leonard de Selva),187 top, 190 top left, 201, 205 top, 218 top, 220 top left, 249, 276 (Bob Krist)
Corbis/Bettmann: 101 top, 151, 167 top left, 208-209, 209, 220 top right
Culver Pictures: 82 top, 131 top left
Decatur House, National Trust for Historic Preservation, photo by Greg Schaler: 58 left
John Easterbrook: 137 bottom
Bill Frei/Pendor Natural Color: 242 bottom
Fruitlands Museums, Harvard, Massachusetts: 116 top
Granger Collection: 64-65,105 bottom, 121, 133 top, 133 bottom, 139 top, 161 top, 177, 191, 199 bottom
Henry Grosinsky: 92-93, 100
Joyce Shea Himka: 225 top right
Michael Hood '67: 263 left
Cadet Kelly Howard: 272 left
Imperial War Museum: 160 top, 202-203
Independence National Historic Park: page 40 top
John F. Kennedy Library: 263 right
Lyndon Baines Johnson Library: 264 top right
Library of Congress: 19 left, 24 top, 48-49, 59 bottom, 60-61, 62 bottom, 93 top, 97 top, 101 bottom right, 101 middle, 105 top, 127 top right, 133 top, 137 top left
Library of Congress, courtesy Northwestern University Library: 175 middle
Library of Congress/Photri-Microstock: 80
Louisiana State Museum: 62 top
Massachusetts Commandery Military Order of the Loyal Legion and the U. S. Army Military History Institute: 92 top middle
Massachusetts Historical Society: 19 right
Metropolitan Museum of Art: 112-113
Inge Morath: 23 top, 258-259, 284-295
Museum of the City of New York. Gift of John W. Campbell: 154
Eleanor S. Brockenbrough Library, Museum of the Confederacy, Richmond, Virginia: pages 63, 82 left
Museum of the Marian Fathers, Fawley Court, Henley on

Index

Boldface numbers indicate illustrations.

Abramovitz, Max, 267
Abrams, Creighton, 264, **264**
Academic Building, **78**
Academy Reorganization Act, 19
Adams, John, 35, **38**
Adams, John Quincy, 38, 43
Air Cadet Memorial, 181
Air Force Academy, U.S., 119, 149, 215-16
Aldrin, Edwin E. "Buzz," 252, 256, **256**, 278-79
Alexander, Edward Porter, 69, **75**, 143
Allen, Hannibal Montesque, 18
Ambrose, Stephen E., 145
American Expeditionary Force (AEF), 135-36, 147, 149-51, **154, 155, 161,** 201
American Society of Civil Engineers, 35, 267
America Online, 15, 279
Ames, Adelbert, 88, 90, **90**
Anaconda Plan, 83
Anderson, Edward, 75
Anderson, Joseph, 269
Anderson, Robert, 67, **81, 259**
Anderson Fountain, **259**
"Anderson Platoon, The," 269
André, John, 22, **24**
Andrews, Lincoln Clark, 135, 148
Appomattox Court House, surrender at, 89-90, 104, **104, 105,** 108-9
Armed Forces Journal, 275
Armistead, Lewis A., 43, 67, **92, 93,** 94, **94**
Army Air Corps, U.S., 180-81, **191, 192,** 202, 204-5, **219, 237**
Army Corps of Engineers, U.S., 25, **51,** 140
Army in Vietnam, The (Krepenevich), 263-64
Army-Navy games, 135, 141, 174, 197, 201, 224, 234, **234,** 236, 238-39, **238,** 239, 240, **243-53,** 243, 245, 251, **256-57, 269**
Army War College, 166, 204-5, 219
Arnold, Benedict, 22, **24,** 39, 258
Arnold, Henry "Hap," 202, **237**

Arsenic and Old Lace, 192, 202
Arthur, Chester A., 120-21
Assault At West Point, 214
Assembly, 217
Association of Graduates of the U.S. Military Academy, 108, 118, 267, 269
Atkinson, Rick, 216
Atlanta, Battle of, 68-69, 79, 94-102, **101,** 121

Baker, Hobey, 216
Baker, Kristin M., 253, 268, 273, **273**
Baker, Newton D., **153**
Baker, Robert M., 273
Baldwin, Alec, 214
Balkan wars, 278
Ball, Charles P., 82
Balling, Peter Hansen, **98**
Baltimore & Ohio Railroad, 53
Bannock uprising, 121
Barclift, Nelson, 189
Barkalow, Carol, 273
Baron, William Amhurst, 24
Bartlett, B. W., 189
Bartlett, William H. C., 52, **67,** 69
Bartlett Hall, 144
Basinger, William Elon, 50
Bastogne, Battle of, **196**
Bataan, Battle of, 163, **187,** 202, 235
Batista, Fulgencio, 174
Battle Monument, 104, 141
Baumer, William H., Jr., 174
Beast Barracks, 174, 185, **211,** 214, 216-17, 273, **291**
Beaugureau, Francis, **219**
Beauregard, Pierre Gustave Toutant, 48, **62,** 65, **81,** 83-84, **89**
Belen Gate, Battle of, 68
Bell, James Franklin, 109
Bell, John F., **41**
Belleau Wood, Battle of, 152-53
Benedict, Jay L., 174
Bentz, Louis, **66**

Bergner, Elizabeth, 192
Berlin Airlift and Blockade, **219**
Berry, Sidney, 272
Best, Marshall, **251**
Beukema, Herman, 174
"Bigger Job Than He Thought For, A," **133**
Black, Frederick, Jr., 269
Black, William Murray, 109
Blaik, Earl H. "Red," 170, 173-74, 177, 194-99, 239, **242, 246,** 247-49, **247, 248,** 251, 258
Blaik, Robert, 247, **247**
Blanchard, Felix "Doc," 199-201, 239, 243, **246**
Bliss, John, 33
Bliss, Tasker Howard, 109, 149
Bliss, William Wallace Smith, **61**
Bloody Angle, Battle of, 69
Blumenson, Martin, 149
Blumner, F., **18**
Blunt, Roger, 269
Bonus Marchers, **167**
Booz, Oscar L., **131,** 134
Borman, Frank, 172, 252, 257, 278-79
Bosnian War, 253
Bouton, Arthur Edward, 148, 153
Bowman, Alexander, 104
Boxer Rebellion, **134**
Bradley, Omar N., **142,** 144-45, **199,** 200, 202, **222, 226,** 242, 262
Bragg, Braxton, 43, **61,** 62-65, **97**
Bray, The, 149
Briggs, James Elbert, 149
Brooke, Richard, **104**
Brooklyn Navy Yard, **55**
Brooks, Leo, 269
Brooks, Vincent K., 267, **268,** 269
Brown, George S., 204
Brown, Reginald, 269
Bucha, Paul, 252
Buckley, William F., Jr., 266
Buckley, William F., Sr., 119

Buckner, Simon Bolivar, Jr., 181, **182,** 187
Buckner, Simon Bolivar, Sr., **84,** 187
Buena Vista, Battle of, **61,** 62-64, **62,** 70
Buffington, Adelbert Rinaldo, 109
Bugle Notes, 143
Bulge, Battle of the, 181, **196**
Bullard, Robert Lee, 136, 151, **159**
Bull Run, Battles of, 48, 88, **89,** 90
Bunker, Paul, 242-43
Bunker Hill, Battle of, 23
Bunting, Josiah, 263-64
Burbeck, Henry, 18
Burma, Burma Road, **188,** 202, 250
Burnside, Ambrose Everett, **98,** 102
Burrows, Larry, **265**
Bush, George H. W., 268, 279
Butler, Benjamin F., 90
Butler, Matthew Calbraith, 141
Butterfield, Daniel, 259, **259**
Butts, Billy, 152
Buzhardt, Fred, 279

Cadet Chapel, 144, 200, 258-59, **258, 259,**
    267
Cadet Life at West Point, (Davis), **69**
Cadet Memorial, 258, **259**
Cagney, James, 213, **214**
"Caisson Song" (Gruber), 143, 207
Caldera, Luis Eduardo, 257
Calvert, Shelby, 253
Cambodia, war in, 282-83
Camp Buckner, 181, 187
Camp Dix, 172, 174
Camp Popolopen, **182,** 184, 187
Camp Smith, **295**
Cantigny, Battle of, 148, 150-52
Capps, Marie T., 259
Carter, Jimmy, 204, 268
Casey, Craig, **272**
Catholic Chapel, 141, 267
Catlin, George, **37**
Cavalry Charge (Remington), **110**
Cedar Creek, Battle of, **103**
Cemetery Hill, Battle of, **92-93,** 121
Cemetery Ridge, Battle of, 69, 89
Cerro Gordo, **62,** 65
Chamberlain, Joshua L., 90
Chambers, Thomas, **8**
Chancellorsville, Battle of, 69, 89-90, **90,** 121
Chapultepec, Battle of, **65,** 67, **92**
Chateau-Thierry, Battle of, 148, 152-55
Chattanooga, Battle of, 104, 121
Cherry Bowl, 267
Chesapeake & Ohio Canal, 53, **55**
Chiang Kai-shek, **188**
Chickamauga, Battle of, **97,** 163-66

China Relief Expedition, **134**
Chippewa, Battle of, 26, **28,** 33, **56**
Christiansen, Bob, 217
Christy, Howard Chandler, **152**
Church, Albert, **67,** 69
Civil War, 15, 35, 43, 45, 48-49, **62,** 68-69, 74-
    75, **75,** 78-79, **78, 80,** 81-105, **84,** 108-9,
    109, 110, 114-15, 118, 121, **131,** 132-33,
    134, 141-43, 145, 149, 158, 171, 173, 210-
    11, 236
Civil War, A (Feinstein), 269
Clark, Mark, **225**
Clark, Wesley, 256
Clarke, Powhatan H., 171
Clay, Lucius D., Jr., 205, **219,** 259
Clinton, Bill, 119, 269, 279
Clitz, Henry B., 104
Cobb, Alma, 253
Cochise, Chief of the Chiricahuas, 121
Cohen, Sears, 204
Cohen, William S., 257
Cold War, 15, **206,** 211, 215-17, **221,** 231,
    275-76, 279, 283
Collins, Mike, 256
Colored Cadet At West Point, A (Flipper), 119
Congress, U.S., 18-22, 24-26, 33-34, 43-45,
    48-49, 52-53, 70, 75, 102-4, 118-20, 129,
    132, 134, 141, 143, 170, 173-74, 184, 224,
    266, 272, 275
Connecticut Yankee in King Arthur's Court, A
    (Twain), 124
Conner, Fox, 135
Cook, Fred A., 162
Corbin, Margaret "Molly," 22, **259**
Corregidor, 163, **187,** 200, 242-43
Cota, Norman D., 259
Côte de Chatillon, Battle of, 162-63
Courtenay, Edward H., 43
Cousey, Bob, **249**
Cowley, Robert, 147-77
Crane, Conrad, 259
Crawford, Samuel Wylie, **81**
Crocker, George, 257
Crockett, Davy, 43-44
Cronkite, Walter, 145
Crook, George, **57,** 68, **98**
Cross, Charles, 89
Crowley, John D., Jr., 205
Crozier, William, 109
Cullum, George Washington, 45, 141-43
Cullum Memorial Hall, **134, 137,** 141-42,
    148, 151, 153, 158, 162, **188**
Currier, Nathaniel, **80**
Cushing, Alonzo, 89, **94**
Custer, George Armstrong, **57,** 74, **74,** 78, **78,**
    88, 90, **98, 103, 104, 105,** 141, 171, 213-

14, 259, **259**
Cutler, Elliot, 177

Dade, Francis Langhorne, 50, **50**
Dade Monument, **50, 259**
Danford, Robert M., 148
Dartmouth College, 19, 24, 45, **45,** 177, 194-
    95, 247
Davenport, Clarence, 268
Davidson, Garrison Holt, 149, 224, 229, 239,
    252
Davies, Charles, 43
Davis, Benjamin O., Jr., 173, **190,** 204, 229,
    268-69
Davis, Benjamin O., Sr., 268-69
Davis, George Breckenridge, 108
Davis, Glenn, 197-201, 239, 243, **246**
Davis, Jefferson, 34-35, 42, 52-53, 62-65, **62,**
    75, **89,** 116
Davis, Jefferson Columbus, **81**
Davis, Theodore, **69**
Davis, William, 119
Dawkins, Pete, 211, 239, **248**
Day, Doris, 213, **214**
Day At West Point Military Academy, New York,
    A, 213
D-Day Invasion, 145, **180,** 181, 187, **194, 195,**
    197, 211-15, **225,** 230, 252, 256, 259, 268
"D-Day Plus Twenty Years," 145
Deane, John, 205-7
Dearborn, Henry, 18
Dearing, James, 89-90
Debating Society, 193
"Deep Night and You," 189
Defense Department, U.S., 45, 86-88, 108,
    144, 167-70, 174, 180, 183, 193, 204, 268-
    69, 277-78
Delafield, Richard, 34, 83, 174
Delafield Pond, 174-75
Dereliction of Duty (McMaster), 263-64
Derussy, Rene, 171
Desert Shield, Operation, 14, **278**
Desert Storm, Operation, 14, 253
D'Este, Carlo W., 107-45
Dewey, George, 136
Dialectical Society, 75
Dickens, Charles, 141
Dickman, Joseph, 153
Dimick, Justin E., 89
Doolittle, James H. "Jimmy," 267
Doubleday, Abner, **81,** 174, 236
Dress Gray, 214
Dress Parades, **127, 169**
Dubner, Stephen J., 259
Duke of West Point, The, 214
du Pont, Henry Algernon, 15, 80-82

Duportail, Louis, 23
Dury, George, **97**

Early, Jubal, 43, **103**
Eaton, Joseph Horace, **61**
Edison, Thomas Alva, 213
Egg Nog Riot, 35
Eglin Field, 224
Egner, Philip, 148
Eichelberger, Robert L., 175-77, **175,** 180,
　　182, 183, 194-95, 199-201
Eisenhower, Dwight D., 14, 33, 129, 132, 135,
　　142, 144-45, **145,** 148, **167, 180,** 187,
　　199, 200, 202, 204, 207, 209-11, 214, 218,
　　224, **226,** 228, **231,** 239-42, 256, 262, 269
Eisenhower, Ida Stover, 262
Eisenhower, John S. D., 187, 207
Eisenhower, Mamie, 145
Eisenhower Barracks, 143
Eisenhower Hall, 257
Eisenstadt, Alfred, **246**
El Molino del Rey, Battle of, 67
Ely, Hanson E., 151-52
Embarkation of the Pilgrims (Weir), 116
Emory, William Hemlsey, **98**
Esquire, 189, 245, **245**
Eustis, William, 24-25, 30
Ewell, Richard S., 48

Fair Oaks, Battle of, 121
Farley, Henry S., 79, 84
Feinstein, John, 269
Fessenden, William Pitt, 103
Field, Kimberly, 274
Five Year Course, 74-75
Fleming, Thomas, 17-44, 172
Fléville, Battle of, 159-62
Flipper, Henry Ossian, 42, 109, 119-21, **119,**
　　174, 269
Flirtation Walk, **137**
Flirtation Walk (film), 213, **213**
Flynn, Errol, 213-14
Foch, Ferdinand, 150-51, 155, 158-59
Foley, Robert, 252
Ford, Gerald, 204, 268, 279
Ford, John, 200, 211, 214, **214,** 251
Forsythe, George I., **264**
Fort Benning, 183-84, 224
Fort Brooke, 50
Fort Clinton, **127**
Fort Dearborn, 19
Fort Donelson, **84,** 187
Fort Erie, 25, **28**
Fort Fisher, 88, 90
Fort Keogh, **110**

Fort King, 50
Fort Lee, 22, 224
Fort Leonard Wood, 175
Fort Putnam, **11, 21,** 141, 200, 257
Fort Sumter, firing on, 48, 75, 78, **80,** 81, **81,**
　　83-86
Fort Thomas, **110**
Fortune, 205
Fort Washington, 22
Foster, John Gray, **81**
Founder's Day, 278
Fowler, James D., Jr., **268**
Fowler, James D., Sr., 204, **268**
Fox Green Beach, **194**
Francis, H. Minton, 268-69
Francis Goes To West Point, 214
Franco-Prussian War, 118, **130**
Freedmen's Bureau, 121, **121**
French, Sam, 62
Furlough Books, **125**
Fussell, Paul, 211

Gabriel, Charles, 242
Gailliard, David Du Bose, 140
Gallagher, P. E., 183-84
Gallico, Paul, 245, **245**
Ganoe, William A., 171-73
Gardiner, George W., 34, 50
Garnett, Richard, **92-93,** 94
Garnett, Robert Selden, **61**
Gavin, James A., 149, **202**
Gettysburg, Battle of, 69, 79, 89-90, **92-93,**
　　94, **94,** 104, 121
Gibson, Channing Wallace, 190
Gibson, James, 25, **28**
Goethals, George Washington, 140, **140,** 258,
　　259
Goethals monument, **258**
Good, Ken, 262
Goodpaster, Andrew J., 273
Gorden, Fred A., 268-69
Graham, J. D., **41**
Grant, Frederick Dent, 108, **259**
Grant, Jesse, 119
Grant, Ulysses S., 14, 48, 51-53, 59-62, **59,** 67-
　　68, 108, **109,** 116, 119, 129, 134, 158, 180,
　　187-89, 193, 235, 262, **276**
Grant Hall, 134, 173
Gratiot, Charles, 43
Graves, Ernest, Jr., 207
Greene, George Sears, 35
Gridley, Oliver, 34
Griffin, Charles, 88-89, **105**
Groves, Leslie R., **205**
Gruber, Edmund Louis "Snitz," 143
Gruenther, Alfred M., 175, 207

Gruenther, Donald Alfred, 207
Gulf War, 230, 268, 276-79, **278**

Haan, William George, 135
Hahn, Herbert, **220**
Haig, Alexander, 200, 266, 279
Haig, Brian, 255-83
Halberstam, David, 262
Hale, Alan, Jr., **214**
Hamilton, Alexander, 18, **19**
Hancock, Almira, 94
Hancock, Walter, **287**
Hancock, Winfield Scott, 49, 90-94, **93**
Hanlon, Tracy, **250,** 253
Harper's Monthly Magazine, 125, 173
Hartinger, James, 252
Havens, Benny, 34-42, **42,** 51-52, 70, 172, 200
Haw, Joseph T., 132, 144
Hazlett, Charles, 89
Herbert, Anthony, 264-65
Herbert Hall, 234
Hill, Ambrose Powell, 49, **82**
Hill, James, 269
Hill 288, Battle of, 162-63
Hilsman, Roger, 207
Hines, John L., 136
Hiroshima, atomic bomb dropped on, 187-89,
　　205
History of the First Locomotive, The (Brown), **52**
Hitchcock, Ethan Allen, 42, 65
Hitler, Adolf, **199,** 204-5, 268
Hodges, Courtney H., 166
Hodges, Harry Foote, 140
Hodgson, P. A., 145
Holland, Cecelia, 22, 33, 39, 44-45, 47-75, 83,
　　116, 119, 121, 124, 129, 132, 140, 165, 171,
　　200, 214, 238, 243, 273-74
Holleder, Don, 249
Hollen, Andrea Lee, 267
Holt, George W., **75**
Holt, Henry, 131
Hood, John Bell, 94-102, **101**
Hood, Michael A., **263**
Hooker, Joseph, 43, **98**
Horne, Alistair, 230
Hotel Thayer, 149, 190
Howard, Kelly, **272**
Howard, Oliver Otis, 75, 94, **98,** 121, **121**
Howard University, 121, **121**
Howitzer, 118, 141, 143, **166, 244, 275**
Howze, Hamilton Hawkins, 269
Howze, Robert L., 143
Hoxton, Llewellyn G., 80-81
Hundredth Night celebrations and shows, 118,
　　132-33, 164-65, **164-65,** 189, 192, 204
Hunt, Henry J., 68

Hussein, Saddam, 273, 276-77, **278**
Hyatt, Mary, 189

Inchon, landing at, 200, **220**, 256
Indian Wars, 44, 48, **49**, 50, **50**, 68, 109, 115, 121, 171
Inside America's Military Academies, 213
In the Men's House (Barkalow), 273
"Intimate Glimpses in the Life of Cadet Joseph X. Funnel, VII," **166**
Iron Triangle, **223**
Italy, World War II and, 173, 180, **190**
Ives, James Merritt, **80**

Jackson, Andrew, 43-44
Jackson, Thomas Jonathan "Stonewall," 14, 48-53, 67, 69, **89**, 90, **90**, 121, 132, **278**
Jefferson, Thomas, 15, 18-19, 23-25, 31, 109, 278
Jewish Chapel, 267
Joffre, Joseph, **148**
Johnson, Andrew, 108-9
Johnson, Harold K., 235, 249, 252
Johnson, Lyndon B., **197**, 207, 224, **264**
Johnson, Robert E., 257, 269
Johnston, Albert Sidney, 35, 71, 94
Johnston, Joseph E., **82, 89,** 94, **101,** 109
Jones, Alison, 274
Joseph, Chief of the Nez Percé, 109, 121
Joulwan, George, 242
Julio, E. B. F., **90**
June Week, 211

Karloff, Boris, 192, 202
Keeler, Ruby, 213, **213**
Kelly, John H., 88
Kelly's Ford, Battle of, **88,** 89
Kennedy, John F., 90, 149, 173, **197, 226, 227,** 257, **263,** 264
Kerry, John, 266
Kilby, Francis B., 183-84
Kilpatrick, Hugh Judson, 88, **98**
Kimsey, Jim, 15, 279
King, Adisa, **240**
Kinney, Peter, 277
Kinnison, Hank, 277
Kirby, Edmund, 89
Kissinger, Henry, 266
Knight, Bobby, **249,** 250-51
Knowlton, William, 256
Koehler, Herman John, 118, 144, 233, 236-37, **236,** 252
Korean War, 15, 144, 166, **197,** 200, 204-7, 210-11, **210, 219, 220, 221,** 222-23 **225, 227, 229,** 242, 244, 247, **248,** 252, 256-57, 268
Kosciusko, Thaddeus, **25, 26**

Koster, Samuel, 261
Krasnaborski, Edward J., 211
Krepenevich, Andy, 263-64
Krzyzewski, Mike, 251
Kuhn, Joseph Edward, 118

Lafayette, Marquis de, 33, 39
Lake Ocklawaha, **49**
Lane, James, 102
Las Guasimas, Battle of, 132
Leary, Timothy, 278
Lee, Fitz-Hugh, 69-71, 78, 84, 132, 141
Lee, George Washington Custis, 71, **105**
Lee, Henry "Light Horse Harry," 69
Lee, Robert E., 14, 33, 35, 43, 51, 53-54, **53, 56, 62,** 65-67, 69-74, 78, 84, 90, **90, 105,** 108, 121, 129, 158, 189
Le Marchant, John Gaspard, 230
LeMay, Curtis, **219**
Lemnitzer, Lyman Louis, 170, 268
Leslie's Illustrated Magazine, **82**
Levy, Simon Magruder, 18
Lewis, Elizabeth, 256
Life, **177, 246, 248, 253,** 268, **271**
Liggett, Hunter, 109, 158, **158,** 163-67, 173
Lincoln, Abraham, 33, 78-79, **82,** 83-86, 89, 104, 108, 121
Linnard, Thomas Beasly, **61**
Lionheads, The (Bunting), 263-64
Little Big Horn, Battle of, 74, 88, **103,** 115, 214, 259
Little Round Top, struggle for, 89-90
Logan, John, 210
Lombardi, Vince, **248,** 251
Lombardo, Tom, 244
Long, Frank S., 162
Long, Stephen, **41**
Long Barracks, **27, 35**
Long Gray Line, The (Atkinson), 216
Long Gray Line, The (film), 200, 211, 214, **214,** 251
Longstreet, James, 67, 90, **97,** 108, 118, 143
Ludendorff Bridge, **199**
Lusitania, sinking of, 148-49
Lusk, James L., 141

MacAlexander, Ulysses Grant, 152-53
MacArthur (film), 214
MacArthur, Arthur, 83, 133-34
MacArthur, Douglas, 14, 33, 109, 131-34 **135,** 141, 143, 148, **148,** 150, 155-56, **159,** 162-75, **162, 167,** 180-81, **180,** 183, 199-202, **201,** 219, **220,** 224, **226, 229,** 234-39, **236,** 242, 244, 247, 250-53, 255-57, **257,** 262, 264, 273, 278-79, **287, 291**
MacArthur, Louise Cromwell Brooks, 173-74

McAuliffe, Anthony, **196**
McBarron, H. Charles, Jr., **28, 56**
McCaffrey, Barry, 277, 279
McClellan, George B., 48-49, 51, 53, **62,** 65, 68-69, **82, 83, 94,** 102, 104-5, 189
McClellan, Nellie, **82**
McCrae, Tully, 78, 82, 84-86
McCree, William, 30
McDonald, Sir Archibald, 234
McElroy, Paul, **42**
McKinley, Barry, **271**
McKinley, William, 134
Mackmull, Jack, 252
McLean, Don, 261-63
McMaster, H. R., 263-64
MacNamara, Robert, **263**
McNarney, Joseph, 144-45
McNeill, William Gibbs, 53
McPherson, James Birdseye, 68, 94, **98**
McRae, Gordon, 213, **214**
McWilliams, Bill, 217
Madison, James, 25-29
Magruder, John Bankhead, 67
Mahan, Dennis Hart, 43, 45, **48,** 52, **67,** 68-69, 83, 104-5, 118
Maher, Marty, 200, 214, **214,** 259
Maihafer, Harry, 222-23
Maine, USS, 109
Malim in Se, 189, 204
Manhattan Project, **205**
Manila, Manila Bay, Battle of, 135-36
Mansfield, Joseph K. Fenno, **61,** 62
March, Peyton Conway, 134, 136, 149, 170
Marcus, David "Mickey," 258-59, **259**
Marmaduke, John S., **75**
Marne, Battles of the, 152-55, **161**
Marshall, George C., 153-55, 162, 224, 247
Maumee Valley, **55**
Maus, Marion Perry, 109
Maxey, Robert Jayne "Moxie," 148, 151
Mayer, Frederick C., 148
Mayo, Virginia, 213, **214**
Meade, George Gordon, 59, **98,** 102, **105**
Meade, R. K., **81**
Mears, Ray, **249**
Meigs, Montgomery C., 48
Menoher, Charles Thomas, 118
Merman, Ethel, 192
Merrill, William Emory, 69
Merritt, Wesley, **98, 105**
Messel, Jacquelyn, **272**
Metz, Battle of, 155
Meuse-Argonne, Battle of, 109, 118, 148, 158-59, **158,** 174
Mexican War, 15, 45, 47, **48,** 53-68, **53, 62, 65,** 70-71, 83, **92-93**

Mexières, Battle of, 159
Meyer, Charles "Monk," 242
Michie, Dennis Mahan, 135, 149, 173, 236, 238, **238, 242**
Michie, Peter Smith, 78, 238
Michie Stadium, 135, 149, 173, 236, 238, **242,** 279, **281**
Miller, Arthur, 282-83
Mills, Albert L., 143
Minot's Ledge Lighthouse, **54**
Missouri, USS, **180**
Monitor, The, 190-92
Monroe, James, 29-30, 33, 83
Monterrey, Battle of, 59-62, **59,** 68
Montgomery, Bernard Law, 145, 211, 230
Moody, Alfred Judson Force, 204
Moody, George "Bliss," 204
Moore, Hal, 262, 264
Morath, Inge, 282, 284-95
"More Than a Ball Game..." (Gallico), 245
Morgan, Charles H., **75**
Morrison, William E., 210
Mosley, Samuel, 256
Mott, Herb, **219**
Mott, T. Bentley, 173
My Lai scandal, 256, 261

Nagasaki, atomic bomb dropped on, 187-89
Nairobi, terrorist attack on U.S. embassy in, 274
Nancy, Battle of, 150
Napoleon Club, 69, 83
Napoleon I, Emperor of France, 18, 59, 69, 83, 230
Nashville, Battle of, **101**
National Color of the Second Battalion, 18th U.S. Infantry, **101**
National Football League (NFL), 177, 249
National Geographic, **169**
National Invitational Tournament (NIT), **249,** 250
Naval Academy, U.S., 109, 121, 135, 141, 174, 197, 201, 224, 234, **234,** 236, 238-39, **238, 239, 240,** 243-53, **243, 245, 251,** 256-57, 269, 273
Nelson, Horatio, Lord, 230
Nesmith, James, 104
Newark Bay, **54**
Newburgh *News,* 177
New York Daily News, 245, **245**
New York draft riots, 79
New York Times, 238, **260**
Nininger, Alexander R. "Sandy," **187,** 202-4
Nininger Hall, 204
Nixon, Richard M., 204, 256, 266
Norfolk, Battle of, 30

Norman, Geoffrey, 233-53
Norris, Ariel, 43
Norstad, Lauris, 173, 279
North Africa, World War II and, 173, 180
North Atlantic Treaty Organization (NATO), 207, 269
Norton, John "Jack," 189, 204
Nugen, John, 57

Offley, Robert H., 207
O'Hara, Maureen, 214, **214**
Okinawa, Battle for, 181, **182,** 187, 204, 250
Olds, Robin, 197, 242
Olympics, 143, 204, **225,** 242, 251
Omaha Beach, 145
Ord, Edward Otho Cresap, **98**
O'Rorke, Patrick, 89
Osceola, 50
Outpost (Mahan), 83
Owens Corning, 279

Palfrey, John C., **75**
Palmer, General David R., 274
Palo Alto, Battle of, 59
Panama Canal, 15, **139,** 140, 258, 267
Pan-American Airways, 204
Pappas, George S., 118, 125, 136-41
Parcells, Bill, 251
Parke, John Grubb, **98**
Parker, Francis H., 87
Parker, James P., 87-88
Parks, Robert W., 190
Partridge, Alden "Old Pewter," 18, 26-34, **28,** 43-44, **56,** 172
Patton, George S., IV, 200
Patton, George S., Jr., 14-15, **124,** 143, 145, 149, 156, **156,** 159, **177,** 179-80, 185, **199,** 202, 210, **227,** 242, **256,** 262
Pawnees, **41**
Peale, Titian, **41**
Pearl Harbor, attack on, 174, 177, **177,** 180, 183, 189, 202, 207
Pearson, Pam, **234,** 253
Peck, Gregory, 214
Pelham, John, 82-83, **88,** 89
Pelosi, James J., 257
Pentagon, September 11, 2001 attack on, 15
Peplinski, Alan, **272**
Pershing, John J. "Black Jack," 14, **108,** 118, **133,** 135-36, 147, 149-50, **151,** 152, **154,** 155, 158-66, **158, 159, 161,** 173-74, 201, 268, 273
Petersburg, siege of, 49, 79
Philippine Insurrection, 132, **133,** 136, 162
Philippines, World War II and, 180-81, **187, 201,** 202

Physical Training With and Without Special Equipment (Koehler), 144
Pickett, George, 52, 67, 89-90, **92-93,** 94, 171
Pike, Emory Jenison, 148, 156-58
Pinckney, Edward, 31
Pinckney, Thomas, 31
Plato, 279
Plattsburg, Battle of, 25
Plimpton, George, 90
Poe, Edgar Allan, 35-43, **39,** 278
Poinsett, Joel, 43-44
Pointer, The, 149, 192, **216, 217, 221**
Pons, Lily, 192
Poole, Barney, 201
Pope, John, 62, 102
Pork Chop Hill, Battle of, 15, **222, 225,** 252
Porter, Cole, 213
Porter, Fitz-John, 68
Post, Justus, 19
Powell, Colin L., 268, **273**
Powell, Dick, 213, **213**
Power, Tyrone, 193, 214, **214**
Prescott, William Linzie, **265**
Prichard, Vernon, 145
Prince, Leonard M., 238
Prince and the Pauper, The (Twain), 124
Profiles in Courage (Kennedy), 90
Public Law 88-276, 224
Pullen, John J., 90
Pusan, Battle at, 200
Putnam, Haldemand, **75**

Quasimas, Battle of, **133**
Quekemeyer, John G., 173

Ramos, Fidel V., 268
Ramseur, Stephen Dodson, 69
Reagan, Ronald, 204, 213, 244, 267
Recognition Day, **268**
Reconstruction, 90, 108-9, 114-15, 119, 121, 268
Reeder, Russell "Red," 211-15, 251-52
Reinecke, Paul S., 144
Remagen, bridge at, **199,** 204
Remington, Frederic, **110**
Reminiscences (MacArthur), 237
Renecke, Lt., **295**
Revolutionary War, 15, 18, **19, 21,** 22-23, **23, 24, 25, 27,** 31, 69, 141, 257-58, **258, 284**
Richardson, Wilds Preston, 118
Richmond, battles against, 88-89
Ridgley, Randolph, 59
Ridgway, Matthew Bunker, 15, 166, **210, 220, 222,** 223, **227,** 247, 262, 269
Riding Club, 129
Riding Hall, 211
Rienzi, Thomas M., 205

Riley, Jack, 234, 251
Ringgold, Samuel, **56,** 59
Robinson, Roscoe, Jr., 268
Rockne, Knute, 173, 244
Rodman, Thomas Jackson, 49
Ronan, George, 19
Roosevelt, Franklin D., **167,** 184, 197, 203
Roosevelt, Theodore, 107, 109, 129, 134-35,
    134, 136, 140-42, **140, 240**
Root, Elihu, 141-42
Rosalie, 213, **213**
Rosecrans, William, **97**
Rosser, Thomas Lafayette, 78-79, 88, **103,** 141
Rough Riders, 134-35
Round Pond, 267
Rowland, Thomas, 77, 82
Rowny, Edward L., 204
Royal Military Academy (RMA) Sandhurst,
    230, 262
Royal Military College of Canada, 234
Ruger, Thomas H., 120, 171
Ryan, George, **75**
Rybicki, Frank, 259
Ryder, Charles W., 144

St. Cyr military academy, 262
St.-Étienne-à-Arras, Battle of, 162
St. Juvin, Battle of, 159-62
St. Mihiel, Battle of, 148, 155-58, **161**
Salerno, Battle of, 230
Sampson, Deborah (Robert Shurtleff), 22
San Cosme Gate, Battle of, 68
Sandhurst Competition, **288, 289**
San Juan Hill, Battle of, 129, 134-35, 149, 238
San Juan River, action at Bloody Bend of,
    132, 135
Santa Anna, Antonio López de, **61,** 62-68
Santa Fe Trail, The, 213
Santiago, Battle of, 132
Saratoga, Battle, of, **24**
Sayles, Andre, 269
Sayles, Tereh, 269
Schaff, Morris, 75, 78, 108-9, 258
Schilling, Charles, 205
Schlafly, Phyllis, 273
Schofield, John M., 94-102, 120
Schofield's Definition of Leadership, 275
Schwarzkopf, H. Norman, 14-15, **14,** 230,
    276, **278,** 279
Schwitzer, Jillian Boice, 253
Scott, James, **161**
Scott, Winfield, 26, **28,** 47, 54, **59,** 62-67, **62,**
    83, 86, 259
Scowcroft, Brent, 200, 266, 279
Sears, Stephen W., 77-105
Seawell, William T., 204

secessionists, 78-88, **79**
Sedan, Battle of, 159, 166-67
Sedgwick, John, 43, 48, **94,** 108
Seminole Wars, 44, 48, **49,** 50, **50**
Seymour, Samuel, **41**
Seymour, Truman, **81**
Shannon, James Andrew, 148, 162
Shaw, Henry A., 144
Shea, Richard, **225,** 252
Shenandoah Valley, Battle of, **103**
Shepler, Dwight, **194**
Sheridan, Philip Henry, **57,** 68, **98,** 102, **103,**
    105, 189
Sherman, Thomas W., 65
Sherman, William Tecumseh, 14, 48, 68, 88,
    94-102, **98, 101,** 105, 109-14, 119, 134,
    173, 189
Shiloh, Battle of, 35
Showalter, Dennis, 209-31
Show Goes On, The, **165**
Sibert, William, 140
Sicily, Battle for, 149, 180, 230
Sickles, Dan, 90
Sidey, Hugh, 200
Sisson, Nathanial, **104**
Skinner, Cornelia Otis, 192
Sladen, Fred W., 174
Slocum, Henry Warner, **98**
Slocum, John McAllister, **98**
Smith, Brian, 269
Smith, Frederick, 207
Smith, Hamilton Allen, 148, 153-55
Smith, James W., 120
Smith, William P., **75**
Snow Plow, The (Weir), 117
Snuffy's Bar and Tavern, 256
Snyder, George W., **81**
Soissons, Battle of, 148, 153-55
Something for the Boys, 192
Spaatz, Carl, **192**
Spanish-American War, 132, **133,** 134-41, 200,
    236, 238, **242**
Sports Illustrated, 244
Spotsylvania, Battle of, 48, 79, 88
Squire, The, 129-30, 132-33
Stanton, Edwin, 104
START Treaty, 204
State Department, U.S., 274
Stevens, John, 140
Stewart Field, 174, 177, 180-81, **190, 192,**
    193, 215
Stichweh, Carl, 224
Stilwell, Alice, **137**
Stilwell, Joseph "Vinegar Joe," **137, 188,** 250
Stilwell, Mary Augusta, **137**
Stimson, Henry, 202

Stockbridge, William, **124**
Strategic Air Force, U.S., **192**
Stratemeyer, George, 144-45
Strictly Personal (Eisenhower), 187
Stuart, James Ewell Brown "Jeb," 68-69, 75,
    89, **89,** 121, 213
Summerall, Charles Pelot, 135-36, **159,** 162-63
Summer Camp, 126-27, **131,** 172, 174-75, **272**
Supreme Court, U.S., 257
Sutton, Bob, 250
Swanton, Donovan, 152
Swift, Joseph Gardner, 18-19, 24, 29-30
Swift, W. H., **41**
Swing, Joseph, 144

"Target Practice at West Point," **131**
Taylor, Maxwell Davenport, 33, 148, 170, 175,
    197, 200, 210, 219, 223, **225, 226, 227,**
    228, 231, 247, 252, 256, **263**
Taylor, Zachary, 54-65, **61**
Taylor Hall, 173
Terry, Wallace, 268-69
Thayer, Sylvanus, 18-19, **18,** 24, 30-45, **33, 45,**
    48, **48,** 51, 68-69, 108, 114, 118, 132, **167,**
    171-72, 218, 224, 259, **259,** 266-67
Thayer Academy, 45
Thayer Hall, 211, **275,** 295
They Died With Their Boots On, 214
Thomas, Brian, 268-69
Thomas, George H. "Pap," 65, **96, 97, 98,**
    101, 163-66
Thompson, Buck, 259
Ticknor, George, 45
Tillman, Samuel E., 121
Time, **226**
Titus, Calvin P., **134,** 141
"To Helen" (Poe), 38
Toombs, Robert, 103
Torrence, Jim, Jr., 262
Torrence, Jim, Sr., 262
Trant, Dominick, 258, **259**
Trent, John, 244, **248**
Trophy Point, **137,** 141, **284**
Trophy Point (Weir), **117**
Truman, Harry S., 268
Trumbull, Lyman, 103
Tucker, Arnold, 199, **246**
Tuskegee Airmen, **190,** 268
Twain, Mark, 124
Twentieth Maine, The (Pullen), 90

Uncertain Trumpet, The (Taylor), 256
United Nations, **220, 222, 229**
United States Military Academy (USMA)
    Archives, 211
Upton, Emory, 88, 108

Vandenberg, Hoyt Sanford, **219**

Vandières, Battle of, 158

Vandiver, Frank, 136

Van Fleet, James Alward, **142,** 144-45, **222, 225,** 242, 268

Vaux, Battle of, 153

Vera Cruz, Battle of, 62-65

Verdun, Battle of, 158

Veterans Against the War, 263

Veterinary Station Hospital, 243

Victory Monument, **6**

Vidal, Gore, 214

Viele, Egbert L., 259, **259**

Vietnam War, 15, 173, 189, 197, 204-7, 224, **227,** 230-31, 242, **248,** 249, 252, 256-66, **260, 264, 265,** 269, 276-78, **278,** 282-83

Villa, Francisco "Pancho," 149

Wade, Benjamin, 102-3

Wainwright, Jonathan M., **187,** 200

Wainwright, Washington, **31**

Walker, James, **48, 59**

Walker, Kirby, 238

War Department, U.S., *see* Defense Department, U.S.

Warner, Susan and Anna B., **259**

War of 1812, 25, **28,** 30, 53, **56,** 69, 172, **258**

Warren, Gouverneur Kemble, **98**

Washington, George, 15, 17-19, **19,** 22-23, **24,** 71, 78-79, **78,** 141, **276**

Washington, James B., **78**

Washington Hall, 148, 174, **221**

Washington Monument, 148

Wasp-Waisted Vampires, **164**

Watergate scandal, 279

Waterloo, Battle of, 230

Watmough, E.C., **28**

Watson, Leroy, 144

Webster, Daniel, 70

Webster, Horace, 108

Weir, Robert W., **18,** 48, 116, **117**

Wellington, Arthur Wellesley, Duke of, 230

West Academic Building, 135

Western & Atlantic Railroad, 53

Western Engineer, The, **41**

Westmoreland, William Childs, 173, **199,** 204, 224, **227,** 230, 257, **260-61,** 263-64, **264, 265,** 273

West Point:

    Academic Board of, 69, 74, 114, 120, 144, 173-74, 267

    Alma Mater of, 144

    Alumni Day at, 143

    bicentennial of, 278

    blacks admitted to, 42, 109, 119-21, **119,** **120,** 173-74, **190,** 204, 214, 229, 268-69, **268**

    blind dates at, 190

    Cadet Leadership Development System (CLDS) of, 275

    cadets' first day at, 14

    centennial of, 107, 141-42, 258

    cheating scandals at, 225-29, 244, 247, **247,** 257, 265-67

    cheerleaders at, **253**

    Color Guard of, **4**

    Commandant's House at, 33

    Congressional Medals of Honor awarded to graduates of, 88-90, 109, 133-34, **134,** 141, 148, 156, 163, 171, **187,** 202-3, 252, 259, 264

    Consultants Board of, 210

    creation of, 15, 17-18, 278

    Curriculum Committee of, 222

    Distinguished Service Crosses (DSCs) awarded to graduates of, 148, 151, 155, 159-62, **159,** 163, 174, 205, 242, 251, 264, 277

    drags at, 189-90, 200

    fires at, **74**

    food at, 190

    historic site designation of, 217

    Honor Committee of, 172, 174, 257

    hops at, **115,** 175, 190, **216,** 273

    Library at, 45, **102,** 120

    mascot of, 141, 243, **243, 253,** 256

    Plebe system at, 274-75

    Professor's Row at, **87**

    standard of the battalion of, **38**

    Superintendent's House at, 33, **291**

    Vigilance Committee of, 172

    Visitors Board of, 34, 43, 114, 118, 175, 215

    women admitted to, 22, 217, 230, 234, **234, 250,** 252-53, 256-57, 267-74, **271, 272,** 277, 279, **279, 291, 295**

West Point (Herbert), 264-65

West Point Annual Reports, 156, 175

West Point Atlas of American Wars (Esposito), 211

West Point Band, **136, 276**

West Point Cemetery, 50, **50,** 129, 200, 258-59, **258, 259**

West Point Club, **42**

West Point Equal Admissions Opportunity Program, 256

West Point Hotel, **59, 115**

West Point Museum, 68-69, **101, 155, 188, 205, 222,** 243, 256

West Point Songs, 148

West Point Story, The, 213, **214**

We Were Soldiers Once and Young (Moore), 264

Wheeler, Earle Gilmore, **264**

Wheeler, George Montague, 108

Wheeler, Joseph "Fighting Joe," 132, 135, 141

Whistler, George Washington, 53, 70

Whistler, James Abbott McNeill, 68, 70-71, **70,** 116, 278

White, Edward H., II, 252, 256, 259, **259,** 278-79

White, Stanford, 141

Whitman, Walter M., 159-62

Whittaker, Johnson Chestnut, 118, 120-21, **120,** 214

Wicker, Tom, 179-207

Wilderness, Battles of the, 79, **94**

Williams, Jonathan, 23-24, **25**

Wilson, Woodrow, 149, **153**

Wofford, John W., 80

Wood, Eleazer Derby, 25, **28,** 258

Wood Monument, **258, 259**

Woodruff, George A., 89

Woodruff, Roscoe, 144

World Trade Center, September 11, 2001 attacks on, 15

World War I, 15, 109, 118, 134-35, 144-45, 147-77, **148, 155, 156, 158, 161, 171,** 180, 183-84, **192,** 200-201, 210-11, **225,** 230, 236-37, 256-57, 282

World War II, 15, 144-45, 148-49, 156, 173-74, **175, 177,** 180-207, **190, 196, 206,** 210-16, 219, **219,** 223, **225, 226,** 228-31, 242-43, 250-51, 256, **256,** 262, 267-68, 276, 283

Worth, William C. "Haughty Bill," 33-35

Wycoff, Marie, 253

Wyndham, John Duncan, 19

Yalu River, **210, 220,** 222-23, 256

Yea Furlo, 189

York, Alvin C., 162

York, Bob, 262

York, Don, 262

York, Duke of, 230

Young, Charles D., 121

Young, Pierce Manning Butler, 88

Zogbaum, R. F., **108, 127**